Jeremy Brett *is* Sherlock H

Maureen Whittaker

Paperback ISBN 978-1-78705-589-6

Published by MX Publishing
335 Princess Park Manor, Royal Drive,
London, N11 3GX
www.mxpublishing.com

Cover compilation by Brian Belanger

Editor & Contributor Gretchen Altabef

With special thanks to Steve Emecz for support in compiling this book.

Contents

Foreword by David Burke

Arthur Conan Doyle was a man at war with his own genius. Detective fiction, a genre he had virtually created, seemed to him an inferior art form. The public knew better and refused to let matters rest. His Holmes was literally resurrected, after which he achieved a sort of immortality and certainly provided Doyle with the kind of wealth few writers are blessed to enjoy. Again and again in his private correspondence, he complained of the treadmill of the Sherlock Holmes stories, but when Doyle died, his creation was still alive and, so far as I know, is still striding up and down Baker Street today.

Sherlock Holmes has continued to make money for others too. There have been feature films and television films based on the stories. In many cases their authenticity is in serious doubt. Many people identify Holmes with Basil Rathbone's impersonation, but those Hollywood based films bear little connection with the original stories beyond the actor's hawkish profile and deerstalker hat.

I was myself lucky enough to be involved as Dr. Watson in the mammoth Granada TV series which began in 1983 and continued long after I had left it. This series owed a colossal debt to its first producer, Michael Cox. It was he who set it up and was responsible for the inspired casting of Jeremy Brett as the famous detective.

At the time I knew Jeremy Brett only by name. He was chiefly famed for two things: his physical beauty, which even in middle age caused grown women to swoon and for being a little mad. The madness I soon discovered was largely a delightful streak of eccentricity and determination to "celebrate" in spite of almost anything life threw at him. He once entertained a lady friend to lunch in the workaday BBC canteen by covering the plastic formica with a fine linen tablecloth upon which he placed a brass candelabra and some sweet-smelling freesias in a fine china vase.

While at Granada Studios in Manchester, I grew used to Jeremy arriving in the make-up room extolling the beautiful day waiting for us outside. "But, Jeremy," I would protest, "It's pouring with rain!"

"Of course, my dear," he would reply. "But the liquid atmosphere will make us both look wonderful."

Jeremy was generous to a fault in celebrating the people who were working alongside him to create this phenomenal successful series. He would use a Polaroid camera to take snaps of every member of the crew and post these up on a notice board for everyone to see creating a warm family atmosphere among all those talented folk. He was also diligent to the point of obsession in ensuring that what the viewer saw and heard on screen was faithful to the word on the page.

The Collected Stories were his Bible and went everywhere with him, and woe betide the writer or director who did not have a good reason for deviating from the original. He once insisted on a retake because he had worn his deerstalker back to front. No one but Jeremy could know which was the back and which the front of this eminently symmetrical hat. But he was not po-faced about these things and was the first to laugh at himself.

He told me how he once accosted a helmeted police constable on Clapham Common and congratulated him at great length and in the most flowery of language on the increase in the number of bobbies on the beat, recently promised by the Home Secretary. He concluded by saying, "We the public will all be grateful to you splendid fellows that we shall be able to sleep more safely in our beds." The policeman replied, "Why don't you p*** off, sir," and plodded on his way. The irony of the situation was not lost on Jeremy, and he could hardly contain his mirth.

I miss my dear friend's passion and humour, qualities which he brought to his peerless interpretation of the world's greatest detective.

David Burke 2017

Introduction

For many people Jeremy Brett remains the quintessential Sherlock Holmes, featured in the Granada *Sherlock Holmes* series for the Independent Television Network, and indeed some people know of him only through this performance. His outstanding success as the unique genius detective would forever link him with the character much as Basil Rathbone had been fifty years earlier. However, his work encompassed much more than this one portrayal. His career covered thirty years on stage, film and television before he accepted the role which brought him international fame as a great actor.

Jeremy's commanding stage presence at the age of 26 made him a "noble and poetic Hamlet" at the Strand Theatre. His interpretation was proclaimed a critical success for such a young and fresh actor. Just a few years later in 1966, his outstanding portrayal as the dashing, passionate hero D'Artagnan in *The Three Musketeers* for the BBC Sunday serial thrust him into the public spotlight. For those who grew up with the *Play of the Month* on BBC Television on a Sunday evening, Jeremy's appearance as the romantic lead was always welcome. His good looks made him perfect casting for the attractive yet dangerous Lord Byron and as a supremely handsome Captain Jack Absolute in *The Rivals,* he revelled in heroic exploits. In contrast, as the duplicitous Joseph Surface in *A School for Scandal* he explored the role of the anti-hero; *"outwardly a paragon of virtue, but inwardly a miserly fortune hunter."* The classics would become a familiar platform for his rich, modulated tones. He excelled as a haunted Maxim de Winter in *Rebecca*; the tortured, yet morally maimed, Edward Ashburnham in *The Good Soldier*; the fervent Robert Browning and the *"fascinating"* William Pitt – all created with authenticity and passion. Through consistently outstanding performances Jeremy had attracted a loyal and firm fan base.

Visitors to the National Theatre from the years 1967 to 1971 would have seen him in the roles of which he was most proud as he worked with his mentor and *"great God,"* Lord Olivier: playing the romantic suitor Bassanio to Joan Plowright's Portia in *The Merchant of Venice*; Orlando to Ronald Pickup's Rosalind, in the modern day all-male production of *As You Like It* and as the first of Shakespeare's great human beings, Berowne in *Love's Labour's Lost*, a part which he *"adored"* and made his own. His portrayal of Che Guevara was perhaps the most significant role at this time. The critics praised him for a performance *"of considerable imagination and power."* His career in the United States was also memorable with his introduction to Hollywood in *War and Peace* in 1955 as Audrey Hepburn's youthful, exuberant brother, Nicholas Rostov, and again playing opposite Audrey as Eliza's romantic suitor, the charming Freddie Eynsford Hill in *My Fair Lady.* Later, he would be praised and rewarded for his Broadway *Dracula* and also for his Doctor Watson in *The Crucifer of Blood* with Charlton Heston as Sherlock Holmes which would be helpful a few years on.

With a career of this length which covered such a wide range of roles, it is no surprise that Michael Cox, an executive producer of Granada Television, chose Jeremy for the role of Sherlock Holmes in the new Granada series, *The Adventures of Sherlock Holmes.* He wanted a man with the voice, the bearing and the presence of a classically trained actor; someone who could jump over sofas or pursue a clue like a bloodhound, often on his hands and knees. In Jeremy he found all this and much more. Not only did he become the definitive interpreter of the role, but he also brought a new army of fans who were intrigued by this new Holmes, and for some reason, spellbound by the chemistry that existed between actor and camera. Many people tell of Sunday evenings kept special for the weekly pilgrimage to Victorian London in the company of Jeremy Brett and David Burke, his first Doctor Watson. The series ran for ten years in which Jeremy "*became*" Sherlock Holmes. When David Burke left the series, Jeremy exchanged his first Watson for Edward Hardwicke. Together they finished the series and wowed a new army of fans at Wyndhams Theatre from 1988-89 when the play Jeremy commissioned, *The Secret of Sherlock Holmes* filled the theatre every night.

As an actor, Jeremy was a perfectionist and set himself the highest standards in his work: his sheer enthusiasm for his art, his professionalism, hard work and commitment would earn him many accolades over the years. When he died in 1995, David Stuart Davies in his book *Bending the Willow*, expressed what many people felt: "Jeremy Brett's sudden death in September 1995 robbed the acting world of one of its incandescent lights and the world of Sherlock Holmes of one of its finest – debatably its greatest – interpreter of that complex creature who dwelt at 221B Baker Street." Many people still feel that this is the case twenty five years after his death. Peter Wyngarde, one of his co-stars in *The Three Gables* an episode of *The Memoirs of Sherlock Holmes* caught the man when he said: "Jeremy's absolute dedication was phenomenal. It was not selfish. It wasn't for him, it wasn't for Jeremy Brett – it was for Sherlock Holmes." Alan Coren who wrote for *The Mail*, said: "Jeremy Brett's performance is still so superlative that no superlatives of mine are adequate to describe it."

In Oscar Wilde's *A Picture of Dorian Gray,* a story that Jeremy played twice, once as Dorian and the other as the artist Basil Hallward who says, "*Any portrait painted with feeling is a portrait of the artist.*" Jeremy was a man of great feeling, and this was a major contribution to his success on stage. In his personal life he suffered too much from life's slings and arrows. Until the age of seventeen he was tongue-tied and suffered from dyslexia throughout his life. His rheumatic fever at the age of sixteen, with its legacy of heart trouble, had changed him from the sport-loving, constantly active young man into a human being of great compassion and warmth. The traumatic loss of the two people he loved the most – his mother and his second wife, Joan – both of whom died too soon, brought a great deal of emotional turmoil from which he never really recovered. Consequently, his response to others showed great sensitivity and understanding; he was a man who was universally loved, and yet he displayed the common touch with a willingness and ability to share his experience. He had a strong desire to achieve his dreams even if it took all of his courage to do so. He became an inspiration to fellow sufferers of manic depression as he movingly and eloquently shared his experience of the condition which dogged his final years. Many who worked with Jeremy talk about his joyful spirit, a life lived as if it were a celebration, or "*a festival*". He always loved to sing and although we do not have any record of the remarkable soprano voice of his youth, we can admire his pleasant baritone in his performance as Danilo in *The Merry Widow* which is available on record. Dancing was also a source of great enjoyment for him. His extraordinary generosity and his exuberant welcome were celebrated by all who visited him and those privileged people still hold him in the highest esteem. They remember every detail of their meeting and sincerely wish he had received some recognition for his extraordinary achievements.

During interviews Jeremy was always self-effacing, always praising his colleagues and never taking the credit for himself, even when it was most deserved. His humility showed the Quaker values of hard work and equality, and he became a reflection of his mother, Elizabeth, whom he described as beautiful inside and out and as a light of great warmth. It seems appropriate to approach a record of his work with his words wherever possible. It also gives the essence of the man who was very much part of a team, even when he led it, as he did in the Granada *Sherlock Holmes* series. In this book I wish to honour his privacy and if he didn't give details of his private life then it isn't included here.

A *TV Times* article on 24th February 1973, gave a resume of his life to date: "On the handsome face of it, actor Jeremy Brett would appear to be the man who had everything: looks, talent, security. Then there's his Eton education, fame at 21, a fashionable marriage at 24 (wedding snaps taken by courtesy of Anthony Armstrong-Jones, as he was then), leading ladies of the calibre of Audrey Hepburn, Ingrid Bergman and Deborah Kerr, and a son and heir on whom he dotes and who has just won first place in an all public schools examination to Radley. Could a chap with the plain, no-nonsense name of Huggins ask for more?" Indeed, he appeared to have taken every advantage that his life had offered and his family life seems to have been ideal.

Sherlock Holmes

"One document which is going to remain a secret for a few more years is my original list of possible actors to play Holmes in the Eighties. There are forty names on the list, and they are not in alphabetical order but Jeremy Brett's name is at the top. He seemed to me then to be the best-equipped actor of his generation to challenge the great portrayals of the past. I had first read the stories in bound volumes of The Strand *and grown up with Sidney Paget's evocative illustrations – they were the benchmark. And I wanted a Holmes with a splendid voice, a commanding presence and the richly varied temperament which Conan Doyle had given him."* (Michael Cox in The Sherlock Holmes Journal Winter 1995)

Writing in the *Sherlock Holmes Gazette*, Michael gave further details of a very wet night in August 1981 in which he and Jeremy had discussed the role of Holmes. David Huggins had accompanied his father to the meeting with Michael and the head of casting for dinner at a restaurant in Charlotte Street and Jeremy would no doubt have felt the contrast with the warmth he had left behind at his home in Los Angeles. Granada had plans to construct a semi-permanent set for a future *Coronation Street Tour,* and Michael had a £5 million budget to create a quality production. The strict control of the character's television representations imposed by the Conan Doyle estate was about to end as the books came into the public domain, and Michael saw an opportunity to return to Conan Doyle's original work and provide the first authentic presentation of Holmes. The decision to use 35mm for the films, the size preferred by the U.S. networks brought the hope of investment from WGBH which was willing to share the financial risk of production in exchange for the right to show it first in the U.S. To ensure advance sales the actor needed to be "of star quality" known to the American market and although Joan Wilson Huggins' position and influence was not mentioned, Jeremy was extremely sensitive about the possibility that he might have been chosen at his wife's request. Above all they needed "a classical actor with a marvellous voice and the appearance of a Sidney Paget illustration from *The Strand Magazine*". Jeremy satisfied all the preferred criteria, but he may not have accepted the role as many actors do not relish the thought of tying themselves too much to a part and Sherlock Holmes had a reputation of being a signature part. Basil Rathbone had been strongly identified with the role long after he had left it. "I was also deeply concerned with being 'typed,' more completely 'typed' than any other classic actor has ever been or ever will be again." (Basil Rathbone In and Out of Character) Jeremy Brett knew it could have meant the end of his career so the decision was a difficult one.

Granada's reputation was exemplary at this time and the company was renowned for its strong commitment to classical drama. Charles Dickens, Jane Austen, H.G. Wells, Saki and Evelyn Waugh's *Brideshead Revisited* had attracted the best actors and earned enormous prestige for the company. Crucially, the talks included the need to be faithful to the Conan Doyle stories plus the determination to achieve the same high standard for which Granada was noted in their drama programming. "(Jeremy) was interested, enthusiastic even, but of course, unprepared to commit himself irrevocably until there were dates and fixtures on paper." (Michael Cox) In the meantime he was producing, directing and playing the lead Prospero in *The Tempest* onstage in Toronto, Canada, *"I was acting Prospero in* The Tempest *and trying to raise money to film the play in Barbados – because it was Shakespeare I couldn't find a penny – and then I did Robert Browning in* The Barretts of Wimpole Street, *I thought, oh phooey, Holmes is old hat, been done to death. He didn't intrigue me at the time."* (Jeremy in Brett Noir)

If he had been successful in bringing *The Tempest* to the screen it is unlikely that he would have accepted. However, Jeremy's attempts to explore the world famous detective were not without some surprises. *"When I tried to buy* The Strand Magazine, *I couldn't find one. I couldn't find Doyle's complete works. I did, eventually find one in Foyles, in London, and it was an American edition, which had been sent over and not been collected, and that's how I got one. Now, Doyle is everywhere..."* The red leather bound *Illustrated Sherlock Holmes Treasury* with his many underlinings and annotations would become "his Bible" to be applied conscientiously to any aspect of the present production which didn't fit with Doyle's original stories. He would carry it with him over the ten years of filming the series.

Jeremy had been reintroduced to the Conan Doyle stories by a friend in the Bahamas where he was on holiday following *The Tempest*. Sherlock Holmes was very different from the romantic heroic figures he had portrayed in his career, yet he was intrigued: *"It was there that I became fascinated with Doyle's tales. I thought, Oh yes, there are things I can do with this fellow! They held me entranced; the late Victorian era, full of gaslit, fogbound streets, the scent of shag tobacco. Then the details began to pop up at me from the page. Holmes chuckled and wriggled in his chair as was his habit when in high spirits... Lighting his long cherrywood pipe which he was wont to replace his clay when he was in a disputatious, rather than a meditative mood... Holmes hunted about among the grass and leaves like a retriever after a wounded bird... Images that I had not seen before. The actor in me was on the hunt. The more I delved, the more I realised there was room for me to be someone else, to do something different... I discovered all sorts of things that I could do if I had the opportunity to do so. So I say 'yes!' with enormous temerity, and a certain amount of fear, and an element of excitement."* (Taken from Armchair Detective and Foreword to Television Sherlock Holmes)

A time of total immersion in Holmes followed which was Jeremy's familiar approach to a new part. He was a classically trained Shakespearean actor with a love of words and the rhythm they created. His approach to a character would be based on his schooling in Classical Theatre plus the training he received at the National Theatre under Olivier and the Stanislavsky method of inventing the man Holmes in which he would live. *"I was talking about becoming. What I mean by that is an inner life. Watson describes you-know-who as a mind without a heart; that's hard to play, hard to become. So what I did was to invent an inner life. I mean, I know what his nanny looked like; for example; she was covered in starch. She probably scrubbed him, but never kissed him. I don't think he probably saw his mother until he was about eight... (she) was just a lady moving through a passageway... Maybe caught a touch of her scent and the rustle of her dress. Probably he didn't actually see his father until he was twelve. I guess college days were fairly complicated because he was quite isolated. He probably saw a girl across the quadrangle and fell in love, but she never looked at him... so he closed that door. And he became a brilliant fencer... and a master at boxing... and many more tiny little details which I have to kind of make up to fill this kind of well... that Doyle so brilliantly left out. To bring it off the printed page for myself, I invented little stories about... the loneliness of his university days, of his brilliance at sports, and his total removal from any kind of social activity... everything to bring a bit more illumination."* (Gunner54.wordpress.com & NPR Interview 1991)

Stanislavsky also suggested, "You study it from the point of view of the epoch, the time, the country, condition of life, background, literature, psychology, the soul, way of living, social position, and external appearance; moreover, you study character, such as custom, manner, movements, voice, intonations." (An Actor Prepares) Sherlock Holmes lived in the Victorian era. *"What you do as an actor, for me anyway, you become a sponge... What you do is squeeze the sponge out. And you learn and assimilate. You read and read and read about the Victorian era. Who was in government? What was the social status of the country? Why was Holmes a bohemian? Then you start to read Doyle and you sort of sniff it through. After a great deal of study, things begin to happen. Like hands. What does he do with his hands? How would he move? And you whisper, whisper, whisper because you have to find the voice. You keep whispering so the imagination keeps going. When you think you've got him – or he's enough in you – you speak. It's an enormously exciting process."* (To Luaine Lee in Scripps Howard News Service)

When filming began for *The Solitary Cyclist* Jeremy had lost a significant amount of weight, around 24 pounds, mostly by swimming, and immersing himself in the part. He reported the effects of his screen tests and described them as a disaster with the choice of white make-up which made his teeth look yellow and his eyes red. *"I started hilariously because I was so embarrassed by feeling miscast and totally inadequate that I did a kind of gargoyle makeup, I put white on my forehead and I put white down my nose and dark violet under here* (his chin). *Trying to look like a hungry eagle, I looked... dreadful. So they said, 'No, we can't do that, that's awful!'"* (SH Behind the Scenes on ITV This Morning) *"Everyone said, 'Jeremy, do you need all that? Where are you under there? Why the funny walk?' I had a painted face, this walk and a ghastly voice. They all went, of course."* (TV Times 19th May 1984) Michael Cox said, "Jeremy is very much an extrovert. He enjoys life, is great fun to be with, is very amusing and has a great way with words. And he saw Holmes as very dark... a rather waspish sarcastic kind of character. I believe the director of one of the first episodes said to him, 'Could you just put a little bit of yourself into this, because the man can't have been quite as black as you're painting him or no one would have ever come to consult him. They'd be frightened away at his doorstep.' Jeremy was persuaded to loosen up a bit and I think his performance improved as a result. He was able to find the moments of humour, moments of warmth, moments when you can see his concern for clients and for Watson in the stories. I think the characterisation has got more interest, has got more flash and fire to it." (Michael in Armchair Detective)

In interview for *Pebble Mill at One* Jeremy said, *"I remember when Sir Alastair Cooke said to me... before we started, he said that the three most memorable people in the last hundred years are Churchill, Hitler and Sherlock Holmes. Now this was meant to encourage me – I was terrified! Well, that's really done it now. I mean, I didn't want to play the part in the first place because I thought I would fail! 'Cause there had been so many people playing it before. But to think that one of those three people never existed at all is extraordinary!"* (BBC One) He was now committed to the role and would make his interpretation of Holmes the very best. Michael said, "From the beginning Jeremy plunged himself into every aspect of production. The scripts had been written during the long layoff, but he had his copy of the original stories, annotated and underlined after hours of reading and rereading and he made a careful comparison."

Jeremy was determined to speak Sir Arthur Doyle's original words in a definitive Sherlock Holmes to attain Michael Cox's vision of "the best Sherlock Holmes series ever". No one had allowed the characters to speak the actual words in an authentic dramatisation of the story before and the prospect excited and challenged Jeremy. *"(When) we approached the* scripts, I said, 'But you've asked me to do Sir Arthur Conan Doyle's Sherlock Holmes. These aren't Sherlock Holmes – Doyle's stories.' I mean, the adaptors had gone so far away. And the script editor said, 'Jeremy, you're here to act. Just get on with it.' And I tipped the table over, and my Dover sole landed in his lap. And that was the beginning of the tussle. I used to take the whole canon with me... (at) the beginning of each film, and fight for Doyle. After about a year and a half I said, 'Listen, if you don't start taking care of me, I may lose interest,' because it was such a tussle. But then Granada Studios stepped in and were so remarkable and wonderful and gave me two weeks rehearsal instead of one. So the first week I could fight for Doyle and the second week I could work with my fellow actors. And that's basically how it's been ever since." (NPR Interview 1991)

Granada Studios set constructed onto the Bonded Warehouse

The thirteen episodes of *The Adventures of Sherlock Holmes* were to be filmed as one complete sequence and depending on the public response Granada would make the decision whether to continue. The first episode recorded ***The Solitary Cyclist* (Dramatised by Alan Plater: Directed by Paul Annett fb: 15th May 1984)** was filmed at Delamere Forest near Chester for the forest scenes of Doyle's story. The Baker Street set had been constructed on the facia of the Bonded Warehouse facing the historical railway at the Museum of Science and Industry in Manchester. *"It was daunting because they'd only just finished the set and it had cost millions and it was all squeaky clean... my clothes were still bristling new, and how do you wear the deerstalker without looking a twit? ... How do I smoke a pipe when I'm left-handed?"* Violet Smith, the sensible, bright and determined young music teacher was seeking help as her safety had been put at risk by the predatory unpleasant Woodley, a friend of her employer who upset her with his unwanted attentions. She was followed each week as she travelled to the railway station on her bicycle to visit her mother and the man on the bicycle behind her wore a beard and glasses. This brought her to 221b Baker Street in fear of her life and seeking help from Sherlock Holmes.

The opening of the story began in the sitting room of the first floor apartment that Holmes and Watson shared in Baker Street. The reading public was first introduced to Sherlock

Holmes and Doctor John Watson in the novel *A Study in Scarlet* where Watson was looking for comfortable rooms at a reasonable price and Holmes, having found a suite of rooms, needed someone to share the expense. The friendship which developed from this arrangement was to be one of the great male friendships in all literature. *"To me, the Sherlock Holmes stories are about a great friendship. Without Watson, Holmes might well have burnt out on cocaine long ago. I hope the series shows how important friendship is."* (Jeremy) *"And then the relationship with Watson began to intrigue. What keeps Watson there? They have perhaps the greatest friendship in literature, and it must be something in Holmes."* (Jeremy in Brett becomes Holmes in the Bryan Times) "These men, totally different, Mr Chalk and Mr Cheese as I once called them, do manage to share a life together because they are complementary to each other. They don't have the same faults or the same strengths. We always looked for the moment at which Holmes and Watson could exchange a glance acknowledging that one had understood what the other was thinking." (Michael Cox in The Armchair Detective 1982)

The way the two men responded to Miss Smith also revealed something of their differing personalities; Watson was always considerate and attentive, a man who was attracted to the ladies; he describes her as "tall, graceful, and queenly" whereas Holmes first notices the effects of cycling on a young lady's body or the *"spatulate"* finger ends of a pianist. However, Jeremy brought another element into Sherlock's response in his "closest" attentions to her hands and her face before disengaging himself. *"I've looked for the cracks in the veneer to allow me to say more about the character. In* The Solitary Cyclist *when I'm holding Violet Smith's hand making deductions about spatulate finger ends, I tried to portray the fact that Holmes found the touch sensuous."* (Jeremy) His willingness to investigate her situation put the young lady's mind at rest and the adventure that followed was full of excitement and confrontation. Holmes's assurance *"Miss Smith, I never guess"* is comforting yet his eyes flash at this seemingly low opinion of his abilities.

The friendship would be sorely tested in this episode when Watson fails to fulfil his task of discovering the identity of Miss Smith's follower and he is told in a forthright manner that he has *"really done remarkably badly"*. Watson is shocked by the severity of the accusation and cannot understand why he shouldn't have returned to London to make enquiries about a To Let sign. The suggestion that he should have visited the *"nearest public-house"* to check up on the *"centre of country gossip"* becomes ironic as that is exactly what Holmes will do.

Jeremy said that he used his physicality as a way to demonstrate Holmes's intelligence. *"He's much faster than any other human being. His brain, when he is working is so fast, that it's blinding to the observer – including Watson. That takes a lot of steam to get up to."* (Sherlock Holmes Review, Interview with Jeremy Brett 16th March 1987) The race through the forest roads in his attempt to stop a horse trailing a runaway carriage and then Jeremy's driving the horse forward in a standing position contribute to the impression of an active horseman, very able to fight for his clients. But, perhaps it is the elegant, faintly humorous boxing scene in the local hostelry which becomes the centrepiece of the episode. It is a compelling dramatisation of Doyle's description of the confrontation made remarkable by Jeremy's balletic movement around the scene; "The dancing footwork at the start of the fight was his; the ripple of applause from the bystanders when the bully is disposed of was the director's contribution." (A Study in Celluloid)

Watching the drunken clergyman staggering from the public house, Holmes deduces that Woodley would also be present and through his questioning of the landlord he lures the blackguard to the bar where he confronts him. Woodley throws a backhanded first punch but as Holmes is a semi-professional boxer he returns to teach him a lesson and defend Miss Smith's honour. The one to one combat will see him defeated but not before Jeremy's intricate footwork with fists upheld in the manner of a Gentleman Boxer, will make his opponent look a fool and the knockout blow sends him reeling across a table.

The cut above Holmes's eye will represent a badge of honour. The impromptu applause from the Pub's regulars gives Holmes a moment of gratification and as he later relates to Watson, *"It was absolutely delicious."*

The final act is pure melodrama with the introduction of an unfrocked clergyman who carries out a forced marriage at gunpoint; the distress of the lovesick employer, Carruthers, who attempts to kill the villainous Woodley and the rescue of the distraught would-be victim Miss Violet Smith who has fainted in her distress. We find Jeremy's masterful Holmes whose dramatic revelations show him in full possession of all the bewildering elements of the case. Dr. Watson tends to the injured with all the skills of his profession and they work together to provide a needy support for the vulnerable Miss Smith with a pistol as deterrent for the villains. "The strong masterful personality of Holmes dominated the tragic scene, and all were equally puppets in his hands." (The Adventure of the Solitary Cyclist) The first film created in the Granada series presented an accurate and visually stunning dramatisation of the Conan Doyle text.

The introduction of the syringe in the final scenes which had been used to inject a 7% solution of cocaine would give Holmes some frailty amongst his many superhuman abilities. However, it is the chemical experiment which results in so much smoke that the fire brigade is called which labels Holmes as an impossible housemate and ends the story on the first comic note of the series at No. 221B Baker Street. Jeremy said, *"Holmes is an impossible man to share rooms with! I think that what I found in what I call the under-bedding of the part is that somehow Watson sees this man's need... He scrapes on his violin, not very well. He does chemistry – nearly blows people to pieces if he's not very careful, or as happens in* The Solitary Cyclist, *nearly sets fire to 221b Baker Street. So he's obviously a problem child."* (Jeremy Brett: The Real Sherlock Holmes by Rosemary Herbert) "Whatever else he achieved in these stories, Conan Doyle gave us one of the greatest portraits of friendship in English Literature and we were determined to put that on the screen more faithfully than it had ever been seen before." (Michael Cox in A Study in Celluloid)

The *New York Times* reported, "Jeremy Brett makes a truly splendid Sherlock: vain, arrogant, imperious, rude." *Sherlock Holmes On Screen* applauded Granada for its faithful interpretation of the Conan Doyle originals, especially the copying of the Sidney Paget drawings, shown at the commercial breaks, or the end of the episode, to become "a fan's dream". Alan Barnes commented on how the interpretation of Doyle created a new, exciting approach to the text. Some of the "finest moments" occur when the writers read between the lines. "The stand-out scene in the first episode recorded, *The Solitary Cyclist*, being a case in point," where Holmes confronts the repulsive Jack Woodley. "The 'delicious' encounter is only fleetingly reported in Doyle; its mechanics here are entirely invented... In just one minor sequence, Peter Cushing's arch superman, John Neville's self-righteous physicality and Basil Rathbone's sharp superiority are fused into a fascinating whole." (Alan Barnes in Sherlock Holmes Onscreen)

"The momentum had begun and I had begun to find things – the cracks in the marble – such as his delicacy with women, his failures, the little human elements... But he's a very isolated, private man; he's removed emotion from his life and that's what makes him so hard to play." (Jeremy to Hilary DeVries in Christian Science Monitor 1988)

The Speckled Band (Dramatised by Jeremy Paul: Directed by John Bruce fb: 29th May 1984) possibly the best loved of Doyle's stories, was the second of the series to be filmed and the sixth to be aired. Arlington Hall, a stately home in Cheshire, became Stoke Moran. The sudden arrival of another young lady in distress to No. 221b Baker Street means that Mrs Hudson woke Holmes at 7.15 a.m. who then woke Watson, so that Miss Helen Stoner (Rosalyn Landor) may be greeted by a fully prepared household with a fire and an offer of breakfast. Holmes shows a sympathetic concern as he recognises her urgent need for advice. The stains he observes on her clothing indicate a long journey by pony and trap and then by train. She is trembling, filled with terror at the actions of a violent stepfather and the intense dismay at his demands that she move into her sister's room. She tells Holmes of the loss of her beloved sister Julia, who prior to her wedding, died in strange and unexplained circumstances. The sound of a whistle and her sister's last words *"The band, the speckled band"* and the lack of precise details of how she died alerts Holmes to the seriousness of the situation, especially with Helen's own approaching wedding. The bruises he uncovers on Miss Stoner's arms provide evidence of her stepfather's abuse and convince Holmes that this case requires his expert attention. *"These are very deep waters."*

Of Conan Doyle's villains, Doctor Grimesby Roylott is one of the worst as he has a vulnerable, innocent and dependent stepdaughter at his mercy. He has deliberately fostered strained relations with his neighbours by inviting gypsies to camp on his land and allowed wild animals, leopards and baboons to roam freely around the grounds. This suggests Grimesby Roylott is a king of his own jungle to whom the usual laws of humanity no longer apply. Holmes points out that when a Doctor goes wrong he becomes the worst kind of criminal and indeed, Roylott will prove a formidable opponent. His sudden arrival to the Baker Street rooms demanding to know why his daughter has been there is delivered with menacing threats, compounded by violence. He calls him, "Holmes the meddler, Holmes the busybody, Holmes the Scotland Yard Jack-in-Office!" The powerful bending of their fireside poker illustrates the danger but contrary to his expectations Holmes sees it merely as "zest to the investigation". The tyranny and abuse of his daughters, from which one will lose her life and the other fears she will be next, resembles a Fairy Tale and it will prove to be one of the most appalling stories in the Sherlock Holmes canon. Holmes tells Watson, *"When a doctor goes wrong he is the first of criminals. He has nerve and he has knowledge... This man strikes even deeper, but I think Watson, that we shall be able to strike deeper still. But we shall have horrors enough before the night is over..."* (The Speckled Band)

The investigation at Stoke Moran, from the outside, reveals that there is no possibility of intruders gaining access which suggests the danger comes from within the walls. Inside, there is a ventilator between two interior rooms; a locked safe and a saucer of milk where there is no cat; a bed anchored to the floor and a bell cord that doesn't work, all contributing to a mystery that only a detective of Holmes's calibre can solve. He alone recognises the implications of what he finds and his presence alone will bring a sense of security and promise of safety for Helen Stoner and in the sincerity of his gaze we have a brief glimpse of the romantic hero of Jeremy's past performances. Waiting in Helen's room for the opportunity to intervene and save her from her own father, the tension shows visibly in Jeremy's shaking hands and on his face. *"I put his fear into* The Adventure of the Speckled Band. *Holmes is quaking, but he's got his back to Watson."* (Jeremy Brett: The Real Sherlock Holmes by Rosemary Herbert) Another reason for the strain on Jeremy's face lay in the need to complete the filming before dawn broke, to avoid the cost of a return the next day. Although the "deadly swamp adder" was reputedly a dangerous creature they had been told the snake was quite tame so the beating was created mostly off camera and the scene not clearly shown until the credits where special lighting was used to lessen the impact on the creature. Here the Granada team again showed a faithful interpretation of one of the best loved of Conan Doyle's stories.

In his role as Watson, David had discovered why so many actors had resorted to humour, like Nigel Bruce's creation of a lovable buffoon. "They had to take refuge in comedy to give them something to do and going for a few giggles was the obvious," he said, "in the story, *The Speckled Band,* I counted the number of words Watson actually spoke. It was 43." (David Burke) By changing Watson's role from Narrator to Friend the dynamic had been changed and some more of the dialogue would be given to David as the series progressed to show his presence throughout the stories. And Jeremy commented on their relationship, *"We make a very good odd couple, because we found we got on so well. David is also debonair with an attractiveness about him that is unusual and appealing in a Watson. That is a bonus and helps to break the traditional mould."* (The New Tenant at 221b Baker Street)

"Holmes is an enigma. There is no woman in his life. There are precious few friends – only Watson. But I don't think Holmes is at all lonely. I think he likes his own time, his own space. I think he has defeated loneliness. I think that's Doyle's great invention. He has created a man who is totally self-sufficient. That's why he is so attractive." (The Armchair Detective 1992) *"The character of Holmes... I have never thought I was right for that... I couldn't understand... why Granada Television were interested. In truth, I was very daunted by it. But, I thought, well I could only fail. But, I didn't want to fail. There comes a time in your life, where you don't want to fail, anymore. It's too painful. Then a miracle happened, people started to like it and the show has been bought and sold abroad, shown in 60 countries. They are asking for re-runs, not one showing or two, but three times. So, it has all happened and it's terribly exciting. But, it has never been easy. I don't suppose I would have liked it, if it had been really."* (NPR Interview 1991)

The Naval Treaty (Dramatised by Jeremy Paul: Directed by Alan Grint fb: 8th May 1984) was also filmed before the official series opener in order to give the actors, the camera men, and the whole team confidence. However, the Granada standard of excellence was established from our first view of Jeremy Brett staring into the fire in *A Scandal in Bohemia*. Indeed, it was there right from the beginning, the moment Holmes was led away from his chemical experiment by the lovely Miss Violet Smith in *The Solitary Cyclist*. Jeremy and David created a wonderful camaraderie between Holmes and Watson. With Rosalie Williams as Mrs. Hudson given a greater role, daily life in No. 221b Baker Street ran smoothly with the occasional interaction showing mutual understanding. Rosalie highlighted one moment from the final scene, "Jeremy wanted to give me a flower. He gave me a little marigold, just as a little gesture. It was very sweet. It wasn't Conan Doyle; it was just something that happened when we were playing (the scene)." She called it "embroidery", a fleeting gesture between them both which would authenticate their relationship and enrich the performance.

The episode begins with Holmes "working hard over a chemical investigation" in order to prove a man's guilt or innocence, and Watson's arrival shows his astonishment at the chaos in their rooms and his friend's eccentric behaviour of indoor gun practice on the wall in the V.R. sign in bullet holes replacing the picture over the mantelpiece. He comes with a request from Percy Phelps, a friend from Watson's schooldays, who has written to ask if Holmes might help solve the mystery of the disappearance of a vital government document. As nephew to the Foreign Minister, Lord Holdhurst, Phelps was given the huge responsibility of secretly making a copy of an important Treaty and the inexplicable disappearance of the document is a potential disaster. The Nation's security has been put at risk and William Baring-Gould suggests that the Treaty could relate to a secret Treaty of July 1887 between England and Italy in which Italy would have a free hand in Libya in exchange for a similar concession in the Sudan and Upper Egypt with implications for Ethiopia, which would interfere with the French ambitions in the area. This could end in war.

Understandably Percy became ill due to the stress of the situation and since that time he had been suffering with a brain fever, cared for by his fiancée and nurse Annie Harrison. Holmes is only too happy to help a friend of Watson's in a fascinating inexplicable case: "*it would be absurd to deny that the case is abstruse and complicated.*" He examines everyone who may have had an interest in the Treaty or who may have profited from it. Ten weeks have passed since its loss but every avenue appears to be a dead end. Holmes faces a particular challenge in this case as there are no clues, or clear avenues of progress and any detective would have felt at a loss on how best to proceed. As he tests every possibility with scientific precision, one is reminded of the aphorism contained in *The Sign of Four* where after all the possibilities are eliminated whatever remains, however improbable, must be the truth.

Jeremy was particularly fierce with the representative of Scotland Yard, Inspector Forbes an arrogant policeman who accuses Holmes of seeking to profit from their efforts and discredit them. Jeremy answers his accuser in a ringing tone, strident in its intensity, dominating him by his use of statistics pointing out that in the last 53 cases in which they had worked together his name had appeared in only four of them, leaving the police force the credit for the rest. He concluded, "*If you wish to get on in your duties you will work with me, and not against me.*" Once Forbes acquiesces, Holmes takes him under his wing and works with him as an equal.

The sick room is full of flowers and as Holmes enters he clasps a rose in order to deliver a lyrical ode to its beauty, introducing another aspect of his character to his friend Watson. However, Percy's fiancé, ever protective of her patient, shows her frustration of his philosophising at the expense of investigation. Holmes may have wished to challenge where Miss Harrison's loyalties truly lay and Jeremy thought that it showed Holmes's understanding of women, *"I was aware of the disturbance felt by Miss Harrison when I talk about the rose."* Her response convinces him of her love for Percy and that she has no hand in the disappearance of the treaty. Michael Cox argued for some editing of the philosophical musings but Jeremy fought to keep the original verbatim, as he wanted to preserve moments like these to fit his interpretation of Holmes as a thinking, feeling man. On this occasion he didn't entirely win. *"What a lovely thing a rose is! There is nothing in which deduction is so necessary as in religion. It can be built up as an exact science by the reasoner. Our highest assurance of the goodness of Providence seems to me to rest in the flowers. (All other things, our powers, our desires, our food, are really necessary for our existence in the first instance. But this rose is an extra. Its smell and its colour are an embellishment of life, not a condition of it.) It is only goodness which gives extras, and, so I say again that we have much to hope from the flowers."* (The Adventure of The Naval Treaty) The brackets provide further effects of the gifts of providence and their removal brings some changes to Conan Doyle's message but the point has been made and the pose of the Sidney Paget drawing retained, to provide evidence of authenticity. The scene in which Holmes and Watson comment on the view from the railway carriage of beacons and lighthouses of the *"wiser, better England of the future"* fleshes out this view of Holmes as a philosophical man but this was edited from the story, because it was impossible to film a Victorian view over the rooftops of twentieth century Clapham Junction.

The episode was filmed in a hot August in 1983 at Pott Hall in Pott Shrigley the private home which was chosen to stand in for the large detached house in Woking. In this rural setting Holmes was allowed to pass the day in pleasant surroundings daydreaming under a tree whilst waiting for his dangerous confrontation with the thief, and with Miss Harrison's help, recover the lost Treaty. The story's conclusion remains very close to how the author told it. The effect is that we can hear Jeremy's voice quoting Doyle through whole scenes, the first time a Sherlock Holmes television or film production had ever achieved such accuracy. *"I managed to persuade Alan Grint to keep Percy's reaction to the recovered treaty much as it was in the script, but it was hard work. I wanted this version to be as faithful as possible."* (Nicholas Utechin, Jeremy Brett: Television's Newest Holmes in The Sherlock Holmes Journal vol 17 1985)

His impression that Holmes didn't laugh was gradually being overturned and Jeremy loved to laugh. He said that this particular episode was his favourite, *"On a difficult case he may build up considerable tension within himself, which explodes in a genial bit of theatricality when the problem is solved. I've tried to get some of that in my Holmes. Of all the stories I've done* The Naval Treaty *is my favourite, it was the first time in which I felt I could be a bit of me as well as Holmes. I wore a beige suit and a straw hat during that glorious summer. I was allowed to laugh, and at the end, when Holmes knew he'd cracked the problem, I made him do a little skip and dance. Some viewers may not have approved, but for me it was a breakthrough."*

The Rose Speech in The Naval Treaty

Jeremy acknowledged his close study of Conan Doyle's stories in an interview: *"I have had this book beside me since we began, because... I wanted to keep Doyle's stories as close to the originals as possible. Now adaptors do have a way of changing things, and so I needed this with me to refer to. When I found something I didn't like I would flip open the book and say, 'Isn't the original better?' I became a bit of a pain in the neck at times, I guess, but it was worth it to get the stories as close to the books as possible."* (Jeremy to Peter Haining) *"I can hear them saying, 'Oh God, Jeremy's brought the book out again."* David Burke explained; "He was a great perfectionist. I mean, he carried his book of Sherlock Holmes stories around with him, almost like a Bible, and woe betide anybody who tried to alter the stories, unless it was absolutely necessary for translation from the page into film. Not merely did he keep a close eye on the dialogue remaining faithful, but also, when we were actually filming, he would concern himself, in the nicest possible way, with making sure everybody was dressed correctly and that the action mirrored what it said in the book." (Scarlet Street)

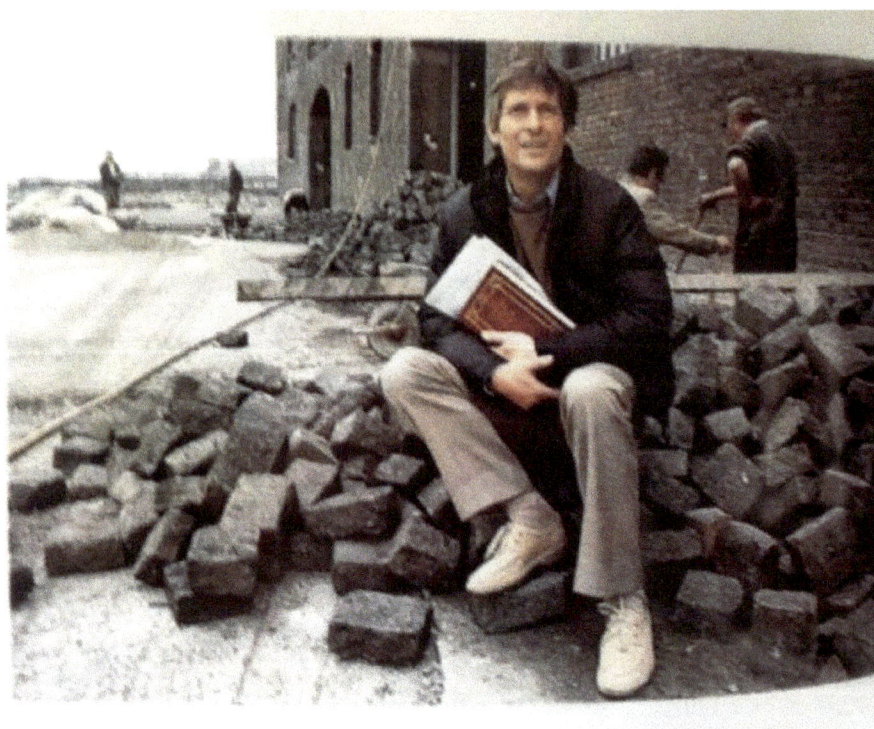

When struggling with some aspect of a scene, Jeremy said, *"I would walk about all over Manchester wrestling with the problem. Sometimes I would discuss it with others or else read the lines over and over again. But in the end I realized the best thing was to go back to the original text by Conan Doyle. So I would pick up my annotated copy, read it, and sure enough there would be the answer staring me in the face."* (The Television Sherlock Holmes)

Jeremy's appearance relied on the deliberate picturing of the Sidney Paget drawings from the original Strand Magazine in which Holmes was perceived wearing a formal black frockcoat with the customary top hat. *"I am quite broad-shouldered and I wear an amazing frockcoat, it's cut two inches in on the shoulder, so I look long and thin. It doesn't fit me, in other words; it's cut so it's snug, right on the bone, so that it gives a length. The waistcoat is pinched very tight to hide my chest, so that I look even more pencil thin. The shoes again giving greater length... Physically, I am much bigger, broader, bigger chested than he is. So, the costume of the black, long, lean look is what I lean on tremendously."* (The Black Box Club)

Paul Annett said he would have the illustrations at his side when they were lining up the shots in order to match the originals. More stills were inserted at the end of the episode, or either side of the commercial breaks so the Sherlock Holmes aficionados would recognise the reverence of Doyle. "We all agreed that if we were going to do this series properly, we wanted it so that people who watched it could actually do a PhD on Conan Doyle if necessary because it was so true to the originals." (Paul Annett in Bending the Willow)

The romantic view of Victorian London was replaced by the reality of the industrial age city with its "peasouper" fogs from the burning of coal; its streets an overflowing cesspool from the horse traffic and lack of cleaning facilities. Granada's realistic reconstruction of Baker Street was built in an area of old railway buildings close to the gasworks in Salford, a hundred yards from the Granada Studios main office in the Bonded Warehouse, its basements originally used for storing tobacco and alcohol. The Street was alive with the noise and constant activity of horse drawn traffic or street workers. "Even Baker Street the elegant desirable residences of Holmes and Watson smelled more like a farmyard than London's fashionable West End yesterday. I keep shouting 'Give me more horse manure,' said Mr Cox who has masterminded the rebuilding of Baker Street on a disused railway just a stride from the Coronation Street set." (Elements of Holmes in Daily Mail 27th September 1983)

Another downside to this authenticity lay in the need to show Holmes using drugs. Conan Doyle had described him injecting a seven percent solution of cocaine intravenously at the opening of his novel *The Sign of Four* and even justifying his actions to an astonished Watson in *"My mind rebels at stagnation..."* This scene was used in *A Scandal in Bohemia* as a means of introducing the television audience to a new portrayal of Sherlock Holmes. It included everything Conan Doyle said about his character: he was a musician wearing a dressing gown, thin, languid, an aesthetic with eccentricities and bad habits. It was the first time he had been portrayed as a complete person and this Holmes was not to be an idealised hero. Drug taking was no longer as socially acceptable as it was to the Victorian public where it was prescribed for babies suffering from colic and this element had not been shown quite so graphically in previous adaptations. *"I have tried to play him as dangerously as possible,"* says the man who shows Holmes for the first time surrounded by his drugs – 16 bottles of cocaine and morphine." (Elements of Holmes in Daily Mail 27th September 1983) Jeremy told another reporter, *"They're pre-Freud, pre-psychology, and much wilder. You realise they're much more destructive and dangerous than you could have imagined. Holmes is his own Special Branch. He's a man who flirts with crime all the time..."* (TV Times 19th May 1984)

Jeremy's career had centred on the classics so he was used to playing characters that *"never stopped talking"* and he found Conan Doyle very difficult in comparison with Shakespeare which has a rhyme and rhythm to aid memory. So he resorted to intensive learning, to know it inside out so he could *"bounce"* on it. *"When we first started I was getting up at 3 am to prepare. It takes a lot of effort to go deeper into a story so that it's not simply a parody. I was bouncing a scene like a trampoline. I'd be polishing my magnifying glass, eating breakfast and making up all while doing twenty-six pages of dialogue. I seemed to have more lines than I'd had hot dinners. By 4 pm when the director wanted fire, my fire was out."* (The Television Sherlock Holmes) "Jeremy himself was a perfectionist. The only person on the team with whom he lost his temper was himself; he was furious if he failed to live up to his own high standards. He had to be word perfect and very well-rehearsed so that he could, as he put it, 'dance on the lines'. The four or five days of rehearsal originally allocated to each film were simply not enough for him. After the first two or three had been shot, he begged me to find him more time in which to prepare. So, we opened up the schedule and, after that, we had a long weekend rest and eight days of rehearsal between films. It was an expensive change and it would be unheard of today, but it gave Jeremy the time he needed to polish his performance." (Michael Cox in A Study in Celluloid)

A Scandal in Bohemia

A Scandal in Bohemia - The Adventures of Sherlock Holmes

The fourth story filmed was to be the first shown as the series launch. *A Scandal In Bohemia,* **(Dramatised by Alexander Baron: Directed by Paul Annett fb: 24ᵗʰ April 1984)**, began with the two most iconic moments in *Sherlock Holmes*: the introduction to Holmes in the opening speech taken from *The Sign of Four* which identifies the detective as a man and the introduction of Irene Adler as *The* Woman. She changed his view of all women. Her intelligence, beauty, operatic voice, and her lifestyle showed him a woman who broke the stereotypical Victorian mould with grace and panache.

The episode begins with Watson's return to Baker Street after a few days in the country, unsure what Holmes's mood will be and the viewer shares his first impressions. Watson's discovery of the hypodermic syringe in the open drawer and the accusation that Holmes is under the influence of drugs brings the information that it is *"a seven per cent solution"* of cocaine. In a brilliant use of breaking the fourth wall, Holmes turns to Watson and the viewing public and asks, *"Would you like to try it?"* This is a memorable moment as the first view of Sherlock Holmes is that of a singular gentleman. *"My mind rebels at stagnation. Give me problems, give me work, give me the most abstruse cryptogram, or the most intricate analysis, and I am in my own proper atmosphere. I can dispense then with artificial stimulants. But, I abhor the dull routine of existence. I crave mental exaltation. That is why I have chosen my own profession, rather created it, for I am the only one in the world... the only, unofficial, consulting detective."* (A Scandal in Bohemia) The delay in which we see only the back of his head before Holmes turned to camera adds a frisson of excitement to a long awaited moment. The image of the great detective with his slicked back hair, his long gaunt face with expressive eyebrows is Jeremy's face transformed into another being, one which is new and intriguing. Jeremy's experience as a romantic lead is used too: he has the intensity of gaze with the ability to let the various fleeting emotions cross his face with the minimum of movement. His distinctive mellifluous voice reveals his inner motivations to his trusted friend and identifies the man whose life is nothing when he is not working at his investigations. Jeremy had been forced to reach up for the character of Holmes, to discover other areas of his talent much in the same way as he created the repressed Edward Ashburnham, a private man behind the cold, closed exterior. This speech presents those findings to us in the first ever glimpse we have of him and in achieving it he had gained maximum impact.

The case begins with the introduction of a masked King Wilhelm of Bavaria who requests the great detective's help in recovering an incriminating photograph of himself with Miss Irene Adler. The acceptance of the case sends Holmes on a mission for information, dressed as a groom, a triumph for the make-up department under Esther Dean. The drunken groom is a close recreation of the Sidney Paget drawing and Jeremy was thrilled to be unrecognisable even to his producer, who when he asked where Jeremy was, found he was standing next to him. "He bounced with joy." (Michael Cox) Jeremy was able to adopt a disguise and be totally convincing and there were several examples in the stories which followed. The removal of the wig, the eyebrows and face packing in front of camera with a couple of wide sweeps, revealed him from behind the mask and although he was concerned that it might be Jeremy who was revealed rather than Holmes, it works well. He described the groom as a *"rough animal which he's not,"* and thought the Non-Conformist clergyman was even less pleasing as it felt more like a music hall character although this had also been a Sidney Paget illustration.

As he works to outwit this resourceful lady, Holmes becomes a witness at her wedding for which he is left holding a small momento she has given him, a sovereign. Later that evening he hires a group of unemployed actors to create a near riot outside Irene Adler's secluded home. Jeremy explained how his own reaction to her perfume would be used in the way Holmes responds to her. *"I was absolutely overwhelmed by it"* and her femininity, *"There was a great shock to him... Holmes has never been so close to a female breast before. She is a beautiful woman with all the sweet essences of her sex. Gayle Hunnicutt wears a scent called 'Bluebell' by Penhaligon. Holmes is affected by this – his senses are acute – and he becomes disoriented. What is going on in his head at the moment? Uncertainty? Is this onslaught of femininity the reason he refers to her as The Woman?... This is the lovemaking of a shy man. He would like to remove Irene, too from his life because he can't waste his precious energies on emotion. But Irene sings divinely, and that means a very great deal to him because he loves music... Holmes changed his whole code of ethics about women after meeting her, but he does this at a cost. The question is, is it worth the cost?"* (Taken from Scarlet Street, The Armchair Detective and The Real Sherlock Holmes)

Gayle Hunnicutt was a perfect and even inspired casting choice for the lovely Irene Adler, charming and intriguing in her dealings with Holmes so it is no surprise that he is enchanted by her. Her intelligence would be fascinating to his clinical mind. Unlike everyone else, she recognises Holmes under his disguise, but only because she has revealed the photograph's hiding place; she had been warned he might be engaged in the affair. Following him home in male disguise as a "slim youth in an ulster" and foolishly calling out to him, "Good night Mister Sherlock Holmes," she displays her true mettle so that she could never be challenged in the role as *The Woman*. *"He fails to get the compromising picture. Holmes covers his error. He says he'll go back. But she has cheated him and gone away. She's a very remarkable woman."* She has succeeded in outwitting the great Sherlock Holmes and that alone is an achievement, but there is the question of her other attractions, those of a sensual woman. Her decision to forego any revenge on the King and destroy her insurance policy, the photograph, is another reason for Holmes to admire her. The portrait of her is his reward and it will remain in his locked drawer to be looked at and cherished over the coming years.

Jeremy was finding out new things about the character of Holmes as he delved deeper into the part. "A Scandal in Bohemia *was when I discovered that Holmes laughed and I went right over the top and never stopped laughing in that one. I was so excited. Before then I had only dared a flicker of a smile.*" (Jeremy in Video Today) He was bringing a new exciting interpretation of the detective and his friend Watson before the public. "*Watson sees that Holmes can't say 'Thank you.' He can't say, 'Good night.' Can't say, 'Help!' But what Holmes does occasionally is rather sweet little things like in* A Scandal in Bohemia *he tells Watson, 'You see, I did remember you were coming; here are your cigars.' And it's the little things that mean a lot. I tried to show how much Holmes does actually need Watson without actually saying it. I think that Holmes would be dead... if Watson weren't there.*" (Jeremy Brett: The Real Sherlock Holmes by Rosemary Herbert) David also had his view of the relationship, "Watson always seemed to me to be a very innocent man, really bordering on the naive. Nigel Bruce had played the part mainly for comedy. I thought it was a very nice characterisation but perhaps went a little too far towards the comic. I tried to bring a balance to it: to be able to play the comic aspect of it; to accentuate the contrast between the rather intolerant, driven Holmes and the laid-back, gentle character of Watson." (David to Daniel Smith in The Sherlock Holmes Companion)

David had transformed the role of Watson. The Granada portrait of Holmes's chronicler was that of an intelligent military man on an equal footing with the man he was writing about. He may have been Holmes's student in the art of deduction but he is a respected doctor who has just returned from Afghanistan with considerable experience of army life and essential knowledge which would become indispensable during his time at his friend's side as he would take care of the injured, the innocent bystanders and the ladies who were in need of sympathy or simply a kind word.

The Guardian gave their full approval, "*The Adventures of Sherlock Holmes* – a seven part series with another to come – is a very posh job indeed. So polished that, if you rub your hand over it, you would leave greasy finger marks, so don't. I can recommend it: as a luxurious, even luscious, way of passing the time. It is the best butter that I can't think why that is not what Sherlock Holmes needs." (Nancy Banks-Smith in The Guardian 25th April 1984) *The Times* agreed. "*A Scandal in Bohemia...* launches Granada Television's season of seven one hour films that shelter under the umbrella title *The Adventures of Sherlock Holmes...* If *A Scandal in Bohemia* is any criterion, Conan Doyle has fallen into good hands... Baker Street and the environs have been ambitiously recreated in line with what appears to be the producer's adoption of the policy that if a thing is worth doing at all, it is worth doing well... Mr Brett adopts the poses that the illustrator Sidney Paget has made familiar (which is not all that vital), and captures the sleuth's eagle sharpness (which is). Mr Burke's Watson is not the pop-eyed bumbler that Nigel Bruce made him but a medical man with the necessary intelligence to be Holmes's Boswell. I don't see how the casting of Gayle Hunnicutt in the role of the adventuress Irene Adler could have been improved upon." (The Times 24th April 1984)

"Jeremy Brett as Holmes is superb from the word 'Go'. His magnificent performance in this episode engaged me instantly, and prepared me for the 40 adventures to follow... during which time, I would come to embrace his Holmes as THE definitive screen characterisation of the world's greatest detective... his presence alone made each and every episode a delight to watch." (IMDb) "Brett portrays a Holmes of a type not seen before; bordering on the arrogant, he will not suffer fools light, be they clients or villains. But his sympathies for those who have real need of him and his abilities are genuine, however brusque he appears on the surface. He is not a social worker, and he presses his clients for the hard facts he needs to do his work properly. It is the solution of a mystery for which they have come to him, not hand-holding. There are many subtle indications at his great trust and affection for Watson. The doctor is not a clown figure, he is Everyman to the remoter Holmes." (Kate Karlson Redmond in The Baker Street Journal)

Baker Street File – Scandal in Bohemia

93 - Had immense faculties and powers of observation

94 - Had a Bohemian soul – but did not miss company

95 - He was the most perfect reasoning and observing machine that the world has seen

109 - Pacing room; head sunk upon chest, hands clasped behind him

110 - Rubbed his long, nervous hands together

111 - Laughed – sometimes heartily and for some time; sometimes till limp and helpless

The Dancing Men (Dramatised by Anthony Skene: Directed by John Bruce fb: 1st May 1984) was third on Conan Doyle's list of twelve best stories. For television it would be close to the top of anyone's list of favourite episodes, including Michael Cox who thought it worked particularly well. It was very effective, firstly due to the chosen picturesque setting in Leighton Hall, Lancashire in the place of Norfolk, but also due to the puzzle of the dancing men *"absurd little figures dancing across the paper"* in the notes strewn around the gardens of the stately home, which for some unexplained reason bring great distress to the mistress of the house. The mystery lies in who has sent the notes and why they cause such unhappiness. William Baring-Gould records: "In the year 1903 Sir Arthur Conan Doyle stayed briefly at Hill House hotel at Happisburgh, near Norwich. Asked to sign an autograph book he saw in it a signature and address written in "dancing men" by G.J. Cubitt, the proprietor's son then about seven. Conan Doyle then and there set to work upon *"The Adventures of the Dancing Men,"* not only the cipher but the name Cubitt for the central character of the tale." (The Annotated Sherlock Holmes Vol. II)

Jeremy remained committed to presenting the authentic Doyle wherever possible and he was eager to include the opening exchange in this episode, although it had not been included in the script. He prepared and learnt it over his lunch break and was justifiably proud to record it in one take, putting the words of Doyle into the mouths of Holmes and Watson. *"I lifted the whole of the first page and a half of* The Dancing Men *straight from the page, and there it was, thanks to John Bruce, my director, who allowed me to do it. I said, 'If I can learn it and bounce on it, can I do it?' And he said, 'Try it.'"* (Armchair Detective). This scene reveals Watson's interests and Holmes's deductive powers with the comment concerning his friend's decision not to invest in South African Securities accompanied by the demand that Watson should not say everything is *"so absurdly simple"* when it was explained to him. The humour of Watson saying these very words when it *"was"* explained to him helps define the relationship between the two men. Jeremy's glance of triumphalism and his *"pom, pom, pom, pom"* represents a challenge. So when Watson retaliates with his own jibe about Holmes being unemployed and the inevitable black moods or an escape into the cocaine bottle, he reaches the inevitable conclusion, "Sherlock Holmes is cheerful, therefore Sherlock Holmes must have a case!" Moments like these would bring further enlightenment to the way the two men dealt with the other and to Watson's tolerance and depth of understanding.

The arrival of Mr Hilton Cubitt at Baker Street with the tale of his three-year marriage which has been spoiled by the strange appearance of indecipherable messages around his home brings little sympathy from Holmes but it does offer intrigue. A letter from Chicago thrown unopened onto the fire may be more puzzling, however, it is the fact that Cubitt had refused to ask his wife for an explanation which most concerns Holmes. This stubborn adherence to "a promise is a promise" on his wedding day will be the cause of the developing tragedy. Translation of the notes is necessary but more messages are needed if the code is to be broken.

Holmes cannot resist the mystery of the childish messages and the blackboard set up in the Baker Street rooms was used to show the progress of the translation, meticulously drawn by Holmes and as more messages arrive, the text is gradually revealed. "By the time of *The Dancing Men* Jeremy and David had established a very good working rapport and they contributed quite a lot of fun about the solving of the code. I suspect they also contributed the moment where Watson is secretly reading Holmes's monograph on cyphers. That was the kind of thing they enjoyed."(Michael Cox in Bending the Willow) The revelation that Watson had not yet read the monograph was kept from Holmes but he would certainly do so later. These scenes represent an illustration of both Holmes's methods and his relationship with Watson as he asks his friend to leave him alone whilst he attempts to solve the puzzle but the demonstration of the end of word flags would offer some relief to an all consuming task and an opportunity for a Jeremy flourish as he mimes the dancing men.

Jeremy was naturally left-handed and he found it difficult to use his right hand on anything they gave him to write. The sheets of paper of the original story were impossible and had been replaced by a blackboard. It has been said that a hand double was used, however, Michael Cox says Jeremy persevered with his right hand for this particular episode and with much practice was successful. This determination is one of his great strengths as an actor and can be seen on several occasions in the series. It enabled him to maintain the authenticity of Holmes even when he was struggling to achieve it.

The discovery that Cubitt's wife is called Elsie provides the essential key to the messages as E is the most common letter of the alphabet. When Watson explained the key to the translation to Inspector Martin in the final scene with his friend looking on, Holmes is rather put out that he might have lost his credibility in the same way as the explanation of his methods in *The Red-Headed League* would earn derision rather than applause. However, the full explanation of Holmes's methods was lost by this substitution which is regrettable as only Jeremy could bring the drama into the situation.

On his close study of Doyle, Jeremy had decided that Holmes was a genius whose powers of deduction were superhuman and he showed these moments by moving extremely quickly, often jumping from a moving carriage or leaping over furniture. His impulsive leap over the back of the sofa which greets the arrival of another telegram containing a dancing men message gives some indication of its urgency: *"Elsie (P)re(p)are to meet thy Go(d)"* is fraught with danger. His mind is swiftly made up and he is ready for action so both Holmes and Watson run from the room snatching the Dancing Men messages as they leave. The deerstalker hat to accompany the light grey suit is a pleasing addition in this episode and a sign that he is visiting the country, as no gentleman would wear a deerstalker in town. This was a decision the team had made to remove some of the trappings which were not part of Conan Doyle's stories yet had been added by others as signature aspects of Holmes' character.

On his arrival at Cubitt's home, Ridling Thorpe Manor in Derbyshire, the news of Hilton Cubitt's death and of his wife's injuries was a complete surprise to Holmes. Inspector Martin's theory was that Elsie has killed her husband and then attempted to take her own life. This is one of only two instances in the Conan Doyle tales when Holmes has delayed too long and lost his client. He was too late to prevent the tragedy but he was anxious to ensure that justice is done. The investigation and the solution is a masterpiece of sleuthing. Holmes has already explored his theories, reached tentative conclusions and through questioning the household staff, confirmed his expectations. The smell of gunpowder from downstairs, the discovery of the bullet in the window jamb, and the search amongst the gravel outside the window, with the precision and grace of a ballet dancer, show him using many of the modern methods of policing and define him as a celebrated master of his trade. The use of the dancing men code to entrap the villain, Abe Slaney and the excitement of the confrontation with this violent member of the Chicago Mafia, is pure melodrama and it is he who provides an explanation of his love for Elsie who had fallen in love with someone else.

When asked to choose between his different Dr Watsons, David Burke and Edward Hardwicke, Jeremy said, *"I couldn't possibly choose. They were both splendid in their own individual way. There are moments I'm fond of. I loved the way David stood up for me in* The Dancing Men, *when the local police didn't know who I was. He stepped forward, 'This is Sherlock Holmes.' I was very touched by his performance in* The Final Problem. *Ted's faint and obvious relief at his friend's return in* The Empty House *was also very touching. He showed such vulnerability. He was so very good in* The Musgrave Ritual, *which is one of the best we ever did. Ted really didn't want to play Watson; he was a reluctant hero."* (Scarlet Street)

***The Crooked Man* (Dramatised by Alfred Shaughnessy: Directed by Alan Grint fb: 22nd May 1984)** filmed at Sandhurst Training College, is a military tale and Jeremy's attitude in the barracks at Aldershot, where Holmes has been called in to investigate the sudden death of the Colonel is rude and overbearing. Jeremy's close connection with the army through his father, Colonel William Huggins, is unlikely to have coloured his responses to this tale as he always showed immense pride in his father's achievements, but his stalking across the parade ground in his long black coat and topper with cane swinging as in a military parade and his hostile approach to Major Murphy suggests that Holmes was antagonistic towards the military. Jeremy seemed to go several steps further and show contempt although the suggestion of a scandal may offer some justification alongside his demand to "*tell me the facts*" which is necessary if he is going to solve this case. His tone of voice and staccato delivery brings drama to the meeting especially for Watson who is deeply embarrassed by the situation. It has been suggested that his hostility may have been the outcome of the discussions over the script which did not follow the Doylean story upsetting both Jeremy and David, but it is certainly a tour de force. Jeremy said, "*I don't like arrogant people and I don't like selfishness. Anyone like Holmes who plays a power trick on people when he meets them is not my scene at all. Holmes is rude and Watson has the compassion to understand why...*" (A new tenant at 221b Baker Street)

This episode begins with the "supposed murder" of Colonel Barclay of the Royal Mallows, one of the most famous Irish regiments of the British Army. Their achievements in the Crimea and the Indian Mutiny were distinguished and James Barclay was rewarded with a commissioned rank. After his marriage to the "charming, vivacious, and spirited" Miss Nancy Devoy, his career had flourished and he had been appointed Commanding Officer. In spite of his success, Colonel Barclay, usually a jovial man, suffered from black moods, sometimes displaying a violent turn of mind and even depression which could last for days. He could be particularly vindictive towards new officers. Added to this, a curious superstition resulted in his dislike of being left alone after dark. The details of a furious quarrel with his wife, Nancy, behind a locked door, became serious when there was a crash, a piercing scream, followed by silence. On entering the locked room through the patio window, the batman had found the Colonel lying dead on the fender with a terrible look of fear and horror on his face with Mrs Barclay lying insensible on the sofa nearby.

There is an opportunity to view a different Holmes in the scenes that follow. Firstly, he responds sharply to Watson's observation that; "mild adultery has always been commonplace among officers and their wives serving in hot climates" suggesting that this might be a feature of the case, and Holmes's prompt reply is noncommittal, *"Thank you Watson for educating me in military morality."* In contrast, the seductive manner of his interrogation of the housemaid is an example of Holmes at his most charming and persuasive; *"Had you ever heard them arguing before?"* suggests that marital upset was a regular feature of the Colonel and Mrs Barclay's relationship. In the role of sleuth, Jeremy's elegant balletic movements around the terrace as he closely examined and traced the footprints would lead to his haring across the lawns following the path of the intruder. The discovery of the canary in its cage contributes to the conclusion that a man had entered and left through the windows accompanied by some sort of animal, *"a carnivorous beast."* Once more we see the speed of the man on a chase and although Holmes's methods may seem fanciful his theories are given substance as the story is revealed, so we know this Holmes can be trusted. We also see Jeremy's instinctive smoothing of his hair as he re-enters the room in a customary gesture which brings subtlety and depth to the performance.

The interview with Miss Morrison leads to the solution and the revelation of the crooked man, accompanied by his mongoose. "I cannot betray a friend, please don't ask me to!" may have been a refreshing sign of loyalty but as Holmes reminds her that her friend is under custody and charged with the murder of her husband, she reconsiders. "I must break my promise of friendship" and true friendship required the sacrifice. The scene in the tavern frequented by members of the military with the discovery of Henry Wood and his pet mongoose, Teddy, is beautifully presented and eloquent. Holmes and Watson stand out as strangers against the military uniforms but the crooked man is eager to share the story of his trials and suffering which have changed him from a handsome, virile young man into a wreck of a human being. The tale told by Wood is a bitter record of the personal cost of those caught up in the Indian Mutiny but more importantly it is one of love and betrayal which was to bring about the death of the Colonel. "It is a heart-wrenching love story which has stood the test of time. The tragic events are brought about by jealousy and misuse of power which allows Barclay to send his rival for the hand of Nancy to his certain death. When we are told the background it is no surprise that Barclay is the unhappy, haunted man who dies of apoplexy." (Lynne Truss in The Times)

The shout of "David", from Mrs Barclay, heard through the locked door was explained by reference to the Old Testament story of David and Bathsheba where Israel's King David had put Bathsheba's husband, Uriah the Hittite at the front of the advancing troops so that he would be killed and she would be free to marry him. Holmes had found the Biblical reference on his return and couldn't help testing Watson concerning the source and implications for this case to which Watson had retaliated. "We are avoiding the clichés and what has been added through the years both by writers and actors. There is no 'Elementary, my dear Watson,' because Holmes never said those four words together. But at the end of the episode we turn that cliché on its head when Holmes and Watson replies, 'Elementary, my dear Holmes'". (Michael Cox in A New Tenant at 221b Baker Street)

There was considerable disquiet over the changes to the story which had been turned upside down, due to the inability of the cameras to record the details as Doyle had presented them. One scene that was changed had upset both Jeremy and David who commented on the lost moment of pathos when Henry Wood had first seen his Nancy under a street light and had called out in recognition of his long lost love, but did not know of her marriage to the man who was responsible for his suffering. "My God, It's Nancy! was replaced by the more mundane mission scene and both David and Jeremy were dismayed: "Blood was almost spilt and tears were shed. I'm afraid we lost the battle." (David Burke) Jeremy was so upset that he went further. *"By the time we got to* The Crooked Man *we were so far away from the story that I despaired. Adaptors would dread me pulling them up on things. I went to them and said that I would lose interest in the project if they didn't stick closer to Doyle's original. I was committed to the first thirteen so I could not have left but my heart nearly broke."* (The Sherlock Holmes Gazette)

This may have been a difficult episode to produce and Michael Cox needed a significant amount of persuasion to include it in *The Adventures* but for the critics this was a very successful episode. "The central part of the investigation, devised by Shaughnessy as a typical Holmesian inquiry, is enthralling and superbly performed. Brett, with his velvet voice, his persuasive tone and his charming smile, conveys the seductive power Holmes can display to draw the truth from a close-mouthed witness. And when he examines the terrace with feline precision before striding across the lawn like a foxhound, he expresses perfectly the animal passion for hunting which spurs on Holmes. As for David Burke, he plays with conviction and brisk energy the active part Shaughnessy has granted Watson. Thanks to the work of the whole crew, this episode, getting the most out of Conan Doyle's short story, retains the fundamental elements of a Holmesian investigation, while its pathos and its exoticism enthral the viewer's sensitivity and imagination." (sirarthur-conan-doyle.com)

"If you are going to buy one Conan Doyle DVD let it be this. If you're going to watch as single episode, let it be *The Crooked Man.* For this is as good as it gets. We have a glorious incarnation of Holmes and Watson here. Brett's Holmes – cantankerous, affected, whimsical, rude, arrogant, precipitous, charming – can only have been drawn from the deepest possible understanding of the text. There have been similar efforts along the same lines, though none so successful. No other Holmes has come close to Brett's portrayal of the brilliant but obsessed mind, teetering on the knife edge dividing madness and genius." (IMDb)

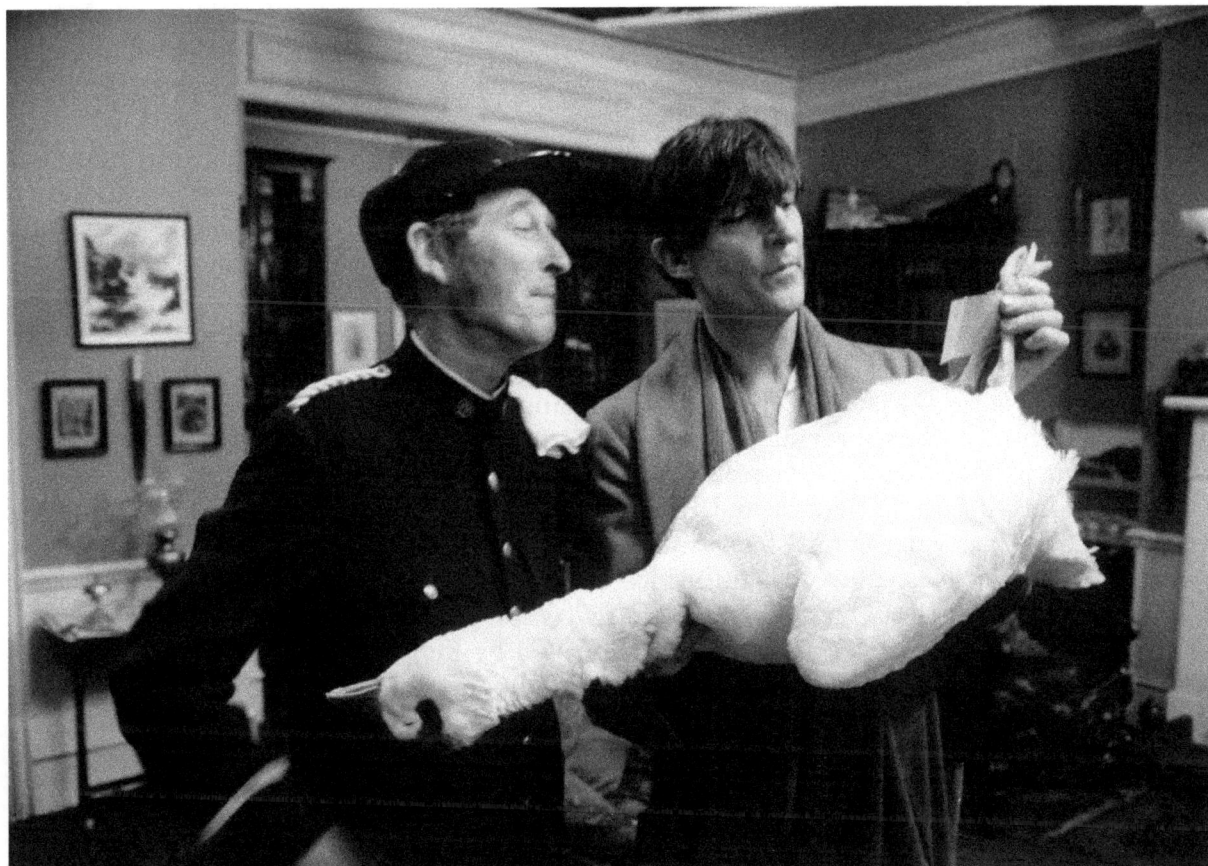

***The Blue Carbuncle* (Dramatised by Paul Finney: Directed by David Carson fb: 5th June 1984)** was a Christmas story shown in June and unfortunately not part of the Christmas schedules. This lack of forethought on behalf of Granada was a lost opportunity to enjoy the Victorian seasonal delights of a goose, holly and the presents bought already wrapped from the Gamages Department Store. The opening credits provide a history of the blue carbuncle, a precious blue gem discovered twenty years before and then lost, stolen from the cold and remote widowed Duchess of Morcar whose screams of outrage are strangely unmoving. The sympathy in the story has been transferred to the man arrested for the theft, the innocent tradesman John Horner, clearly hired for a menial job to take the blame. Thus the setting of a crime is explained with the need of the only unofficial consulting detective to investigate the events.

Watson is the man who is up from his bed and out early to purchase his gifts whilst Holmes is still asleep, only to be awakened by Mrs Hudson as they have a client. It is a unique occurrence to see Holmes being shaken awake when he is usually the one waking his friend. This is humorously followed by a frantic search for a match to light his first essential cigarette, showing Jeremy's shared understanding of Holmes's need for nicotine. His reaction to Peterson, the commissionaire, standing in his living room clutching a goose and a stiff felt bowler hat is full of finely created detail and humour; a Paget illustration faithfully recreated.

The story of how Peterson acquired both of these items sets the scene for the case. It does not concern murder, but poses a question. Why the owner of the goose and the hat should have dropped them and run away, leaving a clue to their identity in the label on the goose which reads, "For Mrs Henry Baker." Jeremy has merged his own humour with the character of Holmes in these scenes to provide a finely judged performance. His generous offer of a drink with "*the season's greetings*," and the gift of the goose, whose condition suggests is in need of cooking without delay, sends the commissionaire home with grateful thanks. He doesn't seem to notice he was almost pushed out through the door.

Conan Doyle's story of the investigation of the theft of the Blue Carbuncle began with Watson arriving at Baker Street the second day after Christmas. To his surprise he finds Holmes lounging on the sofa in his purple dressing gown, with his magnifying glass and pipe rack within reach, surveying a "very seedy, and disreputable hard felt hat, much the worse for wear, and cracked in several places." Granada had decided to bring it forward to a couple of days before Christmas and Holmes's perceptive and detailed analysis of the hat and its prospective owner is full of assurance on his part and non-committal comments from Watson who can see nothing of significance on the hat to justify his friend's deductions. The conclusions that the owner is a "*highly intellectual*" man who has "*fallen on hard times*" and that "*his wife no longer loves him*" is confirmed by his observations at which Watson responds with a mixture of disbelief and delight. "My dear Holmes" is an indication of the depth of the friendship conveyed in this beautiful back and forth exchange.

When Jeremy was asked which episode he found the most difficult he said it was The Blue Carbuncle because of the Sidney Paget drawing, "so marvellous, with Holmes lying sideways on the sofa. I had to actually be in the position for about a day and a half, so I could very nearly not stand up straight at the end of shooting the scene. It was an undiluted piece of brilliant deduction. And one so invariably gets it wrong… a particularly tough film." (zombostcloset.com) In spite of the discomfort he was clearly feeling more confident with the character here with a more obvious blending of Jeremy with Holmes. Some of the distinctive mannerisms appear, for example, the finger before the lips and the ease of smile and laughter that is a generic rather than a measured response. The placing of the hat on his head to cover his ears to demonstrate the size of Henry Baker's head is a memorable choice especially as his intellect surely exceeds that of the owner. The drama of the discovery of the blue carbuncle is the highlight introduced by the hilarious image of a goose coming back to life and flapping off into the heavens. The tracing of the thief is a masterful gathering of evidence and of personal experience as Mr. Henry Baker comes to the Baker Street rooms and confirms much of Holmes's sympathetic analyses of the owner of the hat. Henry Baker is clearly not the thief as the knowledge that the bird has been eaten causes him enormous distress but once in possession of a replacement goose he leaves, a contented man.

Holmes and Watson will finally meet with James Ryder as he tries to locate his missing goose. This section of the episode follows the original story closely and the confidence aligned with the panache with which Jeremy presents Holmes provides added pleasure. Watson also enjoys his moment of triumph as he claims his £5 reward for his wager on the difference in taste between town and country bred geese. The arrival of James Ryder at Baker Street where he has been lured to receive the lost carbuncle changes the tone entirely as Holmes becomes a predator pursuing his prey: first offering him the precious stone as a reward for his persistence, only to take it back and mercilessly berate him for his act of theft. Once the thief is trapped Holmes hears the rest of the sad tale from the beaten man and dismisses him with an uncharacteristic show of anger and disgust. Freeing the innocent man Horner languishing in custody at the local police station awaiting conviction and "seven years penal servitude" is Holmes's sole aim. This is the first instance in the series that we see Holmes acting outside the law; he is in fact "*committing a felony*" although it would probably be more accurate to say he is "*commuting a felony*" in order to save the soul of James Ryder.

Jeremy was a technician as much as he was an actor creating a character. He understood the mechanics of filming and watched the rushes whenever he was given the opportunity. In behind the scenes photographs he can often be seen peering through the camera lens to check how the scene was lit, what was in the shot, where his edges were. In *Stage Struck* he expressed his fascination with the magic lantern and described how the eight member team at Granada worked together in harmony to reveal a stone which would be identified as the Blue Carbuncle "*It's a bonny thing,*" said he. "*Just see how it glints and sparkles.*" (The Adventure of the Blue Carbuncle): the part played by the camera, "*Steve Oxley on camera keeping the stone in focus*" as the "*track goes round*" (Paul and Mike); the sound man and the man with the boom; the perfect lighting (Ray Goode) which could transform a piece of blue glass into *"a zonking great crystal"* which was *"absolutely breathtaking"*. He was as excited by the freedom to create precious moments like this as he was by the closeness of the camera which would bring a new approach to his acting. *"It's like building an enormous mosaic... because the medium is so close you can do so many subtleties and we can build up a relationship with looks, without words at all, and it can be terribly exciting. Suddenly, Watson can look at Holmes on the other side of the room and you, the audience, know that he is concerned, or Oh, he's off on one of his trips..."* The team always looked for the moment at which Holmes and Watson could exchange a glance acknowledging that one had understood what the other was thinking. Added to this new approach to acting, Granada had provided the sense of community and Jeremy had fostered it by his own approach to the filmmaking, bringing everyone together into a close knit community who would all relish the success. *"Filming is magic and I find it thrilling to have as many as 15 people working to the same end to get the moment absolutely right on film. It's a true communication."* (Elementary)

The communication would continue off screen too. "A film crew would do anything for Jeremy and there were two reasons for this. First, because he was absolutely professional in his work, and second, because he knew them all personally. Not only had he memorised everyone's name by the end of the first day's shooting but he also knew whose car had been broken into or whose baby was ill. And it wasn't a trick to curry favour, he genuinely wanted to know." (Michael Cox in Sherlock Holmes Gazette) When his bodyguard, Tony Eyres's son lost his dog, Jeremy made him the present of a new puppy to the boy's huge delight.

On inviting Edward Hardwicke to view the daily rushes with him, Jeremy was surprised by his refusal but the justification was a personal one. "When I'm in the process of working I find it personally very destructive to see the rushes. Jeremy would say, *'Yeah, but you're not just looking at you. All the other people – the lighting man, the sound man – they all want a pat on the back. And if you watch it, you can go up the next day and say, 'Terrific!'"* (The Armchair Detective) In his speech at Granada Television in 1992 Jeremy would pay tribute to each of the experts in their field, not only to the crew and the electricians but also to the film editors, composers, the set designers, system directors, production managers, the researchers, the script editors and paid particular tribute to Sue Milton *"my brilliant makeup artist"* and Esther Dean as *"this country's finest costume designer."* (Charles Allen Granada Television)

The casting of David Burke as Watson was just as important as the choice of Jeremy Brett for Holmes. Michael said, "Very determinedly, I went for someone who could restore the image of Watson to the rather dashing, good-looking, military man who was a believable friend for Sherlock Holmes, who must be one of the most demanding people in choosing his friends, as you can imagine. It seemed to all of us that there was no way in which one could give Holmes as a friend and colleague someone who was a buffoon. So we went for that rather more believable man who also, I think, represents people like you and me in the stories. He is a reasonably intelligent, moderately skilled fellow. Not, of course, anywhere in the same league as the superman Holmes, but he is someone that you and I can identify with." (The Television Sherlock Holmes and Armchair Detective) "David Burke was an instinctive piece of casting... He was able to bring to that ordinariness a degree of charm and intelligence and wit, as well as the flair for getting on with the ladies which Holmes, of course, said was *'Your department, Watson.'* In the final analysis, what one needed was a pretty rounded person – and David fitted the bill perfectly." (The Television Sherlock Holmes and

Armchair Detective) "Jeremy was very kind to me, the junior partner of the series and he made me feel instantly at home, never a cross word between us the whole time, and he was a wonderful leading man because he cherished the crew he worked with... he used one of those instamatic cameras to take pictures not of me or the actors, but of the crew, he even put them up on the walls for all to see! And it was like a very happy family and that was due mainly to Jeremy." (David Burke September 2015)

In spite of his determination to create a happy working atmosphere Jeremy found Holmes a very difficult part to play as his own character was so unlike that of the detective: "*He's chilling... If I saw him walking down the street, I'd say, 'Poor soul... what a tortured creature. He's not a happy man.' Who could be happy who falls apart when he's not working or has to be drugged in order to go to sleep?*" The dark, brooding side of the character worried him and his way of coming to terms with such a superman was to "*look for the cracks in the marble*". "*When I was doing the first five films I used to go back to my hotel room in Manchester and say 'Damn it! I can't play this black figure with a white face all day! I must have a celebration in the evening.' So I would order a half-bottle of champagne. But, of course, I'd wash my hair, and put on something bright and cheerful. Two years go by. That half-bottle has turned into a bottle. Another year goes by. Now it's a bottle and wine at dinner. I realised it wasn't to take me out to celebrate. It's to make me sleep. And that's why Holmes shoots up. To knock himself out... Someone asked me if I dream about him. I said, 'No, and I'm very lucky because otherwise I'd have him all day and all night as well.'*"

The Adventures of Sherlock Holmes

Baker Street

The thirteen episodes of *The Adventures of Sherlock Holmes* were recorded without a break in production, although there was a thirteen month gap between the broadcast of the first seven and the next six on television. This meant there was no feedback from the public to gauge how effective it was, or to give them guidance about the prospects for a new series. The excellence was in evidence from the very beginning, however, the next six episodes seemed to have an added confidence. Jeremy was sharing his interpretation with the press, *"I will never get to the bottom of the barrel. When I get stuck I put my hand in further into the sawdust. Holmes is the most complex, isolated creature – a complete eccentric... He's a man with a brilliant instinct who can be a demented nightbird, driving around the streets of London in the dead of night. He's very gracious to women, but a man with a fear of women - a man who doesn't believe in society or in trivia."* (The Hunt for Holmes Daredevils November 1984)

Nancy Banks-Smith of *The Guardian* had recommended the series as "a luxurious, even luscious, way of passing the time." And Philip French of *The Sunday Times* had agreed: "Jeremy Brett and David Burke are the best Holmes and Watson I've ever seen. For once we can see why Holmes's only passion is detection. The first hint of an assignment galvanises him into a fury of excitement. He takes an inordinate pleasure in dressing up as a labourer and an aged clergyman in order to spy on Irene Adler, and he takes a mischievous delight in the little deductive feats to astound Watson." Another article called him, "one of nature's most engaging extroverts playing the part of the manic depressive detective - a role which nearly destroyed him. Except that he has too much spunk. A more brazenly charming chap you could not hope to meet than Mr Brett, who returns tomorrow as the famous Baker Street sleuth on a new series of *The Adventures of Sherlock Holmes*. Hailed on both sides of the Atlantic as the best ever Holmes, the masterly art of Mr Brett's caustic drawl and cadaverous make-up has even managed to eclipse the memory of the great Basil Rathbone in the role." (Margaret Paton) Jeremy received a letter from his 82 year old grandmother saying, *"Now suddenly this burst of stardom. It's almost frightening! Do you feel the same way? What she was saying is, Are you still humble?"*

***The Copper Beeches* (Writer: Bill Craig, Director: Paul Annett fb: 25th August 1985)**
had an audience of 11.23 million which clearly suggested the studios had a hit after all.
Holmes initially dismisses the request of the young lady who arrives at Baker Street,
seeking his advice regarding the strange requirements of a job as governess as he is unable
to find any challenge in the case. He greets her with extreme bad humour but gradually
thaws as he hears that Miss Violet Hunter, played by a very young Natasha Richardson, is

an orphan. She is poorly treated at Miss Stoper's *Westaways Agency* where the young lady receives no sympathy or protection against the sinister motives of Mr Jephro Rucastle, presented with significant menace by Joss Ackland. Holmes becomes intrigued. It was a mystery why this man should wish to pay her a three figure salary, with an advance of thirty pounds for her expenses, and then ask her "to obey any little commands" and to have her luxurious hair of "a particular tint of chestnut" cut short. As she describes her experiences, Holmes calls it "*a strange fad*", and can't resist touching her hair himself even though this was unacceptable in Victorian times. Jeremy talked about the need to preserve the personal integrity of his clients: "*People in distress – I found them much more emotional when you start putting flesh and blood onto them, when you get actors to play those people, when for example you have a young girl coming in deep distress because she's been told that she's going to have all her hair cut off; otherwise, she won't get the job...*" (Nicholas Utechin in Jeremy Brett: Television's Newest Holmes in The Sherlock Holmes Journal Vol 17, Number 2 1985)

The Copper Beaches has many of the elements of the Gothic genre in the setting of a remote house holding a dark secret. The house, Storrs Hall, near Carnforth, is Gothic in design with a locked turret and as sinister as Miss Hunter's new employer. This atmosphere is also reflected in her unpleasant charge Edward, the boy who enjoys killing cockroaches and the presence of a vicious mastiff dog, kept hungry specifically to keep strangers away, all strike fear in the vulnerable new governess. Jephro Rucastle is a villain and his strange behaviour at the Stoper Employment Agency should have alerted any prospective governess to the dangers in his employment. Miss Hunter should have maintained her original decision. However, as she arrived at Baker Street with her mind made up that she would accept the job it is fortunate that she would have Holmes and Watson ready to help her if things escalate beyond her control.

Violet's call for Holmes's assistance is one of urgency. In a nearby hostelry she tells him of the demands surrounding the wearing of the blue dress and Rucastle's strange antics whilst she sat in front of a window in full view of a man watching from the gate. This was followed by her investigation of the turret room with his violent threats to throw her to the mastiff if she ever returned. Jephro Rucastle may not be in the same league as Abe Slaney or Grimesby Roylott but he is potentially dangerous. Violet Hunter is very much at risk in this sinister pile, and she will have no ally in a sympathetic housekeeper to calm her nerves when events occur to unsettle her. Instead, the guardians of Copper Beeches are a morose couple and the husband is usually under the influence of alcohol making him useless as a protector. The sinister story becomes a tale of terror when Holmes and Watson arrive at the Beeches with the house surrounded by mist and the padlocked but unlocked gates suggesting something momentous had occurred. Jeremy and David are athletic and urgent in pursuit, running swiftly after Rucastle but things become much more dangerous when the guard dog, deprived of food for two days, is released and serious injury becomes inevitable. The revelation of the strange events surrounding Rucastle's daughter Alice, a story of subterfuge and imprisonment, brings light into the mystery. Fortunately, Holmes is able to offer protection to the vulnerable Violet, who has been unwittingly caught up in the events. As Rucastle falls into his own savage trap it is certain that without the intervention of Holmes and Watson the ending would have been very different.

Some of Holmes's more difficult moods are revealed in this episode; his demand for "*Data! Data! I can't make bricks without clay*" and his statement about scattered houses reminding him of what evil may lurk in the countryside. His criticism of Watson's writings brings dismay as he complains about the misrepresentation of his cases which are responsible for a decline in the nature of the enquiries for his services. Watson may complain about the choice of pipe he is smoking being strongly linked to his disputatious mood, but the real source of Holmes's anxiety is the letter from Miss Hunter. *"It seems to be degenerating into an agency for recovering lost lead pencils and giving advice to young ladies from boarding schools."* The detective had solved the cases of the wealthy and influential members of the community so it no surprise Jeremy's Holmes is feeling distinctly peeved that his cases don't reflect his talents or his reputation and his hurt pride floods through the words and baleful tone. Watson may have been hurt at the outburst but he understands his friend's distress and the reasons he feels aggrieved. Furthermore, the companionable humour is regained at the close when Holmes says with good grace, *"My dear fellow, I leave all these things to your excellent literary judgement."* (The Copper Beeches)

Several commentators on this story suggest that Holmes might have had some romantic feelings for Violet Hunter and the manner of presentation seems to agree with this theory. Violet's own comment on the luxurious colour of her hair which "has been considered artistic" in a "singularly brazen fashion" has been highlighted as designed to draw Holmes into her toils. (The Annotated Sherlock Holmes) Holmes's discarding of the strict manners governing the behaviour between a bachelor and a young lady by touching her hair is a fitting explanation for this interpretation. "It's the kind of thing that feels almost reflexive for the Brett incarnation. His Holmes is a tower of fortitude, ostensibly unshakeable to the eye but internally racked by handicapping emotions." (Keith Frankel, Granada's Greatest Detective) Her subsequent letter asking for help, "Do come!" is a personal, almost sentimental one and not in the appropriate terms of client. "...is that a message from a person in trouble to a consulting detective?" (Mr Isaac S, George in Annotated Sherlock Holmes by William Baring-Gould) One (unidentified) news review commented on the appearance of Natasha Richardson in the role of Violet Hunter, as "every inch her mother's daughter – and every speck her father's child too, Vanessa Redgrave's and Tony Richardson's poised and gifted offspring" in her "striking" debut..."

Michael Cox explained the nature of some of the negotiations that took place during filming, "Jeremy would sometimes say to me or to the director, 'My goodness, this is a huge mouthful of words. Do I really have to say this?' I can remember in *The Copper Beeches*, he says something about the great public who couldn't tell a weaver by his tooth or a compositor by his left thumb. He cut that out originally, but I said, 'Oh, it's wonderful, a marvellous illustration of Holmes's observations.' So that went back. It was give and take. I must admit I respected Jeremy when he did defend the stories, and we hammered it out between us." (Michael Cox in Armchair Detective)

Michael also commented on the response to the Granada series in United States when it was first aired on PBS Television. "It was tremendous to walk down the street in New York and see posters on all the bus stops. People would say hello to him in the street and everywhere we went they would congratulate him. They were very forthcoming about what they thought of the series. Usually it was complimentary, and he enjoyed that enormously." (Scarlet Street Number 21)

The Greek Interpreter **(Writer: Derek Marlowe, Director: Alan Grint fb: 1st September 1985)** begins as usual in Baker Street with a domestic scene which provides more personal information about Holmes to his friend, Watson. The fact that he has a brother, named Mycroft, with an important job dealing with government finances was totally unexpected. Watson had come to think of Holmes "as an isolated phenomenon, a brain without a heart" and that his pre-eminent intelligence accompanied by his lack of sympathy and aversion to women, originated from lack of relatives. Watson's ignorance of this element of Holmes's family reveals the detective's closed personality and his desire to preserve his privacy, even from his closest friend.

The meeting with Mycroft took place in the private gentleman's club, the Diogenes Club, which "*contains the most unsociable and unclubbable men in town,*" filmed at Tatton Park, Knutsford. Sherlock has described his elder brother as superior to him in observation and deduction "*but he has no ambition and no energy*" and their skills are put to the test as the audience are invited to share Watson's experience. We see the two brothers either side of a window, listening to them as they compete with each other to provide a detailed analysis of two people in the street below each offering proof for their brilliant deductions. In Granada's version there exists a friendly competition between these gentlemen of equal intellect and consequence. It is clear throughout that the younger Sherlock holds his elder brother in high regard and although they are different in appearance they are similar in interests. They are both a respected expert in their chosen profession. As the visitor Mr Melas is brought into the room to share his story, we are able to appreciate the stylishly framed moment, choreographed and managed by Jeremy, of the younger, slender Holmes stepping out from behind his "much larger and stouter" screen-stealing brother, Mycroft, played by Charles Gray. We also hear of Sherlock's fame due to Watson's publications in "I hear of Sherlock everywhere since you became his chronicler."

The strange tale of Mr Melas, the Greek Interpreter, is a direct contrast with the domesticity of the early scenes and contains elements of Gothic sadism. He recounts a frightening tale of accepting the job of Interpreter unwittingly, being forced to travel in a carriage with blinds drawn under the threat of bodily harm from the weapon carried by his abductor, Mr. Latimer. They journey to a secret location where he is required to question a man who is clearly a prisoner and victim of torture and later he will mention the poor young man with a plaster on his face. As only Mr Melas and his interviewee could understand Greek, he was proud of his ability to gain more information about Paul Kratides with his extra questions but when the victim's sister entered, he was ushered from the room and taken home with the same precautions of secrecy as his arrival had been.

An advertisement appealing for information about Paul and Sophia Katrides, which Mycroft has placed in the newspapers brings more details and provides a link to the house in Beckenham. The need for a search warrant and the difficulties in finding a magistrate who could sign it would bring a significant delay but in spite of his increasing concern, Holmes must wait. When they eventually arrive at the house, an upper room reveals a disaster beyond the imagination; a scene of suffering and death from sulphur poisoning and Holmes once more takes charge, prepared to risk his own safety by dashing once more into the room to rescue Mr Melas and carry him outside. Paul Katrides was found dead and Watson's medical skills were essential in this situation.

Kemp is a soft spoken sinister villain wearing thick lensed glasses, not in the same mould of Grimesby Roylott or Jephro Rucastle who are bullies. However, he is a sadist with a vicious and mocking manner who enjoys hurting his victims with a torture that is slow and exquisitely delivered. Paul Katrides had suffered three weeks of unrelenting torment at the hands of these two infernal villains. His final capitulation will bring about his death in the sulphur attack and murder means that moral justice required them to pay for their crime. Conan Doyle's version had allowed Latimer, Kemp and Sophia to escape but they had all died on the Continent, recorded in the newspaper as two Englishmen travelling with a woman *"had met a tragic end. They had each been stabbed, it seems, and the Hungarian police were of the opinion that they had quarrelled and had inflicted mortal injuries upon each other."* (The Adventure of the Greek Interpreter) Holmes believed that the girl had taken her revenge on her brother's attackers.

However, Granada chose to continue the story beyond where Doyle finishes. The result is an entertaining conclusion which merges seamlessly into the original story and provides a convincing bringing together of the different threads. With the aid of a *Bradshaw Railway Guide*, Holmes, Mycroft and Watson followed the escaping villains onto the train to the continent and confronted them. The scene in the railway carriage where Latimer is told that he is sitting face to face with Sherlock Holmes and Doctor Watson is both tense and ironic as he realises he is trapped. Jeremy's Holmes emerges as the brave and courageous hero who reacts instinctively to the crisis by grabbing hold of Sophia to save her from certain death as Latimer jumps from the carriage into the path of an approaching train. The picture of an inscrutable Holmes holding both Watson and the girl is a heroic one as they seem to be looking into the face of hell. Sophia's behaviour suggests that Latimer has a hold over her, especially as he has promised her marriage. As she is taken away by the police for questioning, Holmes ironically observes, *"It is not a crime to have a cold heart and not a single shred of compassion."*

The episode was filmed at the Bluebell Line at Sheffield Park, Sussex, chosen because it was a, "fine period station, but also because the rolling-stock, impeccably maintained by the Bluebell Railway Preservation Society, includes the London, Brighton and South Coast Railway's directors' saloon where the meal was set up between Mycroft and Wilson Kemp and where he takes the small pistol away from him." Wilson Kemp who was made up with pebble glasses spoke in a manner rather like Peter Lorre in *The Maltese Falcon* "in a jerky, nervous fashion, and with some giggling laughs in between the terror of his face lay in his eyes, however, steel grey, and glistening coldly, with a malevolent, inexorable cruelty in their depths." (A Study in Celluloid) The final image of Jeremy's Holmes walking elegantly and energetically down the platform, in the direction he had just walked, into the mist is a memorable highlight. Jeremy fought for the reinstatement of Holmes's speech about the virtue of modesty; *"To the logician all things should be seen exactly as they are, and to underestimate one's self is as much a departure from truth as to exaggerate one's own powers."* His justification lay in his desire to show more about the man that was Holmes which was *"not just his brilliance but the vulnerability and the... human being that is inside him; lonely, brilliant."* (Jeremy)

The *New York Times* commented on the Holmes brothers, "With eccentricity clearly being a pronounced family trait... Mycroft, played deliciously by the veteran actor Charles Gray, has attained a state of blessed distraction that approaches otherworldliness. Mr Melas finds himself involved with the Holmes brothers in a scenario involving murder, fraud and a heartless woman, who reinforces Sherlock's low opinion of women in general. It's not a very absorbing case but, directed by Alan Grint, Derek Marlowe's adaptation does give Sherlock an opportunity or two to berate the police while flashing his own inimitable powers of deduction. Mr Brett is by now perfectly haughty and irresistible in the role, while Mr Burke's Watson has developed into a splendid partner and foil. Meanwhile, Mycroft, rousing himself from periodic fits of dozing, is only too happy to admit that Sherlock has all the energy in the family." (New York Times 8th February 1986)

In 1989 Jeremy received the award of Pipesmoker of the Year and during an interview for the Morning show *TVam* on ITV Jeremy smiled as he told the presenter Mike Morris of how he had lost one of his valuable pipes during the filming of this episode. Whilst showing the two that he had brought with him, the long thin cherrywood with a curved stem, smoked when Holmes was in one of his disputatious moods and then the long clay pipe which he smoked in his more meditative moods, just like Popeye! He said, *"I was robbed whilst I was doing* The Greek Interpreter. *We had some VIPs round and they stole my pipe. It was either the* Young Conservatives *or the* Royal Ballet. *I bet it was the* Young Conservatives."

***The Norwood Builder* (Writer: Richard Harris, Director: Ken Grieve fb: 8th September 1985)** captures the imagination by so many intriguing elements: an incomprehensible villain with a desire for revenge; a client who seems to be beyond help and a daunted Holmes without the essential facts for so much of the story. The scene of Holmes sitting in his nightshirt and dressing gown, in despair, rejecting food because he *"cannot afford energy and nerve force for digestion"* or his client will go to the gallows, offers a distressing glimpse of the detective. But the presence of his friend who will persuade him to have some breakfast and "go out and see what we can do" together brings further evidence for their dependence on each other. *"I feel I will need your company and moral support today."* (Holmes)

The drama begins with the introduction of John Hector McFarlane, "a wide-eyed and frantic young man, pale, dishevelled, and palpitating," who bursts into the Baker Street sitting room with the assumption that he was already known to Holmes and Watson. Holmes's conclusions that he was *"a bachelor, a solicitor, a Freemason and an asthmatic,"* give evidence once more to his deductive skills. McFarlane reveals the startling fact that he expects to be arrested for the murder of Jonas Oldacre of Lower Norwood and shows him the story in the newspaper Watson has just purchased. The precipitous arrival of Inspector Lestrade, played by Colin Jeavons, prepared to arrest McFarlane for murder brings the threat of danger; Watson facetiously calls him "our old friend," but in this case he becomes a rival for the life of their client. The story told by McFarlane is a strange and incredible one in which he is promised a legacy but is then accused of arson and murder. Although Lestrade is prepared to listen to his account he still takes the accused away in handcuffs with the purpose of having him tried for murder.

Holmes has some possible theories, beginning at Blackheath, which puzzles Lestrade, but which provides a useful introduction to the builder Oldacre to whom McFarlane's mother was once engaged, and she describes him as a cruel and vindictive man. As the villain of the piece, Jonas Oldacre appears to be the victim of murder as human remains have been detected in the remnants of the fire at the timber yard; indeed there is no evidence to disprove the theory until the final scenes where the Machiavellian plot is revealed. Worryingly, further evidence is presented against McFarlane as one of Mr Oldacre's trouser buttons is also found in the ashes of the burnt out building. The housekeeper, Mrs. Lexington, played by Rosalie Crutchley, appears sinister with a manner and appearance reminiscent of Anna Massey's interpretation of Mrs Danvers in *Rebecca,* she seems to dominate her scenes with her unhelpful attitude and latent scorn. Holmes attempts to intimidate her with his close interrogation but he fails and his final salute to her is beautifully done bringing a touch of irony to his manner that suggests a suspicion that she knows more than she is telling. Until the discovery of the thumbprint in the builder's house it appears that the client cannot be saved as the evidence is stacking up relentlessly. Lestrade becomes aware that he now has the young man's life in his hands and he is absolutely convinced of his guilt. His appearance becomes more triumphant with jeers at Holmes's expense as he believes he is finally outwitting the great detective. Even Holmes agrees, "*All my instincts are one way, and all the facts are the other, and I much fear that British juries have not yet attained that pitch of intelligence when they will give the preference to my theories over Lestrade's facts.*" (Holmes in The Norwood Builder)

With the turn in fortunes the tone changes becoming a more celebratory approach to the action. The thumbprint was an error as Holmes was convinced it had not been there the day before and as McFarlane had been in gaol, he couldn't be responsible. Jeremy is once more active and physical in his approach, so that talking is replaced by dancing, running or a leap of joy. The early scene of his sitting entirely motionless, too concerned for his client to find energy for digestion provides a complete contrast. Examination of the dimensions of the house's structure in his most energetic manner is carefully choreographed to highlight the "*serious flaw in this new evidence*" which leads Holmes to the solution of the dilemma.

The stand out scene in this episode concerns the fatal error, which brings the bewildering case to a satisfactory conclusion. The gathering of three police constables, with two bundles of straw and buckets of water standing by, whilst Watson puts a match to the straw and the group shout of "*Fire*" will have a startling effect. Holmes becomes the great magician who reveals the perpetrator with a deadly desire for revenge. It is a scenic highlight as the group are encouraged to shout louder and together, "*We can do better than that. Full voice and together. Fire!*" with Jeremy providing the example in his stentorian tones. The positioning of Holmes, Lestrade and Watson is one of those perfectly staged moments as they peer at the panelling to see "*the witness*" emerge from his hiding place.

The changes made in the Granada version centred on the murder of a tramp dressed in Oldacre's clothes, designed to provide further evidence for McFarlane's guilt. However, Holmes's masterly disguise of a tramp with a blackened face and loose floppy hair, which is clearly Jeremy in *mufti*, helped to reveal the missing information. He spots something the police had missed in his inspection of the fire: a shark's tooth and the signs the people of the road leave for each other when they receive a kindly welcome. The character of an old seaman, the Admiral, may have been familiar to Jeremy due to his mother's unfailing welcome for those who had fallen on hard times at Berkswell Grange. Jeremy's physicality is a positive asset yet again in this episode as Holmes investigates the fire scene balanced on a charred beam with feline precision in the grounds of a large Victorian house in Bowdon to represent Deep Dene House.

Jeremy said he found the character tougher to play than any other in his distinguished career, *"Holmes is terribly difficult to play because he's so private and so much cleverer than anyone else. He's what all men want to be, what all women want to seduce."* (TV Times) *"He keeps me fit. Every time I think I get somewhere, he's a field ahead of me. Can't ever relax, can't pin him down."* He thought he was getting somewhere when he learned how he walked. *"That's largely the result of the shoes, the boots with the pointed toes that are pictured in the books. Then came the hands." "I tried to become him, to sort of find out how it would be if you were a minimalist, an isolationist, not much interest in anything except work. I mean, he should be like a stone, and I tick and twitch all over, I get so depressed when I'm watching myself. I think I'm being still. An eyebrow goes, a nostril goes and the mouth. The thing is; he doesn't."* (Sherlock Holmes Behind the Scenes interview ITV This Morning) "Brett still is a bit of a glamour boy which originally made him surprising casting as Holmes. But he has captured the fastidious theatricality of the master criminologist and given him a neurotic vulnerability that forever eclipses the memory of Basil Rathbone playing him straight. You care about his lonely Holmes like no other incarnation. And he makes you laugh frequently at his answers to everything, delivered with wonderfully dry timing. This is a Holmes with humour and unexpected heart." (Maureen Paton in The Daily Express) Jeremy told *The Calgary Herald* of a moment in a New York taxi; *"And the driver spoke to me out of the side of his mouth, 'When you stood on that burning log and walked across it with your cane and looked down, you looked like a cat.' So I said, 'Are you talking about...?' 'Yes, Mr Brett,' he said. 'I'm talking about* The Norwood Builder (an episode in the PBS series).' *That was a moment! It was terribly exciting that someone, a cab driver in New York has watched the show and picked a moment. I think that's thrilling."* (The Calgary Herald 5th November 1991)

58

***The Resident Patient* (Writer: Derek Marlowe, Director: David Carson fb 15th September 1985)** was another dramatic episode but with a criminal element in the mystery. The opening credits show "Sutton" (Blessington) in the middle of a terrifying nightmare with himself in a coffin surrounded by gold coins. More information is given with the arrival of Doctor Percy Trevelyan to Baker Street who is known to Watson as the author of a renowned monograph on "obscure nervous lesions." Although he was university trained he was grateful when a philanthropist, Mr Blessington, offered to set him up in a Mayfair establishment in exchange for a proportion of the doctor's income and a place in the house for himself as a *"resident patient."* In two years Trevelyan had made him a rich man and Blessington locked it away in a strong box in his own room. Inexplicably, a sudden fear of break-ins caused Mr Blessington to panic; he insisted that locks and bars should be installed and he remained in his rooms in "a state of mortal dread." Two men seeking the doctor's help for a case of catalepsy added to his concern and when they suddenly disappeared there was evidence that someone had invaded his sanctum at which Blessington demanded Doctor Trevelyan call on Sherlock Holmes to ask for his help. Holmes recognises there is a mystery at the heart of the case, especially as he is greeted at gunpoint by a terrified Blessington. However, he senses deep distrust and lack of honesty in this client, without which he refuses to help and leaves.

The detailed analysis of the different types of cigar and footprints in the hallway show he has recorded every detail from the moment he has entered the house. His grim face with which he helps to remove the body from its position is replaced by a sense of excitement at the investigation.   Michael Cox said, "Jeremy Brett always showed great enthusiasm for sequences in which Holmes investigated the scene of a crime. If there was a floor to throw himself on or a mantelpiece to climb, Jeremy would flare his nostrils in anticipation. He was very fond of the scrutiny of Blessington's room in this film, not because it presented a physical challenge but because it was carried out in absolute silence. He called it the Rififi sequence in honour of Jules Dassin's famous gangster movie in which a burglary lasting twenty five minutes is conducted without a sound. Our sequence lasts only two minutes... based on a short paragraph in the story, which is acted out in detail as Holmes collects fibres, dust and ash from different surfaces in the room. This enables him to describe the crime..." (A Study in Celluloid) "That seems to me so very Sherlock. It was also very brave because one of the rules of television is that you don't leave the soundtrack blank for long or you get people ringing up and saying, 'What's gone wrong?'" (Michael Cox in The Sherlock Holmes Detective Magazine) Holmes's monograph on different tobaccos and cigars allows him to see that there were three people in the room and to reach well-informed conclusions about what had taken place just a few hours before. He had even methodically measured the footprints on the stairs on his first visit to enable him to construct a picture of the men. But it is the clean clinical precision of his examination of the room where the man has died that lifts the whole episode into a new realm for detective television. Conan Doyle's account is not only brought to life by Jeremy's well-choreographed physical interpretation but it is also given an elevation to a new sphere of performance. There are no little smiles about the lips to indicate a diverted Holmes, just the bare minimum of detail; he even needs a prompt from Watson, as a reminder to share his thought processes with them.

The friendship between the two men is given further detail in the opening scene in the barber shop where Conan Doyle's humorous short story *How Watson Learned the Trick* of 1924 was included to demonstrate how Watson had learned Holmes's methods of deduction. The original details of the story were still under copyright but Derek Marlowe had created his own version as Watson comments on the way he had observed his friend grinding his teeth and drumming his fingers on the arm of the barber's chair which he supposes is an angry response to Mrs Hudson's spring cleaning of their rooms. He is told every single one of his deductions are incorrect as Holmes was struggling to remember the intricate fingering of Beethoven's violin concerto from the concert they had attended the evening before, but in "*Nevertheless*" he does concede that there was an element of truth in Watson's comment, much to his friend's great delight. The final scene where the choice of title for the narrative is in dispute where comedy is used again to change it from "The Brook Street Mystery" to Holmes's choice of "The Resident Patient".

Back in Baker Street, when Holmes goes in search of a newspaper cutting which will eventually provide evidence for the case, he sifts through all his papers and notebooks scattering paper in pure abandonment and leaving total chaos in his wake. So much mess is created, that Watson leaves the door to their room closed so that Mrs Hudson, who had just completed her spring cleaning, cannot see the results until they are safely away from the house. The villains are not apprehended but in the search amongst his papers Holmes discovers Blessington is one of a gang of murderous bank thieves involved in the Worthington Bank affair which enables him to provide the rest of the details. The picture accompanying the article shows Blessington was in reality Sutton and the worst of the gang who had turned Queen's Counsel and double-crossed his partners in crime prompting them to seek him out and avenge themselves by hanging him from a hook on the ceiling in the enactment of a trial and execution.

"The adventure of *The Resident Patient* is hardly an exhilarating one but scriptwriter Derek Marlowe's humour brightens, warms and livens up the episode. In the delightful opening scene at the barber's and in the final one, when Watson, at first doubtful, ends up appropriating enthusiastically the title Holmes has suggested, of course, but also when Mrs Hudson congratulating the Doctor on the progress of his model ship, he slips away like a guilty kid before she discovers the living room she just cleaned up has been turned into an appalling dumping ground. The upright, likeable and entertaining Baker Street trio act as an antidote against the criminals' loathsome wickedness." (arthur-conan-doyle.com)

"Much of the well-deserved praise this series has received is due to the truly inspired casting of Jeremy Brett as Holmes. There have been other fine interpretations of the role... The fact remains that Jeremy Brett is the definitive screen Holmes and his performances are unlikely ever to be surpassed. This is a brilliant and mercurial Holmes but he is also unstable and neurotic. Playing Holmes in this manner could easily have been disastrous but Brett is in complete control and he does not make the mistake of overly emphasising the great detective's darker side..." (cult-tv-lounge.blogspot.com)

The Red Headed League **(Writer: John Hawkesworth, Director: John Bruce fb: 22nd September 1985)** introduces the arch criminal Professor James Moriarty played with fitting menace by the superb Eric Porter who in the original stories appears only in *The Final Problem.* Michael Cox said he had never thought of anyone else for the part of the master criminal, the man chosen by Doyle to kill off Sherlock Holmes. *The Red-Headed League* is understandably one of the favourite episodes of many, and the story was rated as second in Conan Doyle's "twelve best" list of his short stories. The beginning of the episode features a graceful yet athletic leap over the settee by Jeremy's Holmes in his eagerness to prevent Watson leaving the room. He wants his biographer present at the interview with such an intriguing client. Jeremy said, *"The dashing about is rather me. I loved in* The Red-Headed League *when I was allowed to jump the sofa. My son rang me after that and said, 'Dad, you're obviously feeling better.'"*

The case itself centres on a farcical instance of a Red-Headed League with a bemused and angry red-headed man, Jabez Wilson, engaged to write out a fair copy of the *Encyclopaedia Britannica* in exchange for a respectable salary. The opening scene is full of interest and humour. What began as an elegant leap over the sofa becomes an expert analysis of Wilson's background, as Holmes gives a stunning display of his observation skills indicating that he has done manual labour, takes snuff, has visited China and has *"done a considerable amount of writing lately."* This is what we have come to expect of Holmes but the manner in which the red-headed man dismisses his explanation leaves Holmes quite offended, *"I begin to think that my reputation such as it is will suffer shipwreck if I am so candid,"* and Watson's translation of his Latin, *"omne ignotum pro magnifico"* into "everything becomes commonplace by explanation" is too vague to satisfy Holmes's exacting standards. The exchange of giggles and then howls of laughter between Holmes and Watson at the *"bizarre"* situation Jabez Wilson describes is deliciously ironic as the man feels he has been made to look a fool. However, Holmes is intrigued, *"I wouldn't miss this case for the world. It is most refreshingly unusual."* (ibid) *"It is so joyously comic; this mean pompous chap with ginger hair, the bizarre copying up the encyclopaedia and then the bank robbery, well it has all the elements of a Ben Travers farce. Conan Doyle could be a very comic writer." (Jeremy in Bending the Willow)* More humour is contained in the *"three pipe problem"* and the image is a faithful recreation of the Sidney Paget drawing of Holmes sitting in his chair with his knees pulled up to his chin for *"fifty minutes"* the duration of time needed to smoke three pipes and think through the implications of what he has heard. His dear friend Watson shows a sympathetic understanding and takes a snooze in the opposite chair whilst the great man ponders on the evidence presented so far.

Holmes is the genius of investigation, always making sense of the mysterious. He has picked up on the peculiarities of the man who had come as assistant in Wilson's pawnbroking business on half wages, then encouraged his employer to apply for the position offered by the strangely named League, itself a source of mystery as the organisation was willing to pay a generous amount of money for what seems to be trivial work. The description of the assistant, Spaulding, sounded familiar too, so that he was prepared to investigate the area surrounding Saxe-Coburg Square, to see what reasons lay behind the removal of Jabez Wilson from his shop. *"You see, Watson... it was perfectly obvious from the first that the only possible effect of this rather fantastic business of the advertisement of the League, and the copying of the Encyclopaedia must be to get this not over-bright pawnbroker out of the way for a number of hours every day. It was a curious way of managing it, but really it would be difficult to suggest a better."* (The Red-Headed League) Jeremy's Holmes has the supreme self-assurance and personal charisma to make us believe that these giant leaps of deduction are indeed his. He also has the intensity of gaze to camera to convince the audience of his superior powers. It is no surprise that Watson will write of his own amazement at his methods. "Here I had heard what he had heard, I had seen what he had seen, and yet from his words, it was evident that he saw clearly not only what had happened but what was about to happen, while to me the whole business was still confused and grotesque." (ibid)

The bringing together of the police agent Jones with the Bank Manager Merryweather to test the veracity of Holmes's theories is a tense situation and Watson is forced to defend his friend as the "only private consulting detective who is unique in the annals of crime" and thus worthy of listening to, and more importantly, of respect. Throughout these scenes in the bank vaults, Jeremy is grim-faced and intense as we watch him listening for signs of the audacious bank robbers. The large consignment of 60,000 gold napoleons recently borrowed from the Bank of France, means there is a much larger amount of bullion than is usual in the vault, confirming the idea that it was John Clay whom they were expecting and who eventually emerges through the cellar floor. Once more Holmes has outwitted the criminals and in so doing brought himself to the attention of Moriarty; the central power behind all that is evil in the city and the mastermind of the Red-Headed League. The inclusion of Moriarty was Granada's adaptation to the story as they wished to give him greater substance and danger in preparation for the next story, *The Final Problem*.

Another character development in this episode is the music loving nature of Holmes. Whilst they are waiting for the appointed hour to take up their places in the Bank vault, there was still time to attend a concert provided by the celebrated violinist Sarasate at St James's Hall and Watson marvels at the sight of Holmes "wrapped in the most perfect happiness" with a gentle smile on his face as he revels in the sound. Such contentment suggests that an evil time might be coming upon those his companion had set himself against. Holmes's explanation at the conclusion of the case speaks for his ability to think through every step of the evidence with the reiteration of his watchword, *"I never guess,"* and his attempts to escape from *"the commonplaces of existence"*. Watson acknowledges his contribution: "You are a benefactor of the race". To which Holmes answers in a telling quote from Gustave Flaubert, *"L'homme c'est rien - l'oeuvre c'est tout,"* meaning: "The man is nothing–the work is everything".

Baker Street File – The Red-Headed League

96 - Had a dual nature: swung from extreme languor to devouring energy

112 - Curls up in chair with his knees drawn up to his hawk-like nose. His eyes closed and with his black clay pipe thrust out like some strange bird (while pondering a problem)

The Final Problem was an attempt by Sir Arthur Conan Doyle to kill off Sherlock Holmes. He was finding the demands of the public too great, especially when he wanted to spend more time with his greater interest, writing historical novels like Sir Walter Scott, a great influence on Doyle. He felt this was his chance at immortality. Writing to his mother about the last Sherlock Holmes story he intended to produce (the twelfth), Conan Doyle said: "I think of slaying Holmes... and winding him up for good and for all." In spite of her protests, he did so two years later when his wife Louisa was diagnosed with tuberculosis and he felt the need to spend more time with her. Fandom which had previously only been seen in sports had been created overnight for the death of Sherlock Holmes. The fans wore black crepe and accosted Doyle's carriage in London. They wrote thousands of letters daily to both *The Strand* and to Doyle, they formed Keep Holmes Alive Clubs (the precursors of today's Sherlock Holmes Societies) and they immediately cancelled 20,000 subscriptions to *The Strand Magazine*. It almost folded under the onslaught. "You brute" was the beginning of remonstrance which one lady sent me." (Doyle) "Waiting from month to month for the next adventure of Sherlock Holmes was agony!" exclaimed the poet laureate John Masefield. Nine years later when *The Hound of the Baskervilles* was published as an early Holmes story, the subscriptions immediately returned to *The Strand*. The next year, in 1903, Doyle responded to an offer from an American publisher that he couldn't refuse, of $5,000 for a new Sherlock Holmes story that would bring him back (he wrote 32 more stories) and queues of people stood outside *The Strand* Office to purchase their first copy of his return, to avoid disappointment in the shops.

John Hawkesworth has created an emotional and memorable episode in the Granada version of **The Final Problem (Writer: John Hawkesworth, Director: Alan Grint fb: 29th September 1985)** so that many viewers have said they need to watch *The Empty House* immediately afterwards in order to feel less depressed at the loss of Holmes. "I suspect Conan Doyle knew it would take no ordinary man to kill off Sherlock Holmes. And even though he created a super-criminal to carry out what he hoped would be the execution, he had not bargained for the incredible reaction of the British public." (Eric Porter in Scarlet Street) The episode was filmed on location in Switzerland, for the very first time at the Reichenbach Falls, "a fearful place" tumbling down to "a tremendous abyss", so that the full horror of the situation was given reality. The six takes necessary to record the footage of the one to one struggle between Holmes and Moriarty brought real danger to both Eric and Jeremy due to the specially built slippery ledge above the mist and spray of the 400 foot fall of tumbling water. This spectacular force consisted of three waterfalls with several thundering cascades plunging into a pool of great depth and magnitude. The real heroes of the episode were the two stunt men Alf Joint and Marc Boyle attached to a steel cable and harnesses to ensure they returned alive from the boiling "immense chasm." They were each paid around £2,000 but as they pointed out, if the wire snapped or the platform collapsed there would have been no chance of survival. *"The event quite unnerved me. Eric and I had to film our part of the struggle about eight feet from the edge of the falls – and that was bad enough because every time I looked down I felt quite sick. How those two men went over the edge, I'll never know. You should have seen their bruises the next day. It took six takes to get the fight with Moriarty on the edge of the precipice right... I remember thinking as we slithered around in the mud and grass soaked to the skin that, if we're not careful, we might actually fall over the edge and Conan Doyle would have got his wish after all. There really would have been no return for Sherlock Holmes."* (Jeremy in Television Sherlock Holmes) Jeremy couldn't bear to watch them fall but when the stuntmen returned safely he immediately opened the bottle of champagne he had brought with him to celebrate their courage.

The drama opened with harrowing scenes of Holmes in a series of life-threatening incidents. He had been pursued and almost killed by a runaway carriage, and then providentially escaped a lethal fall of masonry and finally succeeded in fighting off an attack from two determined and ruthless ruffians. His arrival at Baker Street was by a second floor backroom window in personal disarray and covered in dust, tired and irritable. He told Watson of the challenging situations he had experienced at the hands of Moriarty's men and the deadly attacks he still feared from air guns. His comment that he had *"been using myself too much of late"* as he *"was pressed"* was a typical Holmes understatement but his dishevelled appearance told its own tale. The scenes of conflict were filmed at Chethams School of Music in Manchester.

The open hostilities with Moriarty would begin in Paris with the theft of the Mona Lisa from the Louvre, which would become an added spur to Moriarty's push for revenge for the loss of his art copying scam. These scenes were based on the real theft of 1912 when the picture was missing from the Louvre walls for two years and which John Hawkesworth had added to the episode to develop the role of Moriarty for Eric Porter. Jeremy had fought a prolonged battle to maintain the Conan Doyle original story intact and had failed. "Jeremy Brett hated it. The read-through of this episode was not a happy one. Jeremy adopted his fundamentalist attitude to Conan Doyle's work; John was an evil revisionist, I was the devil's advocate. David Burke and Eric Porter wisely kept their own counsel. I tried to explain why it was necessary to add to the original but Jeremy would have none of it. Lunch on the first day of rehearsal was usually convivial but on this occasion I think we all went our separate ways." (Michael Cox in A Study in Celluloid)

The declaration of open warfare between Holmes and Moriarty took place in a confrontation in Baker Street where they openly shared a mutual enmity. Jeremy's Holmes was armed and ready with an unblinking stare of coiled intensity whilst Moriarty's menacing voice and reptilian appearance promised a monumental tussle. Both antagonists reflected what was at stake in their palpable hatred of the other. Moriarty's list of complaints was a long one, headed by the "affair of the French gold" and *The Red-Headed League,* which Holmes judged *"a very ingenious and well-contrived idea".* But the list continued, "You crossed my path on the 4th January. By the middle of February I was seriously inconvenienced by you and at the end of March, I was absolutely hampered in my plans; and now, with this last business in France, you have placed me in such a position by your continual persecution that I am in positive danger of losing my liberty. The situation is becoming an impossible one." (The Final Problem) As Holmes refused to "drop it" and step out of Moriarty's way, a fight to the finish was inevitable. "The verbal exchange between Brett and Porter in Baker Street has EVERYTHING – great dialogue, fantastic diction, beautiful timing, fantastic silences and glances. Any aspiring actor should watch this. It is an acting masterclass." (Amazon.co.uk) In the description of his enemy to Watson, Holmes named Moriarty the Napoleon of Crime and the organiser of half of all the evil in the city, so a holiday in Switzerland appears to be a suitable escape. However, the intricate instructions for the safe arrival at the railway station and the disguise of an Italian priest for Holmes to avoid identification are still insufficient to cover their getaway. Moriarty's hiring of a special train to follow them showed the dogged determination and the cunning intellect of this very dangerous enemy.

Michael Cox records how a peaceful Victorian champagne picnic by the glacier was filmed, although it ended up on the cutting room floor due to time constraints. Only a couple of pictures survive, one with Jeremy arms outstretched in "acknowledgement of the camera" reproduced in *A Study in Celluloid*. The arrival at the Englischer Hof, kept by Peter Steiler the Elder, introduced the climax of the story as the inevitable meeting between the two adversaries, clearly managed by Moriarty, with the merest of reasons to split the two friends, but successfully achieved. The letter of farewell from Holmes and the Last Will and Testament are moving enough, especially when it was anticipated. Only Watson was unaware of the true situation and his final words contain all the feelings of loss as he delivers his eulogy for his friend, the man with whom he has shared so much, and "Whom I shall ever regard as the best and the wisest man whom I have ever known." Jeremy explained, *"Moriarty represents the final element of evil. Holmes is to be erased... you see Holmes facing death... Holmes knows that Moriarty's network will get him. So very sweetly he says, 'Listen, Watson, I'm going to leave the country because I don't want to endanger you.' But then he turns around and says, 'Do you want to come with me?' So the answer is, yes, he's scared. And then he uses the Reichenbach Falls as one of the greatest coups of all times."* (Jeremy Brett: The Real Sherlock Holmes by Rosemary Herbert)

There was a gathering feeling of confidence and even a bravura atmosphere in the studios as Granada had received a wealth of positive feedback from both the critics and the general public, all of which praised the production and the interpretation. Unsurprisingly, Jeremy's Holmes was the focus of much of this attention. By this stage of production, his understanding and commitment to Holmes was so thorough that Eric Porter told *Scarlet Street*, "I found acting with Jeremy Brett a splendid challenge, too, for he was so deeply involved with Holmes that he understood every nerve and fibre of the man. I like to think I gave a good account of Moriarty – though like Jeremy I could hardly dare to watch the two stunt men going over the cliffs."

Whilst in Switzerland the Granada team filmed some scenes for *The Return* in *The Empty House*. Michael Cox issued a press statement, "Just as Conan Doyle was forced by public pressure to bring back Holmes after his disappearance at Reichenbach, so we have decided to go ahead and make seven more stories for the viewers." The critics were pleased, "Jeremy Brett's Holmes has been a striking portrait of an actor: the undulating velvet of the voice, the finger laid like an exclamation mark against the lips and the broad-brimmed hat, turned up a little to one side as though from leaning too long against the waiting room at Crewe." (Every Holmes should have one) Jeremy had accepted the need to wear the iconic deerstalker in this episode, *"I've always thought of the deerstalker as a kind of schoolboy cap that can be scrunched up and put in your pocket... I always wanted to avoid the clichés when playing Holmes and I didn't like the image... I did do the meerschaum pipe for a brief moment in* The Final Problem *because he could have bought it out in Switzerland."* (Jeremy in Scarlet Street) And David's performance had been superb as always. "David Burke's Watson has been most endearing throughout." Michael Cox had succeeded in his aim to create a viable companion for Holmes. "It is unfair to Watson to make him a buffoon and to Holmes who wouldn't have shared an apartment and a friendship with a man who was an idiot. So I decided to do justice to Dr Watson, because if you diminish him, you also diminish Holmes. Without Holmes, Watson's life would be very dull; without Watson, Holmes's life would be disastrous." (The new tenant at 221b Baker Street)

Jeremy and Joan

"We had a once-in-a-lifetime love. She was an incredible person, the best wife a man could have. This was the kind of love where I would start a sentence and she would finish it. Sometimes you can see behind somebody's eyes and feel as if you have known them all your life. That's how it was." (Jeremy to Shaun Usher) *"We were born on the same day. If ever I picked up the phone to ring her, it would be engaged – it would be her trying to ring me. I can't ever imagine having that closeness again."* He says his self-confidence died when he lost his *"Joanie,"* a perfect wife. She had seen him on stage in the Noel Coward play *Design for Living* in New York and decided she would like to marry him. Unsurprisingly, Jeremy points out his dependence on the lady to choose him, rather than the other way round: *"I think she will pick me, just as Joan did, although I'll never know – I'll think I've done it... Women are much cleverer than men; they have this brilliant intellect as well as intuition. They are wiser than men and much shrewder. They can organise a man and make him feel terrific. At least that was true of my wife."* Jeremy and Joan met early in 1975 when PBS Television was showing *The Rivals,* and it was an instant attraction. He was interviewed for the introductory programme on the plays of Sheridan, *"I guess she was keen at organising it because I wasn't the only star in* The Rivals*; there were several others and I was the one that was picked; and we met on camera and she wanted four minutes, and we talked for two and a half hours... and when we got married in 1976* (22nd November) *our best man gave us the bits that were cut out as a wedding present. Luckily we saw them in the dark because we both went bright pink."*

Joan, a former actress, was part Cherokee, four years older than Jeremy and, although she was proud of her candour, refused to admit her age. She had an enormous capacity for work, up to seventy hours a week, and her career was very important to her, especially as she had been the artistic director behind *Masterpiece Theatre* since 1973 and the creator of *Mystery!* the home of British Mysteries for Boston PBS station WGBH. "She was *Masterpiece Theatre,* she chose the dishes with ruthless care and taste. She supervised their service. I was simply the headwaiter." (LA Times 9th July 1985)

Joan was in love with this "debonair, exuberant Englishman, Jeremy Brett about whom she gushed but whom she would not publicly name as her spouse." They both loved dancing and often talked into the early hours of the morning, "she loved to flirt, gloried in marriage and motherhood, yet liked to claim that she placed her career first." They were both workaholics so that when the work was offered, he was often separated from her. In an interview with *Woman and Home* he told the magazine he was pretty demanding of his personal relationships and needed tolerance from a partner. *"I'm not a comfortable person to live with. I tend not to do things by halves. I burst into song at the drop of a hat, or go out disco dancing all night and sometimes I get up at 4 a.m. When I work hard, I'm certifiable."* (Woman and Home 1984)

Whilst making *The Adventures of Sherlock Holmes,* Jeremy and his wife and two step-children borrowed the top flat of a friend's home in Mayfair, although during the week he was living in the Midland Hotel close to the studio in Manchester. "But for now, being so happy makes up for no permanent address. The Bretts' LA house is up for sale. There's a distinct 'devil may care' look in Jeremy's eye and a glowing confidence for the future." (ibid) The same year they purchased the penthouse flat of 47, Clapham Common Northside, the distinctive gatehouse in the French Renaissance style. Joan loved the history with its association to Edvard Grieg, and its placement overlooking Clapham Common which lifted Jeremy's heart too. Unfortunately, they were not to live in it as she became ill before they could move in. The packing cases remained unopened until he finally returned home at the end of July 1985 after her death. He spoke about his children with pride and considered Joan's children his own. *"I have three children, David by my first marriage and two stepchildren, Caleb and Rebekah by my second. They are all absolutely magnificent. David's a painter. Caleb's a lawyer and Rebekah is a brilliant housewife and also a beauty and very intuitive. Only the other Sunday we had a family party, for the older ones."* (ibid)

With a break in filming for the *Sherlock Holmes* series at the Granada Studios, Jeremy flew out to America to be with Joan who had been diagnosed with cancer of the pancreas. He had been told the devastating news whilst filming *The Final Problem* in Switzerland. His explanation to the media was that, *"I wanted a holiday... and it was also to be near my wife... I knew at the end of* The Final Problem *in '84 that she had cancer, and the lights really went out in my life... I didn't want to do it anymore." "I felt so frustrated that I couldn't be with Joan, although actually she didn't really want me around while she was having chemotherapy. She said, 'You're not up to this.' I walked into the treatment room and saw the equipment pointing up at her. I just fell apart. But what really threw me was a two-year-old girl who'd lost all her hair because of the chemotherapy. Seeing Joan and that child together was just too much for me. And I fainted. I was such a dead loss. Joan said, 'You mustn't do any more of this, it doesn't do you any good.' I apologised, and in fact I did go again and it was better. It's taken so much time and energy to come through the grief of losing Joan. After she'd gone, I went into a series of bad states of mind. I kept thinking, Damn it! Why bother?"* (At last I'm free from the shadow of Holmes by Jo Weedon)

Jeremy took the part in *Aren't We All?* on Broadway so that he could be near her as she continued with her treatment. They celebrated the success of the play together on Joan's last good day before her death in one of their favourite activities, dancing: "*The producers had taken the Rainbow Room on opening night. It was April, and the room was full of peach blossoms. Joan looked absolutely radiant, wearing silver and scarlet, and a glorious wig, a facsimile of her hair. And, we danced as the notices flooded by.*" When Joan died Jeremy opened his heart to the press: "*I lost her on July 4th 1985. And I went back to England when the play finished, it didn't finish until the 23rd – I don't know how I did those performances... I staggered on and finished the play, but the lights were out.*" He told *The Star*, "*I still get very angry about Joan dying. Then I get into self-pity, but I know that's not good. I suppose I always thought a miracle would happen and that she would recover. But it was not to be...*" (The Sorrow of Sherlock by Carole Malone The Star 9th January 1986) "*Joan gave me the most enormous confidence – she loved me for being exactly the way I am. The last thing she said to me was, 'Are you going to be all right?' Under the circumstances, that was a pretty stunning question. She was 54 and she had such wonderful things ahead of her.*" (Television Sherlock Holmes)

Photograph by Courtesy of N.S. Johnson

The Return of Sherlock Holmes

Michael Cox called *The Return of Sherlock Holmes*, "The best of times and the worst of times." The confidence which comes with the knowledge that things are good and coming together to create excellence was positively inspiring. At the same time the situation with the star, Jeremy's Holmes was on a knife edge. He had heard that his beloved wife Joan was ill whilst filming the conclusion of *The Adventures*. The diagnosis of cancer was devastating and as many do in these circumstances, they hoped that Joan would survive until the very last minute. *"Well, it was such a shock. She died in '85 on July the Fourth... and I was absolutely lost. And I couldn't see the point really in anything, least of all S.H."* When his commitment on Broadway was over, he returned to Clapham Common to the home he had bought with Joan where his possessions were stored in unopened packing cases.

In September, at the Midland Hotel in Manchester where he lived whilst filming the Granada series, *"I became a recluse. I began to have meals in my room and stare at the hotel walls... when you play Holmes you leave out love and affection. He's a very dark person to play and one of the most uncomfortable parts to wear on a daily basis. Several actors before me in the role have had nervous breakdowns. In television you must live inside your character. Holmes is a very uncomfortable person to live in..." "He became the dark side of the moon because he is moody and solitary where I am gregarious. Holmes is so still and I'm like Jiminy Cricket. I had to wash the part out of me as well as the grease out of my hair." "When Joanie died, all the lights went out in my life. You see, she was my confidence. I didn't want to play Holmes any more. There was no point. But I was committed contractually and started filming two months later, in September. I played the role differently in the second series, but it quite seemed to suit the part."* (Taken from Happy Home from Holmes; The More Elementary Mr Jeremy Brett; A new tenant at 221b Baker Street)

The old bookseller

Footage for *The Empty House* **(Dramatised by John Hawkesworth: Directed by Howard Baker fb: 9th July 1986)** had been recorded in Meiringen Switzerland, exactly where Conan Doyle set the dreadful battle between Holmes and Professor Moriarty. The team's anticipation of the return meant that they were well-prepared. However, the loss of David Burke as Dr Watson meant that further filming was needed to provide a complete story, and as the funding for a return to Switzerland was no longer available, the Welsh mountains became the substitute setting. David had responded to an offer from the *RSC* to appear with his wife Anna Calder-Marshall, who with a five year old son named Tom to consider, was leaving the Granada production. "We were filming virtually solidly for eighteen months in Manchester and I never saw my home and family. I had the chance to join the *Royal Shakespeare Company* at Stratford-on-Avon to appear with Anna, so I took it. It was marvellous fun to work with her and I had the added bonus of playing a real bastard in Maxim Gorky's *The Philistines* – something completely different from Watson." (The Television Sherlock Holmes) Michael recognised the impact this would have. "It was a blow. Jeremy had found aspects of Holmes which no other actor had presented and gradually measured up to his illustrious predecessors. David, on the other hand had completely altered the public perception of Watson. He had given us the Watson that Conan Doyle created and now we had to replace him." Anna was responsible for the suggestion of Edward Hardwicke as David's replacement, as she and Edward had been working together on the Shakespeare play *Titus Andronicus* for radio and she recognised his talents. When Jeremy and Edward were interviewed by Richard Madeley and Judy Finnegan on *This Morning* a few years later, Jeremy was asked if he had been concerned about the change of personality in his co-star and he replied, *"Yes. Truthfully! But then this miracle occurred. Edward is a very gentle person, and very sensitive, and tried very hard not to upset the boat in any way, and succeeded. What could have been a disaster for the series turned into a bonus... David and I had been together for about a year and a half and had built up a great rapport."* He added that he had lost *"my bestest friend"* too.

Edward commented, "One's main concern is not to rock the boat because, as I've discovered, it's such a marvellous atmosphere which is very largely due to Jeremy and all the people working on it. But it inevitably varies a bit because we're different. All actors are limited to some extent by who they are and what they are and how they look." Edward was also given a couple of episodes to create his own version of Dr John Watson before *The Empty House* was filmed. Yet, from the very beginning with *The Abbey Grange,* he proved he would be a pair of perceptive and very capable hands. And then *The Musgrave Ritual* would delight the viewers with a relationship tinged with comedy between these two gentlemen and through twenty-seven films and one delightful play.

"It is now three long years since my dear friend plunged to his death, there deep down under the swirling water, the infamous Professor Moriarty and the foremost champion of law of his generation will lie together for all time. Even now, there is hardly a corner of London that does not remind me of my old friend... the loss of one I shall ever regard as the best and wisest men I have ever known." (Granada's The Empty House) Watson would be the focus of the first fifteen minutes of *The Empty House* and for the first time in the series we see him without Holmes as a local doctor, a police surgeon and medical scientist, making intelligent deductions at a crime scene. Edward accomplished the transition seamlessly and with his impeccable focus on Watson's relationship with Holmes he would succeed in satisfying even the most dedicated audience. As his friend returns, Watson is tested significantly in both the depth of his friendship and in his response to the drama that unfolds before his eyes. However, his grief is soon to be replaced by excitement and the anticipation of new adventures.

The revelation of the living Holmes and the shock of the unmasking was melodramatic notably for Watson's fainting, "the first and last time in my life". And the detective's comment accompanied by his loving touch, "*A thousand apologies, my dear Watson. I had no idea that you would be so affected.*" The hunched up figure of the old bookseller is a masterpiece and Jeremy remained unrecognisable and unnoticed as he crept into the back of the courtroom for the inquest on Adair's death and even sat incognito on the steps as Watson walked down them before making his appearance in the Doctor's consulting room. As he removed the disguise he succeeded in translating Doyle's words, "*It is no joke when a tall man has to take a foot off his stature for several hours on end,*" by elegantly stretching out of his tall frame in front of the window.

The footage filmed at Meiringen of a distressed Watson, of David shouting "*Holmes,*" finding the alpenstock and note, with Holmes watching the "*sympathetic and inefficient*" investigation of his death from a safe concealed ledge would represent a significant display of emotion that lay within the heart of the detective. The moment when he was trying not to call out to his friend emphasised the strength of the bond between them. Jeremy told David Stuart Davies that although the moment was unscripted this was a deliberate choice to show that Holmes's deep affection for Watson went beyond "*his practical mind*" and almost got the better of him. "There is a favourite moment for me when Holmes is tempted to shout to his friend but stifles the impulse and makes his escape into three years of oblivion." (Michael Cox)

Watson would be amazed yet delighted to hear how Holmes had defeated Moriarty in their battle over the spray of the Falls with the rare Japanese style of wrestling, baritsu. How he spent the following three years of oblivion revealed more about the man as he indulged his love of exploration. He travelled undercover as the "*remarkable Norwegian named Sigerson*" through Florence to Tibet where he visited Lhasa and the religious leader the Dalai Lama. He travelled on to Persia and Khartoum to meet with the Khalifa, and latterly, he had been pursuing research into the coal tar derivatives, another of his interests. Jeremy presented Holmes's ever changing moods under the surface as he moved from the troubled memories of the struggle with Moriarty, through his escape from the most dangerous of terrains to pride in his exploits, achievements and challenges in far off exotic places with new experiences. Three long years had been explained in just a few sentences but his command of the past and of what is to come has been established with a new aura of confidence and a new serenity.

Holmes had miraculously escaped with his life but was still very much at risk as Moriarty's deputy had been there to witness that escape. A touching reunion with Mrs Hudson is reflected in the mirror in one of the director Howard Baker's signature moments and the picture of the Reichenbach Falls above the mantelpiece, now shrouded in black drapes to commemorate the tragic death of Sherlock Holmes, reminds us of what had been achieved in his Herculean escape from certain death in "*that awful chasm*". Colonel Sebastian Moran is considered to be Moriarty's deputy and the sniper who had dogged Holmes's footsteps through Switzerland. It is he who had used the powerful air-gun which could fire a soft-nosed revolver bullet of sufficient calibre to kill the Honourable Ronald Adair, a fact that had remained undiscovered, and now Holmes himself was in his sights, informed by the sentinel, watching and waiting under the lamp post.

The entrapment of the man Holmes had waited three years to catch with the specially designed wax model in the window of the Baker Street rooms and the action that follows restores the relationship between Holmes and Watson. The *"old shikari"* with an impeccable military record had expected to take on the mantle of the evil Moriarty, but even he was insufficiently equipped to defeat Jeremy's heroic Holmes. With the *"second most dangerous man"* behind bars, the return of the great detective to Baker Street offered a sense of satisfaction that London was finally safe from the evil deeds of the Moriarty gang. Humour is in evidence too in the midst of the drama as Mrs Hudson is pictured crouched behind the wax figure of Holmes, smilingly changing its position every fifteen minutes and when Holmes and Watson returned safely, it was she who placed the bullet on Holmes's palm; thus providing the proof that would convict Colonel Moran of Adair's murder. The celebratory champagne was a fitting end to the drama. Conan Doyle had successfully resurrected his hero and the public were thrilled.

The twentieth century public were also ready to celebrate. *"The Return of Sherlock Holmes* – For this new series of seven Jeremy Brett again plays Holmes – and it's hard to imagine a better one... Brett has also played Dr Watson on stage. *'They're two halves of the same person'* he said." (Sherlock arises from a fall. The Mail 6th July 1986) "Granada Television, the makers of *The Return of Sherlock Holmes* are, I think, entitled to expect that the television audience that will tonight welcome back the great sleuth after his supposed death at the Reichenbach Falls in last year's episode, will be as glad to do so as were those readers of the Holmes stories in *Strand* magazine who were told in 1903 that the detective managed to survive his Falls fall in 1892 and that he would, in fact be returning in *The Empty House*. The simple truth is that Granada's adaptations of Conan Doyle have been the best to date. The more I see of Jeremy Brett's Holmes, the less fondly I remember Basil Rathbone. The more I see of Granada's successive Doctor Watsons (originally David Burke and now Edward Hardwicke), the more ludicrous Nigel Bruce's Hollywood Watson becomes in the memory..." (The Times 9th July 1986) "Cocksure exuberance underlines all the first seven instalments following *The Adventures of Sherlock Holmes* (1984-5), whereas those episodes were manufactured in the dark, without praise or plaudits, the next set would be produced by a team assured of their own brilliance. And it shows..." (Sherlock Holmes on Screen) "Jeremy was wonderful to work with, such a large talent, the consummate Holmes for me." (Patrick Allen in Scarlet Street 1996)

Baker Street File – The Empty House

90 – Work is the best antidote to sorrow, my dear Watson

103 – I am not a fanciful man

120 – Again in the utter silence I heard that thin, sibilant note which spoke of intense, suppressed excitement

121 – Moran calls Holmes, "You clever, clever fiend!" and "You cunning, cunning fiend!"

Chatsworth House Derbyshire

The Priory School (Dramatised by T.R.Bowen: Directed by John Madden fb: 16th July 1986) is a favourite episode of many. The location of Haddon Hall for the Priory School and the imposing Chatsworth House as the seat of the sixth Duke of Holdernesse is in itself an attractive and commanding backdrop for the story of a missing pupil from his prestigious preparatory school. The opening scenes are workmanlike and driven by the perception and commanding presence of Holmes, here imperturbable and cold. The client on this occasion may not be a King but he is a Duke, who had been a cabinet minister, with money, power and influence.

With the exception of the concluding scene, the episode remains faithful to the Doyle original and opens in Baker Street with the humorous moment of a card placed in the sleeping Holmes's pocket by Watson with the simultaneous, very dramatic arrival of a man, "so large, so pompous, and so dignified that he was the very embodiment of self-possession and solidity." (The Adventure of The Priory School) Dr. Thorneycroft Huxtable M.A. Ph.D., who promptly faints on the hearthrug and then, on his recovery, urges them to return with him to the Priory School where he is principal, to investigate the abduction of one of its most important students, Lord Saltire. The unhappy childhood of the only son of the Duke of Holdernesse may explain the nine year old boy's disappearance and Holmes is pressed into finding him. A reward of six thousand pounds for discovering both the boy and the person responsible for his disappearance is part of the attraction of the case which will become a prestige one for Holmes. His query about a ransom demand is revealing as there has been none and the suspicion of the part played by the German master will provide sufficient spur to accompany Huxtable to Derbyshire to begin his investigation. Holmes challenges the Duke as no one else will, as he broaches the difficult question regarding the real reasons for the disappearance of his son.

As Holmes flings himself into the case with characteristic eagerness he is soon able to trace the events by which the German master followed the young Lord Saltire from the school and onto the moor. Bicycle tyres and horses' hooves are the means by which the mystery is solved; one bicycle for two escaping people is insufficient and horses with new shoes will be significant. Out on the moor as they search for tracks, humour is brought into the relationship in the mention of Watson's hunger, as it is something Holmes hardly ever experiences. Deep in thought, he ignores his friend asking about the possibility of a hostelry even when pressed, but suddenly exclaims as if it is his own suggestion, "*Lunch, my dear fellow, you must be starving!*" Food is mentioned on several occasions in the series and developed by Jeremy and Edward to explore another aspect of the friendship between them. "*They are a great essay in male friendship, which has gone now. Men's friendship has been debased. One of the lovely things about Holmes and Watson is that they do have this great platonic relationship.*" About that "disgusting" lunch, "it was a nice comic moment that we shared." (Edward Hardwicke)

The hiring of two horses first to visit the Hall and then to follow the trail left by the runaways allowed Jeremy to show his skills as an accomplished horseman and to enjoy his favourite pastime. There is one moment when Jeremy's leap from his horse could have resulted in a poor landing but he gracefully avoided becoming entangled in the reins. This skill also enabled Holmes to expertly examine the hired horses with the discovery of, "*old shoes, new nails*", which remains unexplained until the Duke mentions the fact that they were unable to winter cattle outdoors in the district when the significance of the cattle tracks brings enlightenment. "*I have been as blind as a beetle!*" says Holmes. What they find is the body of the dead German master Herr Heidegger who was bludgeoned to death and left for the vultures. Confessions reveal that Wilder is the Duke's son from a previous relationship with the reluctant admission that he has been instrumental in his father's broken marriage and this will represent a crucial aspect of the case.

The music of Patrick Gowers and the choristers of Westminster Abbey under Choirmaster Simon Preston are particularly effective in this episode, especially the refrain *Libera me* which becomes a lament for the missing child. "One of my favourite films was *The Priory School* directed by John Madden... the final sequence filmed in a cavern was very dramatic and I thought improved on the original story. Jeremy was wonderful. It was a bit like playing tennis with a great tennis player. If you manage to stick the racket in the right place he is going to hit it hard enough at you for the ball to just go back." (Edward Hardwicke in Elementary My Dear Watson for ITV) "*The Priory School*, this week's ration of Holmes and Watson, is even better than Conan Doyle's original which has an uncharacteristically lame ending. The adapters, John Hawkesworth and T.E. Bowen have risked being lynched by purists by setting the finale in a cavern, with the villain cornered in classic fashion, in all other respects, though this is Conan Doyle's scrupulously respected tale... Although it has become a commonplace to praise Jeremy Brett's and Edward Hardwicke's definitive Holmes and Watson, potential first-time viewers still ought to have the right to be told what a treat is in store for them tonight." (Choice by Peter Davelle in The Times 16th July 1986). "*Another thing I have found about doing this series has been the people working on it with me. It is very seldom that you get an entire studio of people that have actually read the script before they come to the first shoot. That does help... We need brilliant artistry, great lighting, and pure sound to get the maximum effect.*" (The Television Sherlock Holmes)

***The Second Stain* (Dramatised by John Hawkesworth: Directed by John Bruce fb: 23rd July 1986)** was the third film in the sequence designed to help Edward settle into his role of Watson before his appearance in *The Empty House,* and this is notable for his visit to see Holmes in his retirement, beekeeping in Kent, to request permission to publish the story. These scenes complete with the beekeeper's costume and beehives, ended up on the cutting room floor, probably because of editing and timing issues with the programme. However, some photographs still exist of the missing scenes.

The filming was done around Whitehall and Westminster and although 10, Downing Street was off-limits, the location of the seat of Government is totally authentic. Godolphin Street was also located and used for the Eduardo Lucas scenes. "I can remember at one point we got into a street and Jeremy Brett and I were sitting in a Hansom cab... in which there's a window behind us. The camera was there, and... I can see the yellow lines in the road... And immediately the props department came out with a roll of tape... and you just thought that's fantastic, somebody's actually sat down and thought there may be yellow lines on the road." (Edward Hardwicke in Theatre Archive)

The "*bookends*" introduce the case of a missing document with the arrival of two very distinguished personages in their private capacity at 8.30 in the morning, which requires a rapid clear-up of the breakfast things in the Baker Street rooms. Lord Bellinger, the "illustrious" Prime Minister and his Secretary for European Affairs, Rt. Hon. Trelawney Hope, arrive with a most pressing request for help in finding, "a letter from a foreign potentate and one of immense importance," which had disappeared from his locked government dispatch box. There is no evidence of security issues at home or personal carelessness to indicate how it might have disappeared and only the Cabinet knew of the letter's existence. Both men stress that they are sharing a state secret and that any investigations must be carried out with strict confidentiality as the discovery and publication of the letter could bring a European catastrophe – and war. Holmes is reluctant to take the case without full confidence in him and his methods: his steely smile and dismissal will challenge the men of power to fully confide in him or find someone else.

Their departure is immediately followed by another arrival; of Lady Hilda Trelawney Hope enquiring about her husband. Holmes appears intrigued by her, especially as her coming has no purpose other than obtaining information, which he is unable to give her due to his vow of professional secrecy. He is forced to answer, *"Madam, what you ask me is really impossible."* Holmes scrutinises his clients for clues and motives and he has noted her demeanour, her *"suppressed excitement, her restlessness, her tenacity"* and wonders what her true motive was. This is one of those moments when Holmes shows some interest in a woman and although he tells Watson that *"the fair sex"* is his department, followed by a tirade against women's inscrutability, *"their most trivial action may mean volumes,"* one can't help feeling he is protesting a trifle too much. In fact, Jeremy felt this was the case when he said as much to an interviewer, *"Holmes appears to be this rather cold and distant figure who holds the rest of humanity at arm's length. But deep down I believe – much deeper down – he is a man of tremendous sensitivity and feeling."* (The Bryan Times 8th September 1988)

The three names Holmes suggests as the only possible receivers capable of playing such a bold game, with sufficient money to purchase the stolen document are Oberstein, La Rothiere and Eduardo Lucas. Just as Holmes is leaving Baker Street to investigate their whereabouts he is stopped in his tracks by the news of the murder of one of them and thereafter he follows the connection. The stand-out scene in this episode takes place at the home of Eduardo Lucas of Godolphin Street, one of the eighteenth century houses near Westminster Abbey. Inspector Lestrade is hopeful that Holmes might help to explain the worrying detail of a second stain on the floor of the living room which did not match the one on the bloodstained carpet but neither he nor Holmes is prepared to share what they know, especially as the law is as dangerous to Holmes's investigation as the criminals. The investigation of the scene whilst the constable and Lestrade are purposefully distracted outside is full of humour and tension, as with furious energy Jeremy throws himself onto the floor "clawing at each of the squares of wood," pulling himself along as he seeks some hiding place for the missing document with Edward anxiously looking on, whilst maintaining a watchful eye on the Inspector and his constable. Jeremy was once more copying the Sidney Paget drawings from *The Strand Magazine* as he examined every inch of the wood blocked floor until he finally lifted one piece with a snort, "a bitter snarl of anger and disappointment as it was empty". (The Adventure of the Second Stain)   Jeremy explained, *"And it is fascinating when he takes to the ground – you can read about this and not think it funny at all. But, when you actually do it, actually see him swoop down and hoover the carpet with his nose, searching for a clue, it is hysterical. The speed of the man is my pathetic attempt to show his mental agility."* (Jeremy in Holmes Rule - Video Today)   "The whole mechanism of the rotated rug – Lestrade's finest hour – is beautifully handled and Holmes's feverish examination of the wood-block floor has tremendous tension." (A Study in Celluloid)

When Lestrade returned he was nonchalantly sitting on his chair with the original position of the rug restored. The constable's report revealed that a young woman had visited the rooms on the night of the murder providing Holmes with the link to Lady Hilda. The lady herself is persuaded to tell her story which is one of blackmail and vicious murder, finally revealing that she did it and still holds the document. All that was needed now was to return it to its rightful place in the dispatch box, which remains in full view, yet the illusionist Holmes achieves the impossible by a masterly sleight of hand off camera. This scene displays the bravado that the Granada team had developed as the deed is not shown and no explanation is needed. His almost careless lighting of his cigarette as he once more came into view showed the supreme confidence that Jeremy was feeling in the character in this episode.

The final leap of triumph from the steps with the shout of *"Wa-haay!"* was a fitting conclusion which Michael Cox said was very much a Jeremy flourish but unfortunately, he landed in an ungainly fashion and the scene was cut at the crucial moment. It does, however, recall the earlier comment when he was at a loss on how to proceed with the case, *"Should I bring this case to a successful conclusion, it will certainly represent the crowning glory of my career"* with Jeremy gloating over his puffing pipe. Almost immediately, he accidentally sets fire to his newspaper giving evidence for Jeremy's description of Holmes as *"a problem child"* while providing the viewers with another exquisite moment of humour. *"First of all, Holmes falls apart when he's not working. Well, that's easy to play because actors do that – we all fall apart really, when we're suddenly made redundant. But what does Holmes do? He actually shoots up, straight to the vein, the seven-percent solution. He smokes too much. He scrapes on his violin, not very well."* (Jeremy Brett. The Real Sherlock Holmes by Rosemary Herbert)

"I consider it one of the great privileges of my career to have worked with Jeremy Brett and most particularly in his portrayal of Sherlock Holmes, which was his crowning glory and a definitive interpretation of such a great character. I shall never forget his complete absorption in the role, his meticulous attention to detail, his knowledge of every prop and artefact on set. He also had a stunning concentration on camera." (Patricia Hodge in Scarlet Street)

The Musgrave Ritual - The Return of Sherlock Holmes

"The butler of Hurlstone is always a thing that is remembered by all who visit us."

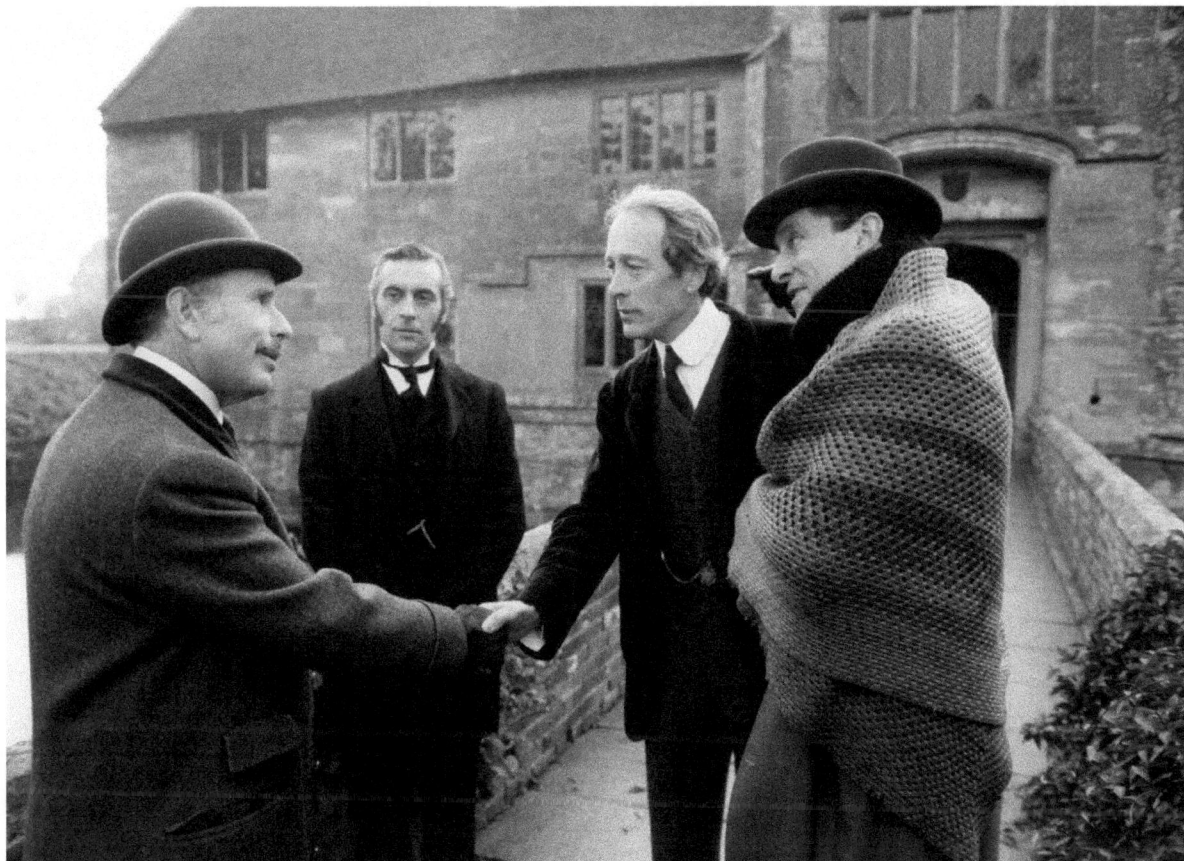

"My friend and colleague, Doctor Watson" The Musgrave Ritual

***The Musgrave Ritual* (Dramatised by Jeremy Paul: Directed by David Carson fb: 30th July 1986)** was the second in the sequence of filming in this series. Holmes is very much centre stage with Watson in the supporting role, and it has been described as a vehicle for Jeremy to mould more closely with the character of Holmes. In this fifty four minute episode he displays a wider range of moods, often changing as on a pin head, with a unique opportunity to explore the effects of cocaine. Holmes's first appearance in the opening scene is on the back of a wagon as he and Watson journey towards Hurlstone Manor in Warwickshire; he is displaying signs of "bad grace", accompanied by complaints about the coldness of the Manor and the grim prospect of hours of boredom in the company of his old friend, the grey Reginald Musgrave. It is no surprise that Holmes finds an escape into cocaine. The next scene is an opportunity to show something not seen before, the effects of cocaine on the repressed Holmes in an outburst of uproarious laughter at the expense of the butler with the memory of an explanation of the *"origins of the picolo"* in French. Watson would at first appear dismayed but soon gets drawn into the high spirits and laughs with him as it is contagious. Jeremy told Peter Haining, *"I was not sure to begin with because Holmes suppresses so many of the emotions in himself. But once I began to* *find the cracks in his armoury I realized there were moments when he laughed. I was also anxious to let a little of my humour into the part."*

Brunton would be at the heart of the story as he had the education and the curiosity to investigate the Musgrave Ritual. He had evidently understood much more than his employer and Holmes will find that at each step of the way the butler has been there before him. His disappearance with the strange actions of Rachel Howells and her own subsequent disappearance will only be solved when the secret of the ritual is finally solved by Holmes. Baddesley Clinton in Warwickshire was the location for the medieval, manor house with its own moat which is a feature of the Musgrave Ritual. Holmes is intrigued enough to ask for the ritual to be read and explores the different elements. He points out "*a patriarch among oaks*", and there is a memorable scene of the three principals with umbrellas shown in silhouette against the darkening sky as they are forced to reject it.

The detective has now recovered from his lethargy. He is in his element as he throws himself into an enthusiastic treasure hunt and with the discovery of the weather vane accompanied by the original position of the elm with the length of its shadow remembered by Reginald, precise measurements can be made and the hunt begins. The search for the treasure is carried out with humour and military precision with the counting out of steps led by Holmes, his baton pointing the direction or tucked under his arm, in his most energetic manner, first one way and then another. And finally, when the ground runs out the three explorers can be seen in a rowing boat crossing the moat with Holmes standing at the prow appearing to walk on water. It is by using his imaginative powers, a crucial weapon in his armoury that Holmes will find the solution to the mystery. The discovery of the treasure trove, the Charles I coin, plus the revelation of the ancient crown that "*once circled the brows of the royal Stuarts*", which emerges from the twisted pieces of metal providing the opportunity for a Jeremy flourish of pleasure at his success.

The scriptwriter Jeremy Paul had achieved an effective turnaround of the original story allowing him to explore Brunton's tangled love life and to interact with Holmes and Watson. Justifiably, he won the prestigious Edgar Allan Poe Award from Mystery Writers of America. "We were lucky in our choice of location for Hurlstone – a magnificent moated house in Warwickshire – but we had trouble in remaining faithful to the stepping out of the ritual. A truthful and exact rendering would have deposited our heroes in a bank of thistles. There was also an 'oak and sun' problem, solved, as if by an act of God, by the fortuitous presence of a weather vane with an ornamental oak on its top. We had fun with the notion that Holmes's steps led him to the edge of the moat, forcing him to cross to the house by rowing boat... Two early scenes depict Holmes clearly under the influence of drugs, to Watson's evident dismay. This is not emphasised in the existing text, but we saw the chance to lay the ground for the moment in a later episode when Holmes is seen to discard the cocaine and clear the matter (contentious in these present times) for good." (Introduction to The Musgrave Ritual script)

Edward commented on their experience solving the riddle, "We actually did it and went around in a complete circle, ending up where we started! Doyle is full of little things like that. But it doesn't really matter because he's managed to convince you, which is what really good writing is about."

***The Abbey Grange* (Dramatised by T.R. Bowen: Directed by Peter Hammond fb: 6th August 1986)** was Edward Hardwicke's first film as Watson and as he has very little to say, it is a perfect vehicle for adapting to his role. The opening scene of Holmes waking Watson with a lit candle is a familiar opening and a dramatic beginning for Edward's Watson. Doyle has quoted from Shakespeare's *Henry V* and *Henry VI* in *"Come, Watson, come! The game is afoot."* And within ten minutes they were both in a cab and travelling to Charing Cross Station for the Kentish train with a letter from the young Inspector Stanley

Hopkins of the local police urgently requesting their assistance. The train journey also allows time for Holmes to criticise Watson's method of writing, by turning his exploits into stories rather than scientific exercises he had ruined what might have been a suitable record of his work. At Watson's bitter remark that he should write his own, Holmes replies *"I will, my dear Watson, I will in my declining years."* Edward was discovering the difficulties of playing a character with so little to say who just needed to react to the more dominant Holmes. "I remember saying to Jeremy, 'I feel I'm disappearing inside my costume.' I just felt everything was too overwhelming..." (Elementary Mr Dear Watson Interview with Edward Hardwicke)

An investigation of the murderers is not needed as Lady Brackenstall has given an excellent description of the Lewisham gang, the three Randalls, and also the fact that they had killed her husband, "one of the richest men in Kent," with a blow to the head with his own poker. She is a beautiful young lady, who had travelled from Australia, with her maid, Theresa, to marry the violent Lord Eustace, and she freely admits their marriage was not a happy one, as he was a drunkard. However, Holmes is not convinced by the lady and the clues which he identifies: the three glasses of port with their crusting (bees-wing) at the rim on just two of them; the cut bell rope three inches below the clasp and the use of a candle from the candelabra need explanation. His request that she should tell him the truth is a typical request from Holmes as his only aim is truth, *"I am convinced that you are a much-tried woman. If you will treat me as a friend and trust me you may find that I will justify your trust."* Her insistence that she has told him everything causes him to withdraw his services and leave the house.

This episode is notable for Jeremy's heightened physicality and accelerated movement around the scene. He jumps confidently from and into carriages whilst they are moving in order to show the speed of his decision-making and the journey back to the Grange from the station reflects how he has recognised the need to reassess the evidence. Jeremy becomes the superhero here, fearless and arrow-like in pursuit. Most impressive is his energetic climbing of the massive overhanging oak mantelpiece of a large deep fireplace which is a dangerous escapade but a necessity when it is so graphically described by Doyle; Jeremy doesn't show any hesitancy and climbs confidently with some style to explore the top of the mantelpiece, even stretching across to examine the cut bell rope, but he was well aware of the hazards in a situation like this. *"The athletic stuff can be extremely dangerous especially when you have to climb up a fireplace and along curtain rails."* (Jeremy in Holmes Rule - Video Today)

Jeremy's Holmes is very much the driving force in the investigation as his honed observation skills identify the position of the stolen silver in the lake, crucial evidence that will unlock the case. He also recovers the buried twice-broken memorial for the Lady's pet dog Fudge by thrusting his arm deep into the mud and bringing up the collar and tag too. By this discovery Sir Eustace will be exposed as a *"sadistic ruffian"* and that the Randall gang were not involved on this occasion. These revelations indicate that Lady Brackenstall has lied to them as burglars would not have thrown stolen silver into the nearest pond. When he has the whole truth in the final scenes, he treats her with extreme care, extricating himself carefully from her impulsive embrace with a degree of dismissal. But is Holmes aware that the lady's charm could be dangerous and is he protecting himself against her feminine wiles, especially as she is acting outside of the expectations of polite behaviour?

With the identification of the chivalrous hero Captain Crocker, Holmes will use all his powers to bring the good Captain on side and with a detailed analysis of the murder of Sir Eustace, he persuades him to tell the full story. The confession will put him at Holmes's mercy but once again the investigator turns from the letter of the law in the cause of justice. *"I'd rather play tricks with the law than with my conscience."* The concluding scene with Watson as a representative of a good British jury brings the expected verdict. Jeremy adjusted the request, *"Now, gentleman of the jury"* to *"gentle man"* to emphasise the compliment to his friend and to show his approval for Captain Crocker. *"Not guilty, my lord,"* is confirmed in *"Vox pupuli, vox Dei.* (The voice of the people is the voice of God) *You are acquitted Captain Crocker"*. He may initially have been reluctant to accept the verdict, revealing his moral integrity, but he is finally persuaded to accept the judgement.

Edward had done a superb job with his portrayal of Watson. *"Well, Edward's a very, very remarkable man. One – probably the nicest... I've ever met in my life. And... he wanted to fit in. So he watched the previous thirteen films... Decided to try and look a little like David Burke, as much as he could, bless him. So he put on a rug, I mean a toupee, and... put lifts in his heels. And the first film we shot together was* The Abbey Grange. *And we were running across a field, and... these heels were too high so he was slipping and sliding. And I said, 'Oh, Edward, take them out! I'll bend my knees for the rest of the film!'"* (Jeremy in Radio Interview 1991)

Baker Street File – The Abbey Grange

92 - I have learnt caution now, and I had rather play tricks with the laws of England than with my own conscience

The Man with the Twisted Lip (Dramatised by Alan Plater: Directed by Patrick Lau fb: 13ᵗʰ August 1986) *"I confess that I cannot recall any case within my experience which looked at the first glance so simple, and yet, which presented such difficulties."* The episode which features two missing husbands, one found by Watson and the other by Holmes, focuses on the picture of a beggar who quotes Shakespeare, Wordsworth and Chaucer, entertaining businessmen in the city centre. In the opening at Baker Street only Watson is at home as Holmes has "disappeared without trace" and a visit from Kate Whitney brings him the task of finding her husband. Isa Whitney has also "disappeared without trace", presumably indulging his addiction in the opium den, the Bar of Gold on Upper Swandham Lane where as an addict he would escape amongst the other ruffians. It is there that Watson finds Isa in a catatonic state, but unexpectedly he finds Holmes as well in another of his disguises as an addict, "a tall, thin old man" carrying out his own investigations. *"Had I been recognised in that den my life would not have been worth an hour's purchase."* (The Man with the Twisted Lip)

Watson sends Whitney home in a waiting cab, and Jeremy's Holmes, once more convincing in his disguise of a poppy addict with long hair and shambling gait joins him soon

90

afterwards. With the removal of his disguise, Holmes suggests that Watson accompanies him on a visit to a villa in Lee, Kent on a case he is pursuing. Once again Watson is asked point blank if he will join his friend on an adventure and he answers without pause, "Of course!" Holmes's investigation had begun with the unexplained disappearance of Neville St Clair who had been missing for several days. A young man of 37 years, "a man of temperate habits, a good husband, a very affectionate father" and as he has no debts there is no valid reason for his disappearance. It is assumed that he has been murdered, however, his wife shows Holmes a newly arrived letter from her husband, accompanied by his signet ring and gives a strange account of having seen him at an upper room window in one of the buildings on Upper Swandham Lane. She had been forcibly removed by the Lascar manager but when she returned with Inspector Bradstreet of the police, they found only "the sinister cripple" Boone, the well-liked professional beggar with a hideous face still quoting Shakespeare and Wordsworth. The evidence of her husband's presence in the room was a box of building bricks, which Neville had promised to buy for his little girl's birthday; her husband's clothes behind a curtain; a bloodstain on the window sill and an overcoat found at low tide on the beach beneath the window with a considerable amount of coins in the pocket so that Boone the beggar, still protesting that he is "an honest trader", is taken into police custody on suspicion of murder.

There are moments of surprising stillness for Jeremy's Holmes in this episode although his body language and facial expression remain a clear reflection of the changing fortunes of the disappearance of a good man. Everybody appears to be telling the truth and there is no pattern which will unlock the puzzling elements of the case. His investigations bring little development until the dramatic moment of revelation for Holmes as he views his own face in the mirror during the morning wash, thus revealing the truth. *"I have been as blind as a mole."* Consequently, Watson is woken at dawn by a tickle to his foot because the detective has a theory he wishes to test at the police station. *"Downstairs in five minutes"* shows little consideration for how Watson might feel after only a few hours' sleep. Now Holmes is in his own atmosphere and confident in his theories. He has the key to the mystery in his Gladstone bag and there is humour mixed with drama in the scene where Neville St Clair is finally revealed under his disguise as a black encrusted beggar. The enormous sponge in the Gladstone bag is the first assault but as more water is poured over his head, each element of St Clair's disguise is removed. "What am I charged with?" His story of how he made a living from begging and "fell among thieves but found honour of a sort" makes an interesting tale and one to evoke sympathy from his listeners. However, the Inspector is prepared to free him with one condition, "there must be no more Hugh Boone."

Jeremy and Edward had become a close team in this episode working separately on their own investigations and then coming together to share what they know and assess how these details might bring them to a solution. After a sleepless night, and the startling revelation that will discover the missing St Clair, Holmes pays his friend the supreme compliment when he tells him he has the invaluable gift of silence. Moments like these underline the valuable contributions Watson makes to his friend's investigations, first by being at his side in the moments of danger as a doctor and as advisor but also in the times when a fresh examination of the evidence can open his mind to the solutions. Edward told Peter Haining how much he had appreciated Jeremy's help: "Jeremy has been absolutely marvellous in helping me into the part. Right from the beginning he was always thinking of new ways of developing the relationship between Holmes and Watson – pushing it into new directions. This I have found immensely stimulating. He also generates such a feeling of team spirit on the set that everyone – not only the actors, but also those working behind the cameras – want to do their best for him." (Edward to Peter Haining in The Television Sherlock Holmes)

The pictures of Sidney Paget feature in this episode much as they do in all the episodes wherever they are available. One newspaper critic pointed out the "uncanny likeness in the vision of the great detective, as imagined by the author. Then he has given the character the tense, nervy, melodramatic fizz which has made the series take off." The creation of these poses was a deliberate choice by the Granada production team to show they were determined to be faithful to the Conan Doyle stories. Jeremy told the reporter, *"I tried very hard to look like the original drawings... I was so nervous of failure that at first I put far too much make-up on, then, I took most of it off again. In the end I got confident and really enjoyed the series."* (The Shaping of Sherlock)

Baker Street File – The Man with the Twisted Lip

97 - Very persuasive manner

***The Six Napoleons* (Dramatised by John Kane: Directed by David Carson fb: 20th August 1986)** is a story of passion and murder told throughout with humour. The scene in Baker Street begins with the three companions around the fire, Holmes, Watson and Lestrade; the two friends sit waiting for the Inspector to explain the reason for his visit. He tells of an unusual series of thefts of Napoleon busts, first from the shop of Morse Hudson in Kennington Road and one from a Doctor Barnicot at Lower Brixton Road and another from his surgery. The fact that nothing was taken other than the busts, later found smashed into pieces, causes Holmes to proclaim it *"singular"* and *"grotesque."* Watson suggests a mania or idée fixe concerning the Emperor Napoleon as the possible reason, but Holmes shows some doubt and his *"My dear Watson, it won't do!"* is wonderfully delivered by Jeremy, showing all the arrogance mixed with tolerant amusement that describe their friendship in this episode. The moment when Holmes is told "two minutes" as he interrupts the lifting of the teacup to his lips brings sweet revenge for all those times when his friend had got him from his bed to catch the early morning train.

The villain of the piece at first appears to be more mad than evil and scarcely suitable for a Sherlock Holmes investigation. Beppo is part of the Italian community and speaks no English so the early scenes are rather difficult to follow. The sustained and passionately fought battle, cheered on by a partisan crowd, is a dangerous affair with flailing knives and swiftly weaving bodies, which will have tragic consequences. With the stabbing of his opponent and the arrival of the police, Beppo's wild behaviour is reminiscent of the madhouse as he escapes into the factory hurling ornaments at the police and leaving carnage in his wake. Thus the backdrop to the Conan Doyle story becomes a violent yet exciting opening for the tale.

As they approach the case from their respective viewpoints the competition between Holmes and Lestrade escalates and it will offer an opportunity for Holmes to show the advantage that following the facts without prejudice can bring. Holmes is always one step ahead and shows a sense of achievement as things fit in with his fact based theories. "*You must have a twinkle in your eye, a naughtiness – and the audience must realise your mind in working faster than your words.*" (Jeremy) Holmes will lead the trio in a series of discoveries about the busts and is good natured and supremely confident that they are the source of the strange and as yet unexplained events whilst Lestrade continues to view them as a mere distraction.

Holmes would finally reveal what he had discovered, with the coming of a visitor to Baker Street. From the moment of Mr. Sandeford's arrival Jeremy had taken control of the space with the use of what Edward called his Victorian signalling much in the manner of a master showman delivering a great performance. His movement about the room was carefully choreographed with Watson and Lestrade moving apart to allow him to carve a passage between them to take the final Napoleon from the mantelpiece. They both looked on in bewilderment as the red tablecloth from a fully laid table was swept away with a theatrical flourish, before being laid as appropriate covering for a side table with hunting crop and bust in readiness. All this was conducted without dialogue or explanation and it must have taken much practice and skill to perfect the feat but it was one of those moments which Jeremy's Holmes achieved with his customary eye on perfection. He appears very much the magician as he miraculously reveals the famous black pearl of the Borgias from the remnants of the smashed Napoleon. The priceless jewel had disappeared the year before, stolen from Prince of Colonna's bedroom at the Dacre Hotel. Lestrade and Watson were amazed and broke out clapping. "A flush of colour which sprang to Holmes's pale cheeks, and he bowed to us... for an instant he ceased to be a reasoning machine, and betrayed his human love for admiration and applause. The same singularly proud and reserved nature which turned away with disdain from popular notoriety was capable of being moved to its depths by spontaneous wonder and praise from a friend." (The Six Napoleons)

The group ensemble effect that was used to focus on the blue carbuncle with such success was once again used here to show off the Black Pearl. The camera followed closely the movement of the pearl as it was handed from Watson, to Lestrade and finally to Holmes who holds it for the camera to emphasise its value and the significant achievement he had made in recovering it. Thus Jeremy has once more brought flesh to the words of Doyle's story, each element is translated into human terms and the drama lives.

The uncovering of the blackboard with its detailed account of the stolen black pearl reveals a model record of the investigation. The essential newspaper articles were pinned alongside photographs of the main offenders, the Venucci family and even included the two halves of the torn portrait of Lucrezia and Beppo.   In the light of such assiduous attention to detail, it is no surprise when Lestrade congratulates Holmes for his unrivalled management of the case and Jeremy's reaction to it is remarkable: "We're not jealous of you at Scotland Yard. No, sir, we are very proud of you, and if you were to come down tomorrow there's not a man from oldest inspector to the youngest constable, who wouldn't be glad to shake you by the hand." "*Thank you!*" said Holmes. "*Thank you!*" (The Six Napoleons) Jeremy's eyes filling with unshed tears and the "softer human emotions" he was trying so hard to control was so effective that our assessment of Holmes was to change as a result of moments like these. Jeremy had proved that his Holmes was not the automaton that people thought Conan Doyle had described. Through his research he presented to us the thinking, feeling man who kept his deeper emotions tightly in check, yet they were still there. "My companion flushed up with pleasure at my words, and the earnest way in which I uttered them. I had already observed that he was as sensitive to flattery on the score of his art as any girl could be of her beauty." (A Study In Scarlet) The offer of his hand to Lestrade as he left the Baker Street rooms is a rare and significant gesture which sealed the relationship and reflected a closer understanding based on mutual respect.

The appearance of two familiar faces in this episode is an added pleasure: one of the best loved comedians, Eric Sykes as Harker and Gerald Campion who was the schoolboy Billy Bunter of the 1950s as Morse Hudson, both in supporting roles. That the stars of past and present were willing to accept a part was a sign that the Granada series was gaining in popularity and although no one would contest Jeremy's position as the star or Edward's role as his friend Watson, they wanted a part of the prestige production. "I used to come in to work on days I wasn't scheduled so that I could watch them at work. He was the greatest of old school actors, and a big proponent of the "less is more" technique of acting. His loss was a tragedy for everyone, and for the profession. Losing Jeremy was the end of an era." (Marina Sirtis, Lucrezia in The Six Napoleons) The critics and the audience agreed with Marina. "Once again it is superbly made, evocative in atmosphere and meticulous in detail. The music is hauntingly beautiful, and the writing is droll and intelligent. Jeremy Brett, Edward Hardwicke and Colin Jeavons couldn't have been more perfect as Holmes, Watson and Lestrade. Brett is commanding, Hardwicke is composed and quietly intelligent and Jeavons is a comic joy... Overall such a fun episode." (IMDb) "To me and clearly a great many others, Jeremy Brett was the man born to play Holmes. No-one else can or will ever come close. The point that struck me about this particular episode above all others is perhaps the most "singular" moment of the entire Granada series... Holmes's tears goes way beyond the "softer human emotions" mentioned by the author. It seemed to come straight from Brett's heart. That he allowed this definitive portrayal of Holmes to be so very human (and caused me to shed a tear in the process) was quite simply extraordinary..." (IMDb)

"Jeremy Brett's portrayal of Holmes on ITV's *The Return of Sherlock Holmes* is nothing short of brilliant: his facial expressions, abruptness, and the tension shown as he perches on a chair, for instance, are faultless. Now, no other portrayal of Sherlock Holmes in films or series will do. All seem a poor shadow by comparison." (Superb Holmes: Berkshire) "Edward Hardwicke seems more than an adequate replacement for the excellent actor David Burke, who played Dr Watson in the previous series. Hardwicke provides an intelligent foil for

Holmes, and the shades of Nigel Bruce, the cinema's best known Dr. Watson are at last laid to rest." (Petersfield) "I deem a critic derelict of duty if he does not express an opinion he has seen fit to change... and I have come to relish that Sunday hour on ITV as perhaps the week's regular best. Jeremy Brett's possessed, capricious, volatile, dangerous but above all convincingly brilliant Holmes wipes the memory clean of all previous portrayals. It is not easy to portray genius. Maybe he has to be one." (Alan Coren in The Mail on Sunday)

A *Daily Mail* article in 1986 recorded the end of filming for series and Jeremy's personal investment in the role with the headline *Why Jeremy's happy to leave Holmes*. Shooting on the third and last Granada series on the Baker Street detective ended at the weekend, and after 20 episodes in the title role... Jeremy Brett is delighted. At last he can abandon the pipe, the deerstalker and the constant dieting that a Sherlock Holmes physique demands. *"I'm longing to do something different,"* he says, *"Each episode of Sherlock Holmes has been like a little polished diamond and each one has demanded its own infusion of adrenalin. I think it makes a great deal of sense to stop while I'm ahead."* (Daily Mail 10th June 1986) Jeremy also told Peter Haining how much he appreciated the new actors coming into the series and how much it had helped him. *"I have enjoyed new directors this time around, new actors in guest roles, even a new lighting cameraman or technician joining the team. On a long series you become terribly aware of new faces, but if you are trying to continue being creative then you need them, for each new face brings in new ideas. All the time the format is changing ever so slightly and that is terribly important, I think."* (The Television Sherlock Holmes)

The Return of Sherlock Holmes

After filming ended on *The Return*, Jeremy was leaving Manchester for a year's break from playing Holmes. His comments on the demands of the part emphasised the cost of acting in a long-running series but also the unexpected discovery of how popular Sherlock Holmes was in the U.S. as a super hero. The Americans considered they more or less invented Holmes since the early appearance in the Lippincott Magazine – "which makes the Stateside accolades ringing in Mr Brett's handsome ears all the sweeter." But the personal cost was enormous. *"It was like being on the brink of a breakdown. They put in millions – and there was no room for failure. The strain was enormous. It was so nerve-wracking that*

I was smoking 60 cigarettes a day... Making the series wound me up to such a pitch that I was trembling like a greyhound before a race. It took me two weeks after filming stopped to sleep at night again." (A case of nerves for Mr Holmes) *"I was on the verge of cracking up several times. I had been living with the part for three years. I saw myself in some rushes one morning, manic, obsessed – a perfect portrait of Holmes, but far too real for comfort. I knew that to play a man who lives on the dark side of the moon was dangerous, but I hadn't realised just how much the part had got to me... I was getting up at three in the morning to go through the script and I started to dream about the part... One weekend I stayed in my hotel room and didn't go out at all. I had my meals sent in to me, and remained totally detached."* (The grim curse of Sherlock Holmes by Brian Whittle in Today 4ᵗʰ December 1986) The complexity of the man, his genius and his isolation could be overwhelming, *"I've played Macbeth, and that's a tricky one to play, psychologically. I've played Hamlet too. But there's nothing as tricky as Sherlock Holmes. Of all the parts I've ever played, it's the most complex. We are in a never-ending maze. You never get to the bottom of it."* (Jeremy)

In spite of the pressures of carrying the show whilst learning to live with his grief at Joan's death, Jeremy was also masterminding the 1987 publication A Centenary Celebration for Sir Arthur Conan Doyle with the release of the *Granada Companion: A Sherlock Holmes Album*. It is a colourful, detailed view of the series to date with an introduction to the first two-hour production, *The Sign of Four* and a collector's piece. The introduction by Vincent Price contains an interesting comment: "Inevitably all productions stand or fail on the casting and playing of Sherlock Holmes. I do not envy the producer who has to choose his Holmes, or the actor who decides to play the part... Michael Cox's choice of Jeremy Brett to play Holmes in this series was inspired. Mr Brett brings just that degree of novelty and differentness to his portrait of Holmes – but not too much – to give the character yet another incandescent lease of life."

Jeremy's own contribution to the illustrated slim volume contains some clues to his interpretation, *"It's difficult for me to say what I may have given to the image of Holmes. Faith to Conan Doyle's text, certainly! I've worked very hard at that, encouraged by Mike Cox, and by Peter Hammond, the director. I carry my annotated volume around with me. Also, I've tried to bring out the emotion that there is in Holmes. On the surface he seems a cold, sometimes dark, rather off-putting figure. But deeper down, I think, he is a man of feeling. He is complex. He loves music – he plays the violin very well – he enjoys a joke, he is vain, maybe a little conceited. He likes to be praised. He can be bitchy when he assesses other great detectives. He can be a bit of a drama queen; he shows off sometimes, he's something of an exhibitionist, especially when he has pulled off a coup. On a difficult case he may build up considerable tension within himself, which explodes in a genial bit of theatricality when the problem is solved. I've tried to get some of that into my Holmes... The things I hate about my performance are when I suddenly see a flare of a nostril or the twist of a lip and I didn't mean that. He's exciting to play because he's such an adventure. I never know where he's going to take me next."* (Granada Companion: A Sherlock Holmes Album) *"My outlook changed. I became a vegetarian and felt better for it. I learned that I'm much stronger than I thought. I must be strong to have survived and that knowledge gave me confidence. Now I'm much more relaxed. I still miss my wife, of course. The worst thing about not being part of a couple any more is that you've got no one to share things with, but at least now I can go forward. I no longer feel the weight of those other Sherlock Holmeses. I'm no longer up half the night worrying about learning my lines."* (Tragedy leads to a new Holmes in TV Times 19ᵗʰ December 87)

The Sign of Four - The Return of Sherlock Holmes

The latest set of episodes to complete *The Return of Sherlock Holmes* began with *The Sign of Four*, a two hour special, the format of which was to be repeated another four times. An article in *The Times* indicated that it had been made to celebrate the centenary of Sir Arthur Conan Doyle but the two hour detective programme was becoming a popular feature on ITV with *The Inspector Morse* series where there was time to develop character and details that were often lost in the one hour format. And after all, Sherlock Holmes was the first great detective so it seemed a good decision to follow the trend.

***The Sign of Four* (Dramatised by John Hawkesworth: Directed by Peter Hammond fb: 29th Dec 1987)** is a very classy and faithful adaptation of the Conan Doyle story. Unfortunately, the first scene of the novel in which Holmes justifies his use of the seven percent solution of cocaine had been used as an introduction to the characters in *A Scandal in Bohemia* and was thus unavailable here. The epic story begins with the arrival of the beautiful Mary Morstan played by Jenny Seagrove, who comes to Baker Street with two puzzles for Holmes: the disappearance of her father ten years before in unexplained circumstances and an annual gift of a priceless pearl together create sufficient intrigue for Holmes to be interested. Her presence brings very different responses from Holmes and Watson: the former remains unmoved by her grief, in fact he is quite dismissive, offering no sympathy; instead brushing his clothes and complaining at the state of their rooms. On the other hand, Watson is clearly attracted by her beauty and shows her the personal support she is seeking. He will go on to marry Mary at the end of the original tale, but not in the Granada stories where Watson remains a bachelor as Holmes's companion in the Baker Street rooms.

The choice of Ronald Lacey in the dual roles of the Sholto brothers, Thaddeus and Bartholomew, is inspired. His appearance is extraordinary, and he captures the poor health and neuroses of Thaddeus, who describes himself as "a valetudinarian", a hypochondriac. It is interesting to see Holmes in the secondary role, listening, watching, and never interrupting the story of the father Major Sholto's return from India with a vast treasure, and his irrational unexplained fear of a one-legged man. The story is intriguing enough, especially as the son tells of his father's greed, the threat from the two strangers and the notes containing the Sign of Four hieroglyph, which appear from time to time. The account of the involvement of Captain Morstan and his death brings Mary grief even though she had been prepared for his loss. Jeremy commented about his desire for stillness in his interpretation which we can see here: *"trying to stay as still as I possibly can when listening, thinking; trying to let it all go through my face without moving, every thought I've had. And then huge physical activity. ... you suddenly jump off the sofa, or you fly down the stairs with Watson running after you, or leap onto a moving cab or whatever. In other words, his mind is made up."*

The party's eventual, long-awaited departure for Pondicherry Lodge is the strangest section in the story with an atmospheric setting providing evidence for the Sholto brothers' search for the treasure in Watson's reaction, "It looks as if all the moles in England had been at work." Holmes cannot wait to meet Brother Bartholomew, to pursue the mystery and Jeremy dominates these scenes as he gains entrance to the house and runs up the stairs swiftly and almost eagerly to view the death scene. *"There is something devilish in this, Watson,"* said he, more moved than I had ever before seen him. I stooped to the hole, and recoiled in horror." (The Sign of Four) The manner of Bartholomew's death is indeed terrible and at first incomprehensible. Nevertheless, Holmes's seeking gaze forensically analyses the use of the coil of rope, the scuff to the window frame, and the entrance of "a child" by the skylight into the roof space whilst Watson identifies the effects of the poison on the rigid body creating *"risus sardonicus"*. Oblivious to the effects on his clothing Jeremy is on his knees crawling through the office desk where the dead man still sits, he examines the floor for any hint of a clue to the murder and the theft of the treasure. It becomes a masterpiece of sleuthing with every detail given relevance. *"How often have I said to you that when you have eliminated the impossible, whatever remains, however improbable, must be the truth?"* (The Sign of Four)

The arrival of the police in the person of Athelney Jones, brings another policeman who needs lessons from Holmes as he bumbles around the attic room, making preposterous theories "weaving a web". The expert Holmes directs him to the poisoned tip of the arrow, the Sign of Four hieroglyph and the stump of the *"timbertoe"* alongside the creature footprint etched in the spilt creosote, all of which will provide the evidence for his theories. Considering that Jeremy was not in the best of health at this time, his energetic exploration of the large medieval building by clambering over the roof area is extremely hazardous and heart stopping especially when he almost slipped on the descent of the water pipe down the side of the building only to be relieved by his sympathetic quick smile to Watson.

The search for Toby, when Holmes had not told Watson that Toby was a dog offers some comic relief from the recent horrors of murder and mystery. The chase along the London riverbank with Toby leading the way is full of excitement and near discoveries, but it ends in disappointment as it comes to a dead end with Toby sitting on a barrel of creosote. But then suspense takes over as Holmes waits for developments and can be seen pacing across the living room floor in Baker Street, uncharacteristically snapping at Mrs Hudson in reply to her question about the time he would like dinner, *"Half past eight the day after tomorrow."* Holmes's very comfortable relationship with young people can be seen in his use of the Irregulars, the street children who assist him, which also brings relief in the tense period of waiting for news of the Aurora. It is fitting therefore that it is by their dedication to duty and watchfulness that the Aurora is located. Holmes's presence is always reassuring even if we don't immediately identify him in his disguise of the old sea-dog in shapeless cloth hat with a racking cough; his dress and manner are totally convincing, every detail is flawlessly presented, even to the weak legs of an old seaman. Watson and Jones respond to his unmasking with delighted applause.

The chase on the Thames was difficult to film, carried out at night, very dramatic and full of incident, with Holmes balancing on the prow of the boat or clinging to the funnel as they gradually catch up with the *Aurora* and the escaping murderers. The Granada team maintained the authenticity of the episode by using an 1874 steel-hulled launch in the pursuit from the Westminster Pier. The death of the islander, Tonga, whose final gesture was to aim a poisoned arrow at Holmes and the capture of Jonathan Small bring a dramatic turn of events and prepares for the disturbing story of the Great Agra Treasure. One of greed and betrayal with Small emerging as the honourable man who had attempted to return the precious gems to their rightful owners: the Sign of Four. Mary Morstan did not receive her inheritance as it disappeared into the depths of the Thames along with Tonga's body, and Small would spend the rest of his life on the chain gang on Dartmoor.

Jeremy said, "*The programme I'm most proud of? Again, personal:* The Sign of Four. *It was very demanding because it's a full-length film with a good number of varied scenes – tremendous action. I wasn't in normal health at the time, and in particular, I had to do a lot of walking about on roofs, and I've no head for heights. I was pleased with myself when I got through that film in one piece.*" (A Centenary Celebration of Sherlock Holmes) *The Mail on Sunday* recorded the details of his illness in the article *Holmes is where his heart is.* "The agony of bringing to life one of fiction's darkest and most complex characters whilst grappling with the loss of his wife, eventually took a terrifying toll on Brett. Last October he was admitted to a mental hospital in London suffering from manic depression. Ironically it was Holmes that rescued him. He recovered at the end of last year, just in time to return to work at Granada Television's Manchester studios in January to make a two-hour Holmes special, *The Sign of Four*, with Edward Hardwicke, John Thaw and Jenny Seagrove. It will be shown on ITV at Christmas to celebrate the 100th anniversary of the creation of Holmes. '*I felt that if I could get on that train to Manchester again, I would be all right.*' Brett says now, '*That is what pulled me through. When I got on to the set I thought: My God, I've cracked it. I am better...*'"

John Thaw, appearing as Jonathan Small said: "I think Jeremy's better than Rathbone now, because he's more; more human. He brings a humanity to the guy that Rathbone didn't." (ibid) R. Dixon Smith in his monograph *An Adventure in Canonical Fidelity* went further when he concluded, "Basil Rathbone *was* Sherlock Holmes, Jeremy Brett *is* Sherlock Holmes." Alan Barnes agreed. "Jeremy Brett's Holmes is the centrepiece, the piercing eyes, brilliantined hair, bat ears and death-mask pallor creating an indelible image of 'true cold reason' personified. Whether clambering around the upper reaches of Pondicherry Lodge (filmed at a Gothic Pile in Harrogate, rather than Norwood) or crinkling in amused fellow-feeling as Thaddeus explains his addiction to the hookah, he is riveting to watch from start to finish." (Alan Barnes in Sherlock Holmes Onscreen)

The vindication of his approach to Holmes came with reference to Conan Doyle. "Jeremy Brett would, I am sure, have warmed the cockles of Conan Doyle's heart... Played with the shrewd neurosis which the character suggests, his manner is as taut as one of his fiddle strings, and at times he resembles a bird of prey, concentrating, twitching, then pouncing, but always with subtlety and eloquence." (Ann Mann in Television Today) "Granada's slightly belated contribution to the centenary celebration is a typically polished production of a little produced Holmes adventure, *The Sign of Four*. Indeed, to get the best possible visible quality, the film unusually for television, shot in 35mm. There has been so much Holmes in the cinema and on TV that there must be a great temptation to find a new approach, or even to send the whole thing up. John Hawksworth's adaptation, directed by Peter Hammond, eschews frills and plays it straight down the line. This also applies to the principal actors – Jeremy Brett who plays Holmes, Edward Hardwicke as Watson – who give notably unmannered, almost self-effacing performances. Brett, of course, is no stranger to the role having made an excellent Holmes in Granada's previous forays into Conan Doyle. Emrys James as the hapless Inspector Jones seems, by contrast, almost to be hamming... once the story proper gets into its stride, there is more opportunity for visual impact, not least in the riverboat chase, that finally nails the thieves of the priceless Indian treasure." (Peter Waymark in The Times 29th December 1987) In another review the critic Antonia Swinson wrote: *"The Sign of Four* was simply magnificent... For two hours, I sat transfixed... But it was, as usual, Jeremy Brett's performance as Sherlock Holmes himself that held me spellbound.... For me, he simply is Holmes. That one flaring nostril, those well-trained eyebrows; who could resist his ice-cold logic and charisma? And yet in this production, I felt there was a new quality; a humour."

In spite of the accolades Jeremy told the *TV Times, "I found him cold, chilling a walking brain without emotion... I didn't like the man but, worse still, I was aware of all the actors who have played Holmes... that knowledge was like a great weight. I was so afraid of doing it badly... but now all that's changed."* Suddenly Brett has thrown away the ghostly make-up, cut his hair and sees Holmes now in a new light. For the first time he feels some sympathy for the man, and for the first time he feels he's got his interpretation absolutely right." (TV Times December 1987)

Rosalie Williams gave some insight into the relationship between Holmes and his landlady, "There's very little in the actual writing for Mrs Hudson, and he used to come up with lovely little inventions... like when he gave me a flower in one episode. There were lots of moments like that where Holmes revealed that Mrs Hudson was very close to him – which isn't in the stories but is something that developed because it was Jeremy and me!... I was allowed to share a twinkle... At 7.00am on recording day I would walk into the make-up room. Jeremy would be sitting in his chair with Sue Milton gently transforming his early morning face into Sherlock. Script in hand and a twinkle in his eye, he'd say, *'I've thought of a lovely moment between us,'* and there and then we'd rehearse a new little piece of action and reaction between Mrs H. and Mr Holmes... Jeremy had spent the previous night after a long day's work going through today's script." (Scarlet Street)   Jeremy told David Stuart Davies about his delight at having Rosalie with him, *"I invented the relationship with Mrs Hudson because I really find it so difficult to have no woman to play opposite. That's a very important little relationship which has come through the films... Rosalie and I love each other so much."* (Dancing in the Moonlight)

Baker Street File – The Sign of Four

59 - He whipped out his lens and a tape-measure and hurried about the room on his knees

60 - He took out his revolver... and having loaded two of the chambers, he put it back into the right-hand pocket of his jacket.

101 - There are in me the makings of a very fine loafer, and also of a pretty spry sort of a fellow

117 - Are you going to bed, Holmes? No, I am not tired. I never remember feeling tired through work. Though idleness exhausts me completely...

127 - Mr Sherlock Holmes, I began; but the word had a magical effect

The Sign of Four – Holmes and Watson with Toby

The Devil's Foot – The Return of Sherlock Holmes

The Devil's Foot (Dramatised by Gary Hopkins: Directed by Ken Hannan fb: 6th April 1988). In the episode, *The Devil's Foot* we were able to admire Holmes's new puckish haircut or reject it as a bad decision. Jeremy had cut it himself in an attempt to avoid the use of gel which made his hair into a hard, immovable cap. It was also necessary sometimes to renew the greasing during the day and altogether it was an unpleasant business that he was pleased to be freed from. It was not popular with Michael Cox, however, who had to wait until it grew back to its original length, which was the end of the series. The increasingly critical Nancy Banks-Smith in *The Guardian* judged it as a savage cut with the "decimated remains standing in protest." She also commented on his scarf-wearing fashion statements, "sometimes under his hat and sometimes over". Whatever the purpose of her words, Jeremy explained the personal cost of playing the part of a genius. *"He was invented in a very dark time you see. A Study in Scarlet was submitted at the same time as* The Picture of Dorian Grey *and Bram Stoker's* Dracula. *Dark people tend to play him best, sardonic, saturnine people. Lee? Cushing? Marvellous actors! Rathbone I imagine could just get in front of the camera and be the man. I can't do that. I have to glue up my eyebrows, slick back and darken my hair, do my face white. It's hard trying to look like a genius."* (Jeremy to Max Bell in 'Brett Noir' Music and Video Insight 1989) In another interview he would explain more: *"But it's the loneliness of the man that one has to find, the isolation of the man, the man who is not alone, but is perfectly happy to be on his own. The privacy of the man; he's private, utterly private. And, therefore, you have to let the camera come in and see you. You mustn't reach out for it, it must come to you. And they – the director, cameraman, and production people – must choose the moments when he's seen and when he's not. Was that the flicker of a smile, was that a moment of sadness, what was he thinking at that moment? He's frightfully difficult to play."* (Arts & Entertainment 1992)

The opening scene of *The Devil's Foot* shows Holmes as suffering from overwork and Jeremy presents an exhausted, ill and out of sorts Holmes dressed in an unusual combination of blankets and scarves to keep him warm. He is protesting at the prescription of complete rest and change of scene in order to avoid a complete breakdown of his health. Holmes's state of health may have been shaken, but it is still a shock to see his use of cocaine, injected intravenously, as the first thing he does on their arrival at the cottage in Cornwall. The following scene is full of unexpected moments of humour due to the influence of the drug, as he makes his typical Holmesian observations about the Reverend Roundhay followed by his great shout of laughter and applause at the response to his explanation, but his ready acceptance of *"dinner at the Vicarage"* and the singing of Wagner's *Isolde's Liebestod* are completely unexpected and may be the result of the drug he has taken or a glimpse of the cracks in the marble. This scene is a dramatic addition to the original story.

The arrival of the Reverend Roundhay and Mortimer Tregennis with a sorry tale of insanity and murder in "a convulsion of terror," brings a halt to any further opportunity for recuperation as Holmes is revitalised in the hunt for a solution. The murder investigation has catapulted Holmes into his true atmosphere as he throws off his outer clothes and with his customary energy examines every detail from the furniture to the remnants of the cigar. His questions for Tregennis show that he is clearly tracing every event of the evening that might account for the tragic outcome; his stepping back onto the man's foot to gain a sample of his footprint will prove invaluable in the investigation. Watson had warned their visitors

that he was unwell and not to be troubled, but seeing Holmes in charge of a case shows the concern to be unwarranted. Just one occasion on the cliff-top where they had been sitting to discuss the details brought a shout of pain to remind us that all was not entirely well. With the second murder Holmes is brought once more to the Tregennis home where Jeremy moved around the living room like a ballet dancer before throwing himself onto the ground outside in search of anything that might reveal what happened to Mortimer Tregennis. On this occasion he would leave with two vital pieces of information.

The relationship between Holmes and Watson is developed further in this episode where Holmes is vulnerable and in need of the Doctor's care due to his poor state of health. The signs of that dependence are touching, but it also shows the lengths to which Watson will go to help his friend with the investigation. The experiment with the lamp, using the crystals taken from the light in the Tregennis house was lunacy. Holmes explained the hazards of what he was planning to his friend, as always, giving him the option not to take part in the experiment and without Watson there could have been tragic consequences. "I broke through that cloud of despair, and had a glimpse of Holmes's face, white, rigid and drawn with horror – the very look which I had seen upon the features of the dead. It was that vision which gave me an instant of sanity and of strength. I dashed from my chair, threw my arms round Holmes, and together we lurched through the door, and an instant afterwards had thrown ourselves down upon the grass plot and were lying side by side conscious only of the glorious sunshine..." (The Adventure of the Devil's Foot) The hallucinatory effects of the poison proved very real in the nightmare visions that Holmes experienced, "all images of death which had obsessed Holmes throughout the episode – Cain, Oedipus, Nebuchadnezzar and Moriarty, orchestrated by the director into a disturbing series of images... When with Watson's help, Holmes recovers, he uses Watson's first name for the only time in the series." (A Study in Celluloid) *"I slipped it in to show that, underneath it all, there was something more than – well what they say, Holmes is all mind and no heart... I tried to bring a little trickle of blood into the marble."* (Jeremy to Scarlet Street)

Holmes now has the method of the two murders in mind and he sincerely apologises to his friend for involving him in the deadly experiment. The murderer on this occasion is pursuing a personal revenge against his own family and in so doing has killed his own sister for which he would be dismissed as a heartless rogue and be condemned to hanging in a court of law. He has also lied to Holmes throughout the investigation and his own murder becomes a just and fitting outcome for the strange and sad tale. Holmes has settled on Sterndale as the guilty party but this time guilty of revenge against the real murderer. If he had reported him to the authorities a greater injustice would have been done so Holmes is prepared to take the responsibility, to act as judge and jury and make the decision that most people would choose if they were in his position. Jeremy said in interview, *"I think he's a very modern person. He's interested in the poor, the street, law and justice."* His comment on Sterndale's love for Brenda Tregennis is made personal when he says. *"I have never loved, but if I did..."* which provides us with some insight into the great detective's personal life. Whether he has ever allowed himself the opportunity to have that experience is not made clear, but there is a certain whimsical longing in the speech which suggests that he may have wanted to be in Sterndale's place, even if only fleetingly.

The Times critic welcomed the new series. "'Mr. Holmes,' says the vicar, "in all England, you are the one man we truly need." To which Dr. Watson, as a good PR man, replies that the great detective "likes nothing better than to sink his teeth into a problem of this sort." Which indeed, embarking on his fourth and final series for Granada, with this episode entitled *The Devil's Foot* Sherlock does with his usual aplomb and uncanny reasoning. Looking not unlike an undertaker, Holmes has departed for Cornwall for the good of his health and finds that the disentanglement of local dark deeds is as good a restorative as he could wish. He even buries his hypodermic on the beach. It's good to encounter once again ringing phrases like "My soul cried out for revenge!" And the investigation itself is vintage Conan Doyle, who wrote his first Sherlock Holmes story more than a century ago. The Cornish locale, the farthest the Manchester crew had travelled, is somewhat falsely embellished with Stonehenge-like emblems, but these only add to some satisfying melodrama... The story is a fine old piece of nonsense which involves a young woman frightened to death and two grown men being scared so witless that they go off, rolling-eyed and foaming mouthed, to the local asylum..." (The Times 6th April 1988)

The dramatist Gary Hopkins told *The Black Box Club*, "I was already familiar with most of the Sherlock Holmes stories, having read and reread them as a teenager.... *The Devil's Foot* was one I'd come back to a couple of times because, as with a lot of the best Holmes, it was dark and scary. If I was going to adapt one, that would be the one... Cornwall was predictably cold and wet in November, and there were times when thick fog added to the problems. But producer June was determined to film *The Devil's Foot* where Sir Arthur Conan Doyle had set it, even though it meant spending extra money and filming a much greater distance away from the production base at Manchester than was usual. Her feeling was that it would have been impossible to make anywhere else look quite like the Cornish coast. I believe she was absolutely right and that the finished result on the screen proves it. *The Devil's Foot* has a brooding, sinister and yet romantic atmosphere all its own... The whole thing works beautifully. And, though I adapted other Sherlock Holmes stories later on, I can't deny that *The Devil's Foot* was – and still is – very special." In 1989, the Granada Team were pleased to visit New York to accept the second Edgar Allan Poe award for The Best Television Teleplay.

Jeremy revealed he had sought permission from Dame Jean Conan Doyle, the author's daughter, for his disposal of the hypodermic syringe in the Cornish sands. *"I wanted to make a little statement to this century that even the great man buries the needle. It doesn't mean to say that Holmes might not pick up the habit again."* The number of messages he received from children thanking him for his interpretation of Holmes had made him aware that he could be a force for good. He commented on his own view of the habit, *"I've never taken drugs. You can't do a good job of acting if you're high on some awful substance. I relieve the pressure of my profession with yoga or meditation. I used to fall over drug addicts in the street outside the theatre on Broadway. I got to know them so well that they started waving to me."* (Private sadness of a super sleuth in The Daily Express 24th March 1985)

At Jeremy's Memorial Service Denis Quilley shared some memories of filming in Cornwall, "After a day's shooting, we sat in this small private hotel in Cornwall singing our way through the score of *A Most Happy Fella*. 'Joe-ey! Joe-ey!' we crooned into each other's eyes. The other diners, who tended towards the elderly and respectable, stopped in mid-mouthful. June Wyndham Davies was sitting at the same table trying pathetically to pretend she wasn't with us. When we finished, instead of receiving rapturous applause as we would have done in a black-and-white Frank Capra movie, there was a stunned silence.

Jeremy whispered in my ear, *'I think we've just lost the contract.'"* (Denis Quilley) Both Denis and Jeremy were very competent singers and had both starred in the role of Robert Browning in the stage production of the musical *Robert and Elizabeth* in the 1970s so the concert would have been a professional one. Maybe the audience were stunned by the intimacy of the performance and would not have been used to such exuberance. Denis also commented on Jeremy's response to his wife's death, "he was in a very fragile mental and physical state... despite all this he managed not only to soldier on but give that extraordinary, electrifying performance of Sherlock Holmes under the most intense physical and emotional pressure. He could easily have packed it in... Far from doing that, it even, it seems to me, deepened his interpretation of Holmes." (Scarlet Street)

Silver Blaze – The Return of Sherlock Holmes

Silver Blaze (Dramatised by John Hawkesworth: Directed by Brian Mills fb: 13th April 1988) Jeremy's Holmes had been undergoing a transition from the cold, repressed man who was incredibly difficult to play, to gradually let more of his own personality flow into the performance so that every move, every expression appears totally natural. It is also interesting to realise that he has been building the jigsaw piece by piece and as the series progressed each piece seems to fit more securely into place. *Silver Blaze* is an episode in which Holmes and Watson visit the Kings Pyland Stable on Dartmoor to investigate the disappearance of the famous racehorse, Silver Blaze, the odds-on favourite to win the upcoming Wessex Cup. The brutal murder of the trainer John Straker brings a challenge for Holmes to piece together the events of that night, find the missing racehorse and the murderer. Watson's reading of the sporting paper provides more details about Silver Blaze, of Isonomy stock in his fifth year of racing with an excellent record. Baring-Gould notes in the *Annotated Sherlock Holmes* that Isonomy was a real horse with a remarkable record which won the Manchester Plate and the Ascot Gold Cup in 1879 and again in 1880 and went to stud in 1881. He also gives evidence that Silver Blaze was possibly Compass, another successful horse. Holmes's amazing powers can be seen on the train journey to Dartmoor, in the unforgettable image of the detective holding his watch, side-stepping the other passengers, counting telegraph poles and thereby calculating the speed of the train.

Jeremy's Holmes takes on the role of interviewer as he first speaks to the principal witnesses, Edith Baxter, the maid; and Ned Hunter, the stable boy. With Watson's help he soon identifies a series of important clues to what happened on the fateful night; the unexpected visitor seeking information about the horses, the stable boy who was drugged with powdered opium and the dog which didn't bark in the night time. Holmes recognises that Inspector Gregory has no imagination and is therefore restricted in his success. In contrast, Holmes displays his ability to use his imagination and reach inspired conclusions. Just as in *The Musgrave Ritual* where he constructs the events that led to the death of the butler Brunton, here he can uncover the facts behind the disappearance of the horse. He examines the scene of the crime to find every last detail of the events of that night. Holmes's close scrutiny of the murder scene was made more dramatic by Jeremy's throwing himself onto the mud, by his "stretching himself upon his face" as he made "a careful study of the trampled mud in front of him". He is seemingly oblivious to the effects of the mud on his long, light grey hooded coat as he reveals a couple of items hidden in the soil; a half burnt wax vesta and a piece of candle that the police had missed or failed to trample on. He tells the Inspector he had found the items because he was *looking for them."*

His imaginative powers will lead him to follow the missing horse across the moor towards Mapleton and Lord Backwater's stable. Taking one of Silver Blaze's horseshoes with them he can justify his theory with finding a matching print, so it is with confidence that he seeks and finds Silas Brown, the sneaking bully of a trainer who is quickly outmanoeuvred by Holmes's commanding tone and the missing horse is recovered. But instead of taking it home to Kings Pyland he decides to have a little fun at the Colonel's expense to pay him back for his earlier *"cavalier"* attitude. Although all of the filming took place in the North of England, possibly the Peak District, the *Wessex Cup* was filmed at the Bangor-on-Dee racecourse. It was only there that Holmes revealed Silver Blaze to Ross, *"There, Colonel, is your horse! I found in the hands of a faker and brought him to the course just as he was."*

There are two criminals in this episode: first, the trainer who is prepared to injure his own horse in order to make money from those who would pay for such information and secondly, the trainer Silas Brown who is ready to take the opportunity of a wandering stray horse and conceal its identity by painting out its distinguishing marks. His motive is similar to that of Straker in that the community in which he works will make it worth his while. Both these men are very different from the other criminals we have seen in Doyle's stories and may have been familiar in the horse racing community. Ellery Queen wrote in his anthology *Sporting Blood*, "Silver Blaze belongs prominently to any list of the five leading Sherlockian short stories. It represents the great Holmes at his incisive, dynamic best; despite its author's biographical apology, it reveals no obvious turf errors at least to the lay reader; and we could find no finer yarn to head our parade of The Great Sports Detective Stories." (Quoted in The Annotated Sherlock Holmes by William Baring-Gould)

The Granada team had decided to have Holmes reveal all the details of the case at dinner at the Colonel's house and not on the train journey back to London as in the original story. The dinner presented the opportunity for sharing out details of the investigation between both Holmes and Watson and as such was more effective; it is interesting to note that Holmes remains abstemious and rejects most of the food he is offered whilst Watson is happy to enjoy all the pleasures of the occasion. The amusing manner in which Jeremy suggested the role of the sheep in the story and his request for an amnesty for the nearby stables is sensitively achieved so that Colonel Ross has no alternative but to thank them for a successful solution and drink to his new friends, "Sherlock Holmes and Doctor Watson."

There are several moments in this episode which show Jeremy's flair and flourishes suggesting that he was once more enjoying himself in the role of Holmes. As the two friends leave for London, he calls Mrs Hudson in a singing voice; he waltzes back into his room and the music of Patrick Gowers is particularly effective here. The long grey coat enables him to move about the moor as if around a dance floor, and helps him to dominate the scene, which Jeremy's Holmes cannot fail to do. He also thanks Mrs Hudson for bringing his telegrams with the whispered endearment, "*Thank you, my dear,*" which surely doesn't appear in the original tale. His show of concern for the distressed maid as she tells of finding Straker's body is a sensitive gesture which reflects Jeremy's own personality. This series would provide instances where he allows more of himself to creep into his interpretation of the cold more repressed Holmes.

His love of horses can be seen again, especially in the scene with Silver Blaze where he seems to whisper that the sponge and water will not hurt him, but merely restore his beautiful appearance and understandably the horse was reluctant to be dismissed. "The solution to it all is satisfying as well. Jeremy Brett reminds us yet again as to why he is the perfect actor to play Arthur Conan Doyle's legendary sleuth and Edward Hardwicke makes for a Doctor Watson of equal perfection." (IMDb) The *New York Times* commented on Jeremy's performance, "When not flinging himself on the dank moors to search for overlooked evidence, Holmes is delivering tidy lectures on the necessity for imagination. Pointing out the difference between himself and the well-meaning but unimaginative inspector, he says: '*We imagined what might have happened and acted on our supposition and find ourselves justified.*' Holmes has his tricks for keeping others off balance. While they might be walking away from a site, Holmes will hesitate for one last, clearly significant look. Or, conversely, while they dawdle, Holmes stalks out impatiently. It's an ingeniously clever act. Little wonder that the initially sceptical Colonel Ross eventually gasps, 'Good heavens, you take my breath away, Mr. Holmes.' Mr. Brett has developed his impersonation of the character to the point where it is capable of doing just that." (New York Times 18th November 1988)

The Baker Street File – Silver Blaze

118 - Holmes cocked his eye at me... like a connoisseur who had just taken his first sip of a comet vintage

The *TV Times* listing asks, "What is the secret of *Wisteria Lodge*? Holmes and Watson enter into one of the most baffling and intriguing cases of their career. A foreign tyrant, an English governess and an unorthodox police inspector lead them on a wild goose chase which starts with murder." (TV Times 16-22 April 1988) **Wisteria Lodge (Dramatised by Jeremy Paul: Directed by Peter Hammond fb: 20th April 1988)** is a *"grotesque"* story which is brought to Holmes by Mr Scott Eccles. The telegram sent by Scott Eccles read,

HAVE JUST HAD MOST INCREDIBLE AND GROTESQUE EXPERIENCE. MAY I
CONSULT YOU?   SCOTT ECCLES, POST-OFFICE, CHARING CROSS (Wisteria Lodge)

The opening chapter of the story is entitled, "The singular experience of Mr John Scott Eccles" and it explains what has actually happened but with little information of why he was chosen for this experience. The flourish with which Holmes welcomes the flustered and distressed Mr Scott Eccles suggests he is missing the heady days of adventure and would welcome some distraction from his boredom. *"My mind is like a racing engine, tearing itself to pieces because it is not connected up with the work for which it was built. Life is commonplace, the papers are sterile; audacity and romance seem to have passed for ever from the criminal world."* (The Adventure of Wisteria Lodge) The flustered and distressed Mr Scott Eccles first solicits Holmes's help and then immediately insults his profession as a private detective to which Holmes responds with a masterful assertion of his position.

When Scott Eccles was able to organise his tale into an intelligible order, it was indeed a "singular and unpleasant" tale of a night spent at Wisteria Lodge in the company of Garcia, a brief acquaintance who had invited him to stay for a few days. The dinner itself had been a strange affair and not what he had expected, notable for the nervousness of his host and the gloomy servant; the lack of good food and wine served by foreign staff. The evening was interrupted by a sudden unexplained disturbance caused by the delivery of a note which was crumpled up and thrown onto the fire by Garcia. "He gave up all pretence at conversation and sat smoking endless cigarettes, lost in his own thoughts..." He remembers being awakened by his host at one o'clock in the morning, asking if he had rung for something, but in the morning the house was empty: "Foreign host, foreign footman, foreign cook all vanished in the night." The explanation of how Scott Eccles came to accept such an invitation is also rather strange, especially as he didn't know Garcia before this event took place, so one can't help feeling he had been rather foolish or simply too trusting.

This episode becomes a contest between the two investigators, the Inspector of Police and Holmes as they each pursue the true reason for the night's strange events which had ended in the murder of Garcia, the host. Freddie Jones as Baynes enjoys showing off before Holmes with his analysis of the note that Scott Eccles had said was thrown into the fire the evening before: he had "overpitched it" and the Inspector relishes sharing every last detail as a personal challenge to Holmes who looks on fascinated by the performance and the competition. In spite of this show of bravado the real detective, Holmes, finds a few more *"trifling points"*. As he examines every area of the room, Jeremy amusingly investigates the contents of the fireplace with more vigour than usual, proving that no further evidence would escape notice before he finds the gun case for two pistols, one of which is missing. It is interesting that Watson is the one who sees and chases the mulatto who has been looking through the window, leaving the two detectives still in personal competition with the other. Inspector Baynes has a considerable ego and as another of those over-confident representatives of the law he has an enormous regard for Holmes's methods, but in this case, he would like to outshine the master. In spite of the sabre rattling, surprisingly, they reach the same conclusion that Scott Eccles is innocent. Michael Cox described Freddie's interpretation as "smug": "He certainly gives us the vain, ambitious character described by Conan Doyle. He embroiders it with a few actor's tricks – the mittens, the outrageous hat and the boiled sweets – and sits up and begs for words like rich and ripe to be applied to it. I would describe it as smug. It is certainly such a big performance that it nearly throws the picture out of balance." (A Study in Celluloid)

By using his usual methods of investigation Holmes has discovered information about the local residents and identified the suspect, Henderson at High Gables. Watson on his own instincts has accidentally discovered the person who can provide the backstory of events and bring them together. Don Juan Murillo/Henderson is an extremely dangerous villain, a savage dictator responsible for endless cases of murder and torture who had escaped from justice. It is assumed that Conan Doyle was influenced by accounts of Dom Pedro II; "The Emperor of Brazil was deposed in 1889 and spent the rest of his life in Europe, where he died (December 5th 1891)" (Dr Julian Wolff in The Annotated Sherlock Holmes) It is even more surprising when both Holmes and Baynes independently identify him as Garcia's murderer and, in spite of Baynes's attempt to steal his rival's limelight, they join forces. This is an example of Holmes's magnanimity towards another detective as the search for truth comes before all other considerations. The story of the once dictator of San Pedro, Central America *"A lewd and blood-thirsty tyrant"* is finally revealed along with the plot for revenge *"for the rivers of blood,"* on behalf of the families of his victims, led by Garcia and Miss Burnet, which had ended in tragedy.

Miss Burnet's rescue from the railway station by Holmes and Watson arriving at speed on hired bicycles becomes one of the highlight scenes where Jeremy merges with Holmes. It is a remarkable vision of Holmes in full regalia, long black coat, hat and scarf flying, making pursuit on a bicycle. They arrive just as the train is leaving, almost too late to make any attempt at a rescue. However, Holmes leaps onto the engine footplate in a brave yet vain attempt to stop the train whilst Watson, ever the ladies' man, successfully catches the imprisoned governess as she opens the door and escapes from the railway carriage helping her away to safety. Holmes's vicious attack on the villains with his cane, breaking the carriage window, is an unusual display of anger but a legitimate response from a man who stands for justice. But then we see his smile as he recognises the men sitting in the next carriage who will bring about that justice. It is Miss Burnet's description of life under the dictatorship of Don Murillo, the Tiger of San Pedro, which confirms the events that Scott Eccles was unwittingly caught up in.

The *TV Times* provided an assessment of the success of the series to date with the headline, *Detecting a good series*, "Thanks to ITV's Sherlock Holmes dramas... a new generation of fans has discovered the pipe-smoking violin-playing sleuth. And enthusiasts for Sir Arthur Conan Doyle's detective stories have praised the TV series for its authenticity. The Swedish Academy of Detection which encourages higher standards of crime literature, recently gave the series a special award for faithfully rendering the text and successfully capturing the period atmosphere and distinctive nature of the classical stories." Jeremy Brett who plays Holmes, tries to explain the character's appeal – to readers and viewers. *"He shows you can live your life according to your own code of ethics. And he combines the logical thinking men are supposed to have with the intuition of women."* (TV Times 23-29 April 1988)

The Bruce Partington Plans **(Dramatised John Hawkesworth: Directed by John Gorrie fb: 27th April 1988)** is based amongst the backstreets of London and Holmes solves the case of the murder of Cadogan West and the missing submarine plans by his detailed knowledge of the city's railway system. The *"bookend"* of this episode shows Holmes in a state of boredom with no cases needing his attention and fog plus the dull London criminal is to blame. The piece we hear him singing is *Palestrina's Psalm 42 "Sicut cervus desiderat ad fontes aquarum, ita desiderat anima mea ad te, Deus"* (translated as "As the deer longs for running waters, so my soul longs for you...") Rosalie as Mrs Hudson would bring more "embroidery" to their relationship, as she says she must have a word with him, but his reply, *"I apologise for the state of my room,"* feels like a Jeremy led addition. The telegram announcing Mycroft's visit to Baker Street brings some relief and is of particular interest as it is such a rare occurrence, *"Once and only once he has been here... But that Mycroft should break out in this erratic fashion. A planet might as well leave its orbit... Jupiter himself is descending upon us today."* (The Adventure of the Bruce Partington Plans) The death of a Government employee, Cadogan West, explains Mycroft's presence.

The appearance of Charles Grey as the benign Mycroft Holmes is always a pleasant addition to an episode. The brotherly relationship created by Charles and Jeremy is based on mutual respect; there is no rivalry as one would expect from two men of equal intelligence. As a government official, on this occasion accompanied by Inspector Bradstreet, Mycroft brings his concerns about the Bruce Partington submarine plans (probably the British built E-class submarine) found on the brutally murdered body of Cadogan West, left lying beside the railway track. Holmes's observation of the murder scene can be seen in Jeremy sitting cross-legged on the side of the railway track, in full Holmes finery with top hat and scarf, oblivious to the effects of the dirt upon his pristine clean black coat. *"Points and a curve"* in the railway track is of interest to Holmes and he goes away laughing loudly, as he can see *"possibilities"* where the others cannot.

This is a workmanlike, almost textbook investigation with the keepers of the keys at the Royal Naval Patents Office at the Woolwich Arsenal being the initial focus beginning with Sir James Walter, the official guardian. In the Granada version there were two people in possession of a complete set of keys; Sir James and Sidney Johnson, the senior clerk which enabled the scriptwriters to suggest other possible suspects for the robbery. On arrival at his home, they are informed Sir James has just died which brings more questions than answers, and interest too, as Holmes and Watson, dressed in their usual formal attire are mistaken for the undertakers, an amusing addition by Granada. Watson is also given an opportunity to introduce his friend Sherlock Holmes to a stranger with immense pride.

With no crime scene to search for missing clues Holmes follows his usual approach of following the clues and never assuming guilt until it's proven by fact. Cadogan West will be the focus for investigation and Miss Violet Westbury, his fiancée provides a picture of a loyal "patriotic man." The street on which West left her on the night of his disappearance faces the office at the Woolwich Arsenal where the plans are kept. Holmes's visit gives him an opportunity to learn more about the security: the keys necessary to enter and the window shutters that don't meet in the centre, all of which raises questions about what West had seen and his involvement in the theft. We can also see Holmes's need to understand the plans of the submarine and the full implications of the drawings that show the double valves with the automatic self-adjusting slots one of those found on West's body.

No one has noticed the implications of the double valves and these observations will prove helpful in trapping the criminals. Holmes has discovered enough evidence to question West's guilt and he is building a picture of the night's events. The station master at the Woolwich Arsenal, played by Robert Fyfe, Howard from *Last of the Summer Wine*, remembers the frantic hurry of West to catch the London train on the day of his disappearance but can give no explanation for the cause of his hurry or of loss of his ticket.

This is an international crime and the names of foreign spies who might trade in the submarine plans are the same as those mentioned in *The Second Stain* and with the death of Eduardo Lucas there are only two remaining. Hugo Oberstein lives at Caulfield Gardens, an address which Holmes knows backs onto the Underground where two other lines meet and trains are frequently held motionless. Seeking further information, Holmes suggests *"A spot of amateur burglary"* and the request for Watson to accompany him on his criminal exploits brings confirmation of the theory on how West's body ended up on the railway line. The relationship between Holmes and Watson appears particularly strong on this case where they work as a team and each show their dependence on the other. He must know that he is asking his friend to risk his reputation, so Holmes makes his request on patriotic grounds: Mycroft, the Admiralty, the Cabinet with *"the exalted person Herself who waits for news... We are bound to go."* It becomes a necessary act of public service and as Watson, replies, *"Of course,"* Holmes's pride and relief is reflected in Jeremy's wide grin: *"I knew you wouldn't shrink at the last."*

It was Watson who found that Oberstein was burning newspaper in his fireplace without wood or coal. This led Holmes to discover the messages from Pierrot in the agony column of the *Daily Telegraph* and this same method of communication would be used to capture one and convict both criminals. Colonel Walter is not the person Holmes anticipated at Caulfield Gardens but he was coerced into writing the letter which would entrap his foreign collaborator as reparation for his wrong doing. The final scene is a well-orchestrated drama with the three protagonists sitting nonchalantly at a restaurant table in the lobby of the Charing Cross Hotel, whilst the police and the spies move purposely in front of the observers, every move noted and responded to, so that Oberstein is taken into custody and although Walter had slipped away unnoticed, Bradstreet promises to "keep him on a long lead." One feels that Sherlock and Mycroft Holmes with the indispensable John Watson make a perfect team of investigators. Holmes's willingness to turn to crime is responsible for the success of the investigation and the earlier scene with Jeremy eating his breakfast in his nightshirt and dressing gown twinkling at the suggestion that he would have made an excellent burglar is a reminder that the police could never be quite as effective.

Jeremy was a master in front of the camera. Edward said of him, "He was a genius. Sometimes the director would say, 'Would you do so and so?' And I would think, How can you do that? And Jeremy would do it in a gesture!" A current reviewer thought his performance encompassed all the qualities of Holmes. "Sly, camp, exuberant, melancholy, savage, trite, pompous, sensitive, manic and loyal – all the qualities that defined Holmes seemed to run across Brett's face in a flickering slideshow, his muscles twitching and jerking, as if he could not bear to suffer any one emotion for more than an instant." The writer thought that Jeremy was "too good. His understatedly intense Sherlock Holmes brought the Victorian menace of the stories to life on screen" and he concluded "Brett outshone every actor who had ever portrayed the Great Detective." (Christopher Stevens in Daily Mail 10th March 2015)

The Hound of the Baskervilles

The Hound of the Baskervilles appeared in *The Strand* magazine in August 1901 nine years after Holmes's death in *The Adventure of the Final Problem* and Holmes fans around the world had waited all that time with considerable dismay for the next Sherlock Holmes story from Arthur Conan Doyle. ***The Hound of the Baskervilles* (Dramatised by T.R. Bowen: Directed by Brian Mills fb: 31st August 1988)** is Doyle's best known work, probably because it has been filmed the most over the years. The mystery set on the wasteland of Dartmoor concerning a mystical hound brings intrigue and death, perpetuating the legend of "Sir Richard Cabell, Lord of the Manor of Brooke, in the parish of Buckfastleigh. A gentleman of ill repute and on the night of his death, black hounds breathing fire and smoke raced over Dartmoor and howled around his manor house." (The Annotated Sherlock Holmes) In Conan Doyle's story Sir Hugo Baskerville abducts a young girl "who escaped across the moor at night, cursing. He unkennelled the pack of hounds and hunted her down like a wild animal": the girl was found dead from exhaustion and Sir Hugo's throat had been torn out by *"a huge demonic hound."* He would dedicate his story to his friend Fletcher Robinson who brought the original idea to Doyle. "Robinson and I are exploring the Moor over our Sherlock Holmes book. I think it will work out splendidly indeed I have already done nearly half of it. Holmes is at his very best..." (Conan Doyle)

Jeremy told the *TV Times*: "*I remember how I felt as a child. We would drive across the Moor on the way to family holidays in Cornwall, and to this day I can remember the fear coming from it, the fear of the legends, the bleakness, the prison, and obviously of the Hound. There is danger here. That's what the story draws on so brilliantly. There is the very smell of the supernatural. Then add in the lamb to the slaughter, in the shape of young Baskerville returning to his inheritance. The threat to him runs right through the story, so that you have no idea what is coming at him – whether it's human, animal, metaphysical or supernatural. Is the Hound real?*" (TV Times 27th August 1988) Whilst standing on the scene of the Grimpen Mire where the story reaches its climax, Jeremy shuddered and said, "*How brilliant Conan Doyle was to keep – at every moment – the Hound bounding through the story, gleaming and salivating.*" But this hound was not scary and the Great Dane, the size of a donkey nuzzled up to him, recognising his love of animals. "*If you can't get the Hound right, it's better you don't see him. We didn't get it right.*" (Jeremy)

A story where "the powers of evil are exalted" and detection attempts to investigate the supernatural begins in the Baker Street rooms with Holmes observing Watson who is seated behind him, in his examination of the silver-topped cane left behind in their rooms the night before. Jeremy explained how difficult he found presenting this simple detail, however, after a great deal of thought and rereading of Doyle, he found that by lifting the lid on his "*well-polished, silver-plated coffee pot*" he was able to view his friend. The arrival of Dr James Mortimer will confirm Holmes's deductions of a young doctor in Hospital medicine with his walking stick, a gift from Charing Cross Hospital and the possessor of a dog. Watson's assessment might have been different to Holmes's own, but he does receive some recognition for his efforts, "*Watson, I am bound to say you habitually underrate your abilities*". Although his conclusions are "*erroneous*" Holmes finds ways in the Canon of praising his friend's qualities and in *The Last Bow* he points out, "*Good old Watson! You are the one fixed point in a changing age*" a recognition of the value of their friendship to him.

Jeremy's unique humour is in evidence when the enthusiastic scientist asks, "Would you have any objection to my running my finger along your parietal fissure?" and Holmes replies with a twirl of his chair amidst uproarious laughter, "*Behave and sit down.*" Jeremy has maintained the image of Holmes as someone who relishes such diversions in much the same way as he had with Jabez Wilson in *The Red Headed League* and in his meeting with the butler Brunton in *The Musgrave Ritual*. Mortimer gives the reason for his visit as the recent death of Sir Charles Baskerville who suffered a heart attack brought on by sheer terror and with all its supernatural overtones Holmes is intrigued in spite of his initial conclusion that the story of the hound was no more than a fairy tale. The Granada team had made the decision not to film the first appearance of the hound which was at the heart of the mystery leaving Doctor Mortimer to deliver the mystical phrase "Mr Holmes, they were the footprints of a gigantic hound!" Holmes turns away from a supernatural explanation and finally asks sympathetically, "*How can I assist?*"

Further mystery is brought into the case with the recent arrival of the next of kin, Sir Henry Baskerville the last of the Baskervilles from America and Holmes will need all his skills to unravel the tangle. It becomes clear that he has been followed by someone who knows who he is when he complains of two *"inexplicable"* thefts of shoes from his hotel room and then a worrying note, unsigned and put together from newspaper cuttings taken from *The Times* which reads:

AS YOU VALUE YOUR LIFE OR YOUR REASON KEEP AWAY FROM THE MOOR

Breakfast with Sir Henry at the hotel provides an opportunity to provide an expert, detailed analysis of the writer of the note which Holmes delivers in his usual methodical and assiduous manner with the conclusion that this was a friendly warning. However, he is interrupted when a mysterious bearded observer is brought into the frame and although Holmes and Watson give chase, his identity remains a mystery as they were unable to catch him. The fact that the Baskerville estate is worth *"close on a million"* could represent "a stake for which a man might play a dangerous game." Holmes further admits to Watson, *"it is an ugly, dangerous business"*.

The tension of the action slackens as Watson is sent to Dartmoor and the moor itself looks bright and attractive in daylight hours, with no hint of mystery or threat of a raging sinister hound. His role is to protect Sir Henry Baskerville and to be the eyes and ears of his friend, to observe behaviour amongst the country folk and *"simply to report facts to me in the fullest possible manner"*, but above all, he has instructions to *"avoid the moor where... the powers of evil are exalted"*. Watson is no detective but he is a reliable narrator who responds to events as any normal person would and he concentrates on the people and the realities of country living rather than on the need for detection. However, he is swiftly tested as Watson's first concern becomes the news of an escaped convict, Selden "the Notting Hill Murderer" deemed "insane" and roaming the mist covered moors. The dreadful Grimpen Mire brings further danger with its risk of perishing in the deadly bog. A series of further concerns unsettle Watson: Beryl Stapleton, assuming he is Sir Henry, advises him to leave for his own safety; the suspicious behaviour of the butler Barrymore and afterwards the revelation of Selden's relationship with his wife causes Watson to cry, "I wish to God Holmes was here. Why does he not come!"

There is the possible hiccough of the relationship as Holmes finally returns and Watson realises that he has sent letters when they were not required, but Holmes provides the much needed assurance that they were *"well thumbed"*. There is humour in the *"meagre refreshment"* he serves Watson, a "quite disgusting" stew for which the boy Cartwright had provided the ingredients and another example of the joke surrounding food, created by Jeremy and Edward. Holmes then tells Watson that Beryl Stapleton is in fact Stapleton's wife and not his sister. Stapleton will emerge as the villain of the story when he is recognised as a Baskerville; Holmes identifies the relationship in the portrait of Sir Hugo Baskerville hanging in the Hall and concludes that he may have ambitions to inherit the estate. When a trap is laid with their proposed visit to London, we are not surprised to see Holmes and Watson entering, then immediately leaving the train to return to Grimpen. In the final scenes Holmes shows an unexpected concern for an upset Laura Lyons, who is forced to accept that Stapleton's offer of marriage was only a fairy tale. We see him cradle Beryl Stapleton sympathetically in a dramatic rescue from her brutal imprisonment and his concern for Sir Henry is just as caring as he receives a savage mauling from the phosphorous coated hound before it is killed with Holmes's revolver.

The enthusiast might also notice that there are two scenes within this episode which have been taken from *The Greek Interpreter,* one where Holmes takes a carriage to *The Royal Observatory* and another when he can be seen walking down a deserted railway platform swinging his cane and disappearing into the mist, which points to serious cost cutting resulting from an overspend on the earlier four episodes of *The Return.* Jeremy had told David Stuart Davies that he was *"terribly unwell"* whilst filming this episode. Yet, he gave a brilliant performance, hitting all the notes, and even brought a more compassionate Holmes to the screen. The only problem with this Hound was the Hound.

The critics gave a mixed response to the episode. Jeremy's interpretation of Holmes had been a triumph and there was enormous expectation on the Granada team to present the very best version of Conan Doyle's most famous story. Overall it was welcomed. "Though many mystery fans think that this is not the definitive version of HOUND, it does have Jeremy Brett, which makes it good enough for me. It also has a superb performance by Hardwicke, who actually has more screen time on this particular outing than Brett." (Sean Farrell in Scarlet Street Winter 1996) "Brett's Holmes is by now justifiably celebrated. The actor brings a calculated touch of 19th century melodrama to the role. If Brett had a moustache, he would be twirling it shamelessly. His Holmes is cold, arrogant, smug and infuriatingly brilliant..." (New York Times)

Nick Smurthwaite in *The Stage* found the pace "predictable and plodding" but was full of praise for the "ravishing camera work" and especially for Jeremy's "outrageously mannered performance, alive with ticks and grimaces". "There is one extraordinary scene, in a hotel coffee lounge, where Holmes applies his scientific mind to dissecting an anonymous letter, while Brett applies every piece of ammunition in his actor's armoury to make the scene appear as riveting and sexy on screen as it must have appeared dull and dry on the page. How can you help but admire the resource of such an actor? Brett does not have the advantage of Basil Rathbone's traditional Holmesian looks... but he compensates with a look of crazed intensity and an actorish charisma. It might not have been what Conan Doyle had in mind, but works a treat nevertheless... Its biggest let down is the hound an 11 stone Great Dane...which looks more silly than menacing..." (Nick Smurthwaite Barking up the wrong tree in The Stage and Television Today 1st September 1988)

The Times praised the episode for its style and polish, "Style is the keynote of *The Hound of the Baskervilles,* the climax of Granada's polished series of Sherlock Holmes adaptations. Deciding, perhaps, that the story is not one of the strongest of the Conan Doyle canon and that it will be familiar to many viewers, the makers have decided to go all out for production value. This means strong locations (with Yorkshire and Staffordshire doubling convincingly for Dartmoor) supplemented by a spooky, studio-created Grimpen Mire, and a standard of camerawork in which no opportunity is lost to squeeze the maximum effect out of lighting and composition. Happily, this attention to form does not mean a smothering of content and my only complaint is that, after steadily pacing for most of the time, the denouement is wrapped up all too quickly. Having enjoyed the bulk of a leisurely and satisfying meal, it is a pity to have to wolf the cheese and gulp the coffee." (Peter Waymark 'The dogged detective' in The Times 31st August 1988)

When he was asked about the effects of living with the character for so long and whether he thought Holmes was taking over his life Jeremy replied, *"I used to think he was. I can't bear to look at old photographs of me looking strained and ill on location. But I no longer feel threatened by him and for the first time I'm really enjoying playing him."* (TV Times 27th August 1988) *"I began to feel better with Holmes, and I wasn't quite so cross with him... 'cause I blamed him a little... I was working, you see, so far away from Joan, and it had taken up so much of our last – what we – I discovered to be our last few years."* However, it wasn't quite as simple as that. *"I have to be sure to get rid of him. It's rather like washing. I mean if you really wash. I had to really shower, because the thing about Holmes is it's like walking a magnesium tightrope of blazing brilliance. You're up. You have to reach for him."* (ibid)

The fan letters he received also helped him make the decision to carry on, *"...the fan letters I have received – about 200 a week from all over the world – have moved me so much I have decided to carry on... I've changed my make-up now so I don't look quite so bloodless and in the current series I play him more of a heroic figure than a neurotic. I think he is still quite an isolated figure but I've warmed him up a bit."* He felt so confident about Holmes that he said, *"I have this feeling that* The Return of Sherlock Holmes *is better even than the first 13 series. I can't quite tell you why that is – it is to do with some shift of emphasis, some confidence, some chemistry between Edward and me. But there is definitely something."* (The Television Sherlock Holmes) When he was told by a taxi driver: *"Sherlock Holmes is our hero, you know"* he was amazed because *"I'd never thought of Holmes as a hero before. But as I thought about it I realised that Holmes works for the poor and can't be bothered with the rich, and so he really is a sort of hero."* (TV Times 19th December 1987)

Baker Street File – The Hound of the Baskervilles

108 - My simple wants: a loaf of bread and a clean collar

125 - Never have I seen a man run as Holmes ran that night. I am reckoned fleet of foot, but he outpaced me...

The Case of the Abbey Treasure

A short feature was made in 1988 to coincide with Jeremy's unveiling of a bronze plaque on the wall of Abbey House in Baker Street, the location which had been chosen as the most accurate address for 221b. At the unveiling ceremony Jeremy stated that Sherlock Holmes had lived at that address and later it would become the Abbey National Building Society. The whimsical short film ***The Case of the Abbey Treasure*** was produced by the Granada team and filmed at the conclusion of *The Hound of the Baskervilles,* in which Jeremy and Edward had just discussed the final details of the case. In this short film Watson is reading a letter addressed to them both saying that in 1898 they were in funds at the Bank to the tune of £917 for Watson and £988 for Holmes which with interest would total £100,000 in 1988. They humorously discussed the need to invest in the Building Society and subsequently in the future. HOLMES: "Our memory may linger on, or your writings may still be read. I suggest we may send Billy our page boy to collect it on our behalf. Or... his grandson." WATSON: "What a splendid idea. Do you think it will work?"

The feature ends with LOVE FROM THE GRANADA PRODUCTION TEAM

The Secret of Sherlock Holmes 1988 - Wyndham's Theatre

Jeremy by courtesy of Marcus Tylor

When asked whether the stage or film was preferable for his interpretation of Holmes, Jeremy said, *"The thing about working on the stage that makes it harder is that film is so instantly near it can see right into the person's soul. With someone so unbelievably isolated and closed, as Holmes is, it's sometimes easier to see the internal workings of the private man across on camera. He is such a private creature... and with the camera you can slide in and see the flicker of things across his face... little disappointments, little angers, little changes of mind. Of course, the other things you can get across on camera are his brilliant deductions and observations, but also his amazing intuition. And that's easier to do on film. On stage I try not to look at them for the first fifteen minutes... I don't even look at Watson very much either... I kind of gradually open up to them. That was the hardest part of moving into the theatre. But my director, Patrick Garland, helped me with that. He said, 'put a pane of glass down between you and the audience and don't look at them, ignore them, and then after about fifteen minutes warm through let them in...'"* (sherlockbrett.blogspot.com)

The Secret of Sherlock Holmes was on stage at Wyndham's Theatre from 22nd September 1988 and ran for more than 300 performances as a two man show with Jeremy in the role of Sherlock Holmes and Edward Hardwicke as Watson. Jeremy had personally commissioned Jeremy Paul to write the play in 1987 as a response to the centenary memorial for Arthur Conan Doyle. He recorded on audiotape more than eight hours of material from his study of the character, including his background inventions which he had come to rely on in his interpretation of the role. *"I sent him eight hours of tape. I just rattled off my ideas, and so when it comes to moments of leaving the canon... Jeremy (Paul) has taken them directly from the tapes. The thing I love about the play is that it gives Watson much more to say than the Canon does, because naturally, it was in the first person. I remember David Burke, when we finished* The Speckled Band, *saying, 'I had only thirty-six words to say in the entire film!' And this play does give Watson a platform to speak. Which I think is vital."* (sherlockbrett.blogspot.com) Jeremy wanted to concentrate on the friendship which existed between the two men in the course of their adventures and to develop the character of Holmes both through the tales of Doyle and beyond. None of the stories were done in whole but the play was faithful to Conan Doyle's dialogue *"taken and fashioned into an original mystery which I hope will intrigue Conan Doyle himself if he is looking in."* (Jeremy Paul) The ending was a *coup de Theatre*, an unexpected surprise for the audience yet fully justified. With his customary generosity, Jeremy refused acknowledgement as co-author of the play.

The play began with a one night performance under the title *A Case for Sherlock Holmes* at the Mayfair Theatre to which family, friends and colleagues from the acting world were invited and also included Dame Jean Conan Doyle. Edward Hardwicke was not available so the part of Watson was played by Sebastian Stride, who appeared as Cadogan West in *The Bruce Partington Plans* and the parts of Conan Doyle and Moriarty were played by Jeremy Paul. In this first performance of the play, a narrator was also included. The evening was a success and with the return of Edward Hardwicke as Watson the two man play opened at the Yvonne Arnaud Theatre in Guildford on 30th August with the new title *The Secret of Sherlock Holmes* under the direction of Patrick Garland. It was booked for a six week run at Wyndham's Theatre in the West End and with its Box Office success the play ran for a year in London before touring the major cities of Bradford, Hull, Cardiff, Birmingham, Aberdeen, Brighton, Manchester and Bath for a further eleven weeks. It also appeared in the Chichester Festival Theatre in November 1989. Consequently, Jeremy and Edward were on stage from 30th August 1988 until the beginning of 1990 for six evenings and two matinees a week. Thankfully there were some welcome breaks because it was a punishing schedule.

The main focus of this play was the relationship between the two men who shared the lodgings in 221b Baker Street. Jeremy's Holmes describes his need of Watson to the audience: *"Without Watson, I would have been dead within two years. A man needs a companion, he cannot sit alone... With his silent reproaches, his hurt look, Watson controlled my addiction. And our walks, our conversations, the sheer breadth and enthusiasm of his mind on any manner of subjects kept me sane... when the black fits were upon me. There was never a better friend. And I treated him abominably.*" Jeremy's six year study of Doyle had convinced him that, "*Watson and Holmes are two parts of the same person... It's a brilliant creation, their friendship and it needs both, you can't have one without the other, it's impossible.*" Dr Joseph Bell, the exceptional person on whom Conan Doyle based Holmes, would agree with Jeremy. In a letter to Conan Doyle he said, "*You are yourself Sherlock Holmes and well you know it.*"

"*The play is about friendship, which I think is terribly important, because it's a bygone thing. It's a Victorian thing, it's a Greek thing. But in the eighties it has lost its way through the rise of feminism – nothing wrong in that... But, men have lost all dignity in their personal friendships. And therefore, I think it's quite foreign to the young... I mean two gentlemen sharing. It's immediately suspect, or the 'odd couple.' So, that's really what the play is about... it's about love actually. I am so glad that several of the critics have managed to tune into that... not in a jaundiced sense... That's what we were aiming for, to show these two remarkable men.*" On another occasion he said, "*...But this play is really a thank you to Dr. John Watson, since behind every great man there's either a woman or a Watson, and Holmes finds to his amazement and a certain amount of horror that Watson has become indispensable. Holmes feels lost without his Boswell.*" (Brett becomes Holmes by Gregory Jensen)

Jeremy's interpretation of the enigma Sherlock Holmes still fascinated the public and the press. "Jeremy Brett's portrayal of Holmes is equally masterful, as one would expect. He entrances his audience with a projected voice and arm gesticulations worthy of Lord Olivier. His skill at changing Holmes's moods is compelling, as he leads the audience through his mental torment brought about by cocaine, his jovial quips with Watson; through Holmes's own exposition on Moriarty, where he leaves us dangling as he pauses for effect until he chooses to bring the audience down. Brett has the versatility of character to produce Holmes's many guises with the mere change of stance or gesture of hand, and the awesome ability to place an audience on the edge of their seats or roll them in the aisles..." (Review Gazette) It was refreshing to see Watson coming into focus, "Watson... comes across as an interesting personality in his own right, a doctor whose vocation was lost during the Afghan War and who has astute detection powers of his own. But it is to Jeremy Brett's mesmeric portrayal of Holmes, fascinatingly reptilian, to which we are drawn as he looks into his own soul, hinting at an unhappy family background, confessing his inadequacies and finally revealing..." (The Stage 29th September 1988)

Audience reviews commented on the magic that Jeremy created by his stage presence, his voice and the movements which were extraordinarily effective. He could move between the cruel, sardonic egotist to the concerned and friendly companion with a move of the hand or a raised eyebrow and bring about a complete transformation with just an alteration of tone or gesture. Edward was the perfect companion; his dependability conveyed in a low-keyed and naturalistic manner. "Edward Hardwicke... stalwartly genuine... not a touch of falsity in his performance." (The Independent) They made a perfect whole in this unique and unforgettable experience. The critics were full of praise: "Jeremy Brett... a brilliantly sculptured piece of exhibition acting... a spellbinding performance." (Daily Telegraph) "We are more preoccupied with this lonely Holmes than with any other interpretation. And he makes us laugh too, because he has an answer for everything and he strikes out with a marvellously dry sense of reason. It is a Holmes with humour and an unexpected heart." (Daily Express)

"In many ways Jeremy Brett is an old-fashioned, barn-storming sort of actor who appears to revel in strutting and fretting his hour upon the stage. Watching him on TV, you sometimes feel he is unhappily constrained by the smallness and intimacy required of screen acting. On stage he is larger than life, pacing around the elegant Victorian set like a caged animal, yet he knows exactly when to tone down the bravura style in order to invest the merest look or line with significance. You may be able to see the cogs turning in Brett's performance, but it's such a marvellous machine you don't really care." (The Stage 15th September 1988) David Stuart Davies said: "Jeremy's real home was the theatre. It was here where his flame burned its brightest, its warmest, its fiercest, its truest... He had the fine intellect necessary to analyse, dissect and intercept a role truly and definitively..." (Bending the Willow) Michael Cox agreed, "I had never seen Jeremy Brett in the theatre before and hardly expected such a powerful presence. Some film actors disappear on the stage, but Jeremy positively flourished, like a genie released from a bottle. Edward, of course, was the perfect Watson for this situation, giving us the most admirable, ordinary man in literature without being overshadowed by his mentor." (A Study in Celluloid) Initially, Edward was *a reluctant hero*. (Jeremy) "I remember that before we started to rehearse *The Secret of Sherlock Holmes* I went to the phone several times with the intention of telling Jeremy that I couldn't do it – I hadn't been on a stage for several years and found the idea of a two-handed play somewhat daunting. In fact I never picked up the phone. I knew Jeremy wouldn't hear of it. Jeremy was always positive, optimistic and so encouraging." (Edward Hardwicke)

Jeremy was still discovering new ways to play Holmes. *"I'm so steeped in playing Holmes now that a new idiom comes every day, without my choosing it, and I suddenly have another illumination. Why, just last night I found a new way of doing Holmes's soliloquies. I looked up toward the balcony, let myself open up, and let the audience flood into the words I was speaking. Suddenly I had found a new vulnerability in Holmes. Another essence. Another clue."* (Brett becomes Holmes) One observer recorded these differences, "I saw the show many times but always relished the matinee performances... as he would always push the envelope with left field acting choices. Once, out of the blue, he strutted around the stage, squawking like a demented rooster, flapping his coat tails like wings... brilliant. Two days later on the Saturday matinee, in the same scene, he simply squatted at the edge of the stage and spoke the same text quietly. Equally affecting. To watch the pair of them was a true master class in acting..." (Anon on jeremybrett.info)

Jeremy said of Edward, *"Ted is the nearest thing to a saint I have met on two feet. If it was not for him, I wouldn't be doing the play and I probably wouldn't do the television either. I haven't been on stage for 15(10) years. But I love the theatre."* The last major stage production of Sherlock Holmes had been *The Crucifer of Blood* in New York and Los Angeles with Charlton Heston in the role of Holmes, with Jeremy playing the role of Watson. This had made him one of the very few actors who had presented both Holmes and Watson in this medium. "I always used to think how sweet Watson was, and then I played him on stage and discovered he was a much better part for me. He's so full of love, and outgoing and reassuring, a loyal friend, so marvellous. If it wasn't for Watson, I think Holmes would be dead."

"The relationship which Edward Hardwicke and Jeremy Brett have built up between Holmes and Watson that has captivated audiences on screen becomes electric on stage. The two actors' scholarly performances produce a rare clarity of character. Hardwicke's dignified Dr Watson becomes a more familiar general practitioner as if in a living room with friends rather than an auditorium with an audience... Watson's true compassion and humility and devotion to Holmes in a delicate, intense manner that is perhaps too intimate for the screen but on stage the gestures and words seem to be more meaningful. There is a closeness with literally, just the two of them, that is lost on television... Watson is the stability that Holmes needs..." (Gazette)

Jeremy was thrilled to discover that there were a lot of children in the audience, "*I used to say to the house manager that there are so many empty seats. He'd say, 'Mr. Brett, just look again. The lights are on, now. Look again.' And, of course – children! Little faces! Absolutely unbelievable! They adored him, and I think I know why... a little boy, called Michael McClure II, age 8, of St. Louis gave me a picture of Holmes killing a dragon and he said, 'Oh, he kills my dragons. I don't have nightmares anymore!'... So, he is a hero to the children. Three-year-old Solomon, is there in Dallas, a little aficionado, has all my films, and knows every word! I couldn't believe it.*" They were often invited backstage after the performance to see the reality behind the theatre and Jeremy loved sharing his view of Holmes with these "*little aficionados.*" He would also keep in touch with some of them in lengthy correspondences in much the same way as he did with his older fans.

Wyndham's Theatre was an intimate and friendly space ideally suited for a two-handed production like this. However, when the play toured the larger cities with large theatres, such as Manchester and Bradford, with two thousand seats it brought new concerns of projection and filling the theatre with their personalities. It became rather an ordeal with necessary adjustments, but immensely satisfying. One observer said, "Manchester Palace Theatre had a production line around the front, round the side along a passage to the stage door of the theatre where Jeremy and Edward were signing autographs. A grey haired lady commented on her way out 'Good grief, you'd think they were royalty!'" (Rosalie Williams)

During the run Jeremy reconnected with the viewing public and thoroughly enjoyed the experience. Jeremy Paul commented on his performance and on the Green Room: "Holmes was a poseur, full of theatrical gestures, and I think Jeremy's high style of acting, though not terribly fashionable today, is in keeping with the period. There aren't many actors around who move around the stage as he does, he's incredibly light on his feet for such a big man, almost balletic. During the run there was one abiding memory: the star's dressing room door was always left open. Jeremy called it the Green Room – and at any time you could wander in and find people – the mighty and the lowly – completely at their ease. He had time for everyone – to laugh with, to share a glass of champagne or simply to listen to their troubles over a cup of tea." And they came from all over the globe; Australia, Japan, and India. One fan recorded the thrill of the opportunity to meet Jeremy after the performance, "We descended from street level, the stairs were fairly steep..."

Jeremy was sometimes overwhelmed by the dedication of the fans, especially from the ladies. *"It's quite tragic, really. They see wedding bells because I'm a widower. The whole of the front row of the stalls used to be women who had seen the show more than 100 times. At one stage I was getting 3,000 letters a week and my dressing room was like a flower shop. The fans also send me clothing – jackets, jumpers – the only thing I've got on today that's mine is my underpants."* Jane Robbins sent hundreds of red roses to his dressing room every week for 15 months inspired by the "Rose Speech" (here delivered in its entirety) from *The Naval Treaty*. She sat on the front row during the run of the play and was thrilled when Jeremy pointed to the rose he was wearing saying *"this is one of yours, Jane."*

Another view of Jeremy in the play of *The Secret of Sherlock Holmes* can be found in the book of photographs by Marcus Tylor in *A Roll with Jeremy Brett*. They are a very fine example of portrait prints and represented a special photo-shoot executed at Wyndham's Theatre in October 1988. In black and white, the medium Marcus was most comfortable with and in keeping with his exhibition of backstage pictures at the Palace Theatre for which the photos were needed – Jeremy was serious in each of them. Marcus said they represented a special record of "such a beautiful man." At the front of his book, he gives a detailed account of the meeting in which Jeremy was "wearing red socks. And in a buoyant mood to match" and struck him as an outstanding presence of "pure charm... his abundant energy making his television appearances seem tame. The story of how he threw himself into the task of posing with a mirror as the only prop gave further evidence of his self confidence. On his next visit, Jeremy displayed even more extremes of energy in his response to the prints, loudly demanding that one of them, number 30, should appear in the *Evening Standard* that very day, which was impossible as the paper had already gone to press. The outcome of those brief meetings was that some of the very best photos of Jeremy had been captured for all time, although Marcus regretted that he would not have the chance to meet him again.

"In the theatre, when he appeared in *The Secret of Sherlock Holmes* in 1988 he came into his own in a tour de force for him and Edward Hardwicke as Watson. At the end of a triumphant first night, a friend said to me, 'What an evening! The curtain calls alone were worth the price of admission.'" (Michael Cox)

"Women love Holmes. I was astounded when I realised how attractive he is to them. You'd never suspect it for one moment from the books. Girls long to seduce him. I know from experience that quite simply he is the man who has power over women. They lust after him because he's a challenge. Holmes is unattainable and that acts as an enormous turn-on. He treats women as objects of interest, not as objects of desire, and gets to them. Women *throughout the world identify with what's going on and see me as Holmes. I know because it's my body they're after! It's all very flattering and frightening at times. I just have to realise I'm in the fantasy business, but I do feel responsible and I get very concerned about the power this character wields."* (Jeremy to William Hall) *"...you have to risk showing the flesh underneath. If he's going to be flesh, then you've got to take a gamble and bring in a little humour, bring in a little vulnerability, bring in a few faults and pray that doesn't offend people."* (Jeremy. Kate Tyndall posted 29th March 1990)

Whilst on set Jeremy would often take "a one o'clock catnap on a bed adjacent to Holmes's consulting rooms, and wore Holmes's uniform – a black frock coat, waistcoat, fob watch and chain and black lace-up boots even to rehearsals." (Today 4th December 1986) *"Queues stretch right around the block in Manchester. I can't believe it. There on the back lot is Baker Street and we have to pay to get on it. As I dart into 221b I turn into a pizza parlour. Mrs Hudson's Pizza Parlour. It's a huge success but I think it's absolutely ghastly. I haven't done the tour, I must be absolutely honest. Those who have are sometimes startled when they turn into Sherlock's tiny bedroom. I sleep on the bed during the lunch break because I only ever eat an apple and sometimes people come through and see this* dummy *lying on the bed. And they talk as though I were a* dummy. *And I suddenly go 'HUL-lo' and they go 'Aaaaaaaaaah!' and I looove that."* (Sherlock Holmes in America –The Morning Call 10th November 1991)

However, there was a personal price to pay for his appearance as the aesthete Holmes in the series; the need to be on a permanent diet. Several of his colleagues had commented on the occasions when he had lived on "a lettuce leaf and a carrot" and could not join his friends for a good meal at the end of a day's shooting. It is no surprise he would want to eat normally in between but then dieting became a necessity for each new series. Jeremy told one reviewer: *"I love nosh but the trouble is Holmes has to be gaunt because he's supposed to be a workaholic and a junkie. When I'm not acting I gain so much weight I have to book into a health farm for a few weeks just to fit into Holmes's suits."* (Chris Hughes in Brett Binges Junk Food Then Diets to Play TV tec.)

Jeremy was also having a significant effect on some of his viewing public in a beneficial way. *"I have a mountain of mail to cope with, which I do very happily."* One letter from a teacher in Wichita Falls, Texas, thanked him for encouraging her students to read the Holmes stories. And another, an unforgettable one, came from an 11 year old girl in Chicago. Jeremy told one reporter the story of how it came about: *"A friend of mine, an actor rang me at the theatre I was playing and said, 'Can you ring tomorrow this number? Little Louise Ann is your greatest fan. She likes you and Bette Midler.' I love that. So I don't know why I did it, but I picked up the phone then – it was about half an hour before the curtain went up – and spoke to her aunt. The girl was asleep, but her aunt promised to tell her of the call. I sent love, and she woke, received my message and died from leukaemia. I then had a letter written about three weeks before she died. And it was a letter of such unbelievable care and cherishment, saying she was concerned about me... she saw a dangerous light around me and was concerned for my well-being. That is part of the amazing side of playing this creature, this man (Holmes). It has unbelievably jettisoned me into a place I wasn't in before. Because romantic heroes weren't really in."* (Calgary Herald 5th November 1991) *"One letter had my name on it, and underneath it simply said, 'Somewhere near Clapham Common. Dear Postman, please help.' And it reached me! I found that very sweet indeed."* (Jeremy)

The Disappearance of Lady Frances Carfax
- The Casebook of Sherlock Holmes

***The Disappearance of Lady Frances Carfax* (Dramatised by T.R.Bowen: Directed by John Madden fb: 21st February 1991)** picks up the story of Sherlock Holmes after a three year hiatus during which Jeremy and Edward had been on stage electrifying the theatre audiences with their nightly performances of *The Secret of Sherlock Holmes*. An adventure tale set in the Lake District is an attractive prospect with its stunningly beautiful scenery and opportunities for such pursuits as sailing and horse riding which would have delighted Jeremy, but the Granada team had chosen to make some significant changes to the original script and thereby lost some support.

This episode features the story of a daring modern woman who would be considered one of the New Women of the day. She is pursued by a very clever trickster and consequently is in danger of nearly losing her life. Her disappearance is the central action and the Lake District makes an appealing substitute for the original Lucerne, Switzerland, where Watson is on holiday at the same picturesque hotel in the shadow of Skiddaw, the impressive mountain overlooking the scenic Derwent Water, and therefore he would be on hand to assist the distressed Lady Frances. Holmes receives a letter from his friend with details of his walking activities and also the people staying at the hotel. Watson continues to show his special regard for the ladies and Lady Frances Carfax attracts his attention by her adventurous spirit. Sailing her skiff across the lake to church (St. Beda's on the shores of Bassenthwaite Lake), or in heated exchanges with her brother the Earl of Rufton, plus her extreme reactions to the bearded man, who seems to threaten her by his presence. Cheryl Campbell plays the firebrand to perfection. Watson also introduces the missionary, Shlessinger and his nurse and "disciple", Miss Calder, and it is he, the man in the wheelchair who rescues Frances when her sailing skiff overturns and saves her from drowning. However, Shlessinger is not the hero he seems as the innocent young lady is lured into selling her inheritance of extremely valuable gems and her saviour proves to be "a bounder." The other adaptation Granada had made to the story was to give her a part in the action at the beginning of the story. In Conan Doyle's original story Lady Frances had already disappeared before Holmes and Watson had heard of her.

As there is no client requiring his assistance or crime scene requiring investigation, Holmes is not there for the first 15 minutes of the episode and he is missed as Jeremy's relationship with the camera always brings excitement to the action. Instead, there are fleeting glimpses of him examining the details of Watson's letters, visiting Scotland Yard or staring at chess pieces to gain inspiration. He hardly speaks in these scenes and his dynamism is much needed where a crime is unfolding and the lady's life is in danger. In the original Conan Doyle story Holmes follows Watson in secret and even saves him from a fight in another of his disguises as a French labourer, but here he is searching the press for crucial information. A newspaper account of the tragic death of another victim of the man who calls himself Shlessinger reveals his unscrupulous methods thus Holmes uncovers dual identities and the seriousness of the situation. His telegraph reached the Hotel at the same time as he did, and from then on the search for the Lady Frances becomes a familiar business with an authoritative Holmes once more at the helm.

Once in the Lake District, he visits the Earl of Rufton, the Lady's brother played convincingly by Michael Jayston, and there Holmes is told that he does not have the funds to meet her demands but that she has her own inheritance. Holmes and Watson pursue her to the Oxford and Lombard Maritime Bank in Pall Mall in an attempt to intercept her before she does anything foolish, but they arrive too late and thereafter the lady disappears completely, taking her gems with her. The dramatic scene was shot at the ornamental Port of Liverpool Maritime Building where Watson makes an instinctive, boisterous challenge of the Hon. Philip Green, the penniless poet whom Lady Frances had become close to until her brother had intervened, sending him away to Australia. Watson plays the lady's champion as he tackles him to the ornate tiled floor, watched helplessly by Holmes from the gallery above and the French labourer of Montpellier who rescued his friend with a cudgel was sadly lost in this interpretation. Thereafter, Philip Green joins forces with Holmes and Watson and carries out surveillance on the activities of Major Shlessinger and the gems, as the only way to locate the trickster, now identified as a career conman.

With the arrival of a coffin Holmes and Watson are forced to take action but the lady remains hidden until the very last minute, a situation more suited to a horror film with a rescue from the grave in circumstances too horrible to imagine. Holmes contributes his reliable, caring arms to the trapped young lady, whilst the would-be murderer is disabled by Watson. The ending of the Granada production is darker and more tragic than the original story. It remains uncertain whether Lady Frances will recover her mind from the *"terrors of the grave"* needing the constant care of the man who wanted to be her husband. It is for this reason that Holmes considers the case to be one of his failures, *"I have to say, I have failed"* and in his estimation he does fail. He saves her life but it is a damaged life. And he cannot accept a reward from Green. *"I refuse to be rewarded for fostering a tragedy. I have never suffered such a complete eclipse of my faculties."* One critic gave his approval of the changes made: "There are times when an original short story can be enhanced when adapted for the screen and, on this occasion, T.R. Bowen has produced a dark and quite powerful adventure..."

An article entitled *Sherlock – The Casebook* put his presentation of Holmes into context, charting his success and the onset of his illness; "In 1984 Jeremy Brett was cast as Holmes, and he brought a passion and determination to the role that frequently had the sides of your television set expanding. Determined to be the best, most accurate screen Holmes ever seen – a notion brought out of obsession rather than arrogance – Brett compiled exhaustive notes on the character and lived the part with a ferocity that was perhaps not altogether healthy. Brett had long been friends with Robert Stephens... with his own experience in *The Private Life of Sherlock Holmes*, Stephens tried to persuade him not to take the part... 'You will have to go into such a pit to get into that man that you will self-destruct.' Brett was diagnosed with manic depression in 1986, and he spent the rest of his life in the role becoming more and more unwell... *'I am bloody well trying to shake him off, but Holmes seems to haunt me these days.'*... that he still managed to excel in the role is testament to his skill... a masterful run of adaptations." (Sherlock – The Casebook)

The *New York Times* announced, "Jeremy Brett has become television's quintessential Sherlock Holmes... One curious development: the more the actor painstakingly refines and enriches his portrayal, the more he tends to suggest in his increasingly chilly cerebrations the interpretation of another actor closely associated with the role, Basil Rathbone. Even if unintentional, the effect is perfectly on target." And in another article the publication thought the story was rather like a "penny-dreadful... but the hour, produced with the usual polish and attention to Victoriana, has its pleasures. Jeremy Brett's Holmes grows more entertainingly neurotic as the seasons go on, and Edward Hardwicke's Watson is as solid as ever and even more gallant. Imagine Holmes referring to his upright old pal as "a dangerous ruffian!" (New York Times 25th August 1992) Lynne Truss in *The Times* was equally complimentary. "In this week's *The Disappearance of Lady Frances Carfax* even Conan Doyle's brief-but-exact reference to Kennington was hurtfully omitted. And the London scenes were filmed, in any case, in Liverpool and Preston. This has always struck me as the one false note in the Jeremy Brett *Sherlock Holmes*. Everything else is marvellous – the faithful dramatisations the tasteful sepia hue, the Virtuoso viola theme-tune and, above all, the flamboyance of Jeremy Brett. The whole project was well-conceived and has been brilliantly executed... Jeremy Brett is a magnificent Sherlock Holmes. Not only does he grasp each "Hah!" as an entirely new vocal challenge, but he has banished forever the notion of Holmes as a brain on a stick. It is, of course, a great help that the Granada writers and producers have given him a refreshingly companionable relationship with his Watson (David Burke originally; now Edward Hardwicke). But what makes Brett's Holmes so special is a quality that is strangely easy to overlook – his superb physical performance, which is graceful and seductive. And the way those little smiles play on his lips – well, I could go on." (The Times 23rd February 1991)

"The later stories, I think everyone agrees are less substantial than some of the earlier ones. With *The Creeping Man* and *Shoscombe Old Place* we added elements which have increased the mystery and given them more texture. I suppose the most changed one is *The Disappearance of Lady Frances Carfax*, which is originally a story about Holmes sending Watson to the Continent to look for a lady who has mysteriously disappeared. We've changed that, and Watson is on holiday in England when he meets the lady. He's puzzled by her behaviour and her fear of certain people." (Michael Cox in The Armchair Detective 1992)

The Problem of Thor Bridge **(Dramatised by Jeremy Paul: Directed by Michael Simpson fb: 28ᵗʰ February 1991)** Michael Cox thought the opening of this story was probably his "favourite in the whole Canon... because it is such a fine example of Conan Doyle's wit and invention in fleshing out Holmes's career." (A Study in Celluloid) However, the contents of a dispatch box with its intriguing contents didn't fit the requirement for action and mystery for the viewing public. Filmed at Capesthorne Hall this episode opens with humour in the Baker Street rooms, firstly in Watson's perceptive observation that Holmes has a case after a month of trivialities, deduced from the smile on his lips. Secondly, his dismissal of breakfast of two hard boiled eggs because Billy the page is not a good cook, and Watson's irony in, "I hope Mrs Hudson is enjoying her holiday." The hunt for a letter shows Holmes emptying first his desk drawer, then his cabinet, and throwing everything onto the air in wild disarray. He locates the missing note in his breast pocket which he turns his back and hands to Watson over his shoulder with the name Neil Gibson. His wife has been found murdered with a note in her hand incriminating the governess, Miss Dunbar and the murder weapon, a revolver, was found hidden at the bottom of the girl's wardrobe.

This is a stylish episode with a crucial case of a woman accused of murder but with no one making a real effort to find the truth or to rescue her. One may say it was the lack of information and co-operation which causes the two main players, Gibson, the Gold King, and Sherlock Holmes to distrust the other. Daniel Massey, Jeremy's brother-in-law, fits the physical description that Doyle provides, "His tall, gaunt, craggy figure had a suggestion of hunger and rapacity... his face might have been chiselled in granite, hard-set, craggy, remorseless, with deep lines upon it and scars of many a crisis." (The Problem of Thor Bridge) Gibson's arrival at Baker Street in a "*new-fangled*" motor car announces his importance and the expectation of getting his own way. Money and reputation accompanied by "*Booming*", are the rewards he offers Holmes if he succeeds with the case. His first comment is that Miss Dunbar is innocent and that Holmes must be the one to clear her name, however, the question concerning the "*exact relations*" between Gibson and the governess was deemed too personal and he resorted to threats. With a fiendish look the millionaire raises his arm to strike Holmes who is not intimidated, remains totally immobile whilst issuing the warning, "*Don't be noisy!*" a restraint, which is sufficient to stop him in his tracks, take command of his anger and leave.

When Gibson doesn't return Holmes realises he has made a serious misjudgement but Watson's practical suggestion that they apply for an official permit to visit Miss Dunbar in the Winchester cells (filmed in Chester) provides an opening. Although the unexpected arrival of Gibson interrupts the fact-gathering exercise, the involvement of his assistant, Ferguson, finally brings Holmes an invitation to Thor Place which enables the detective to make his usual meticulous, detailed investigations. This scene differs from the Doyle original as a chastened man returns to the Baker Street rooms to give his version of the relationship between himself, his wife and Miss Dunbar.

At Thor Place, filmed at Capesthorne Hall, the sight of Holmes and Watson, accompanied by a police sergeant on bicycles riding across the park onto the bridge is novel and further developed by Jeremy's carefree hop onto the bridge parapet, in itself a risky action and reminiscent of earlier films where Holmes climbed buildings or jumped from carriages with no regard for his safety. Michael Cox went further, "One of the qualities which made Jeremy so right as Holmes was his particular bearing. He was a public school boy in the choir at Eton with Daniel Massey and an actor in the old theatrical tradition. He brought that theatricality of voice and gesture to the part over and over again. It meant that even the most familiar piece of exposition in the sitting room at Baker Street crackled with danger. In the heat of the chase he would leap over the furniture or jump onto the parapet of a bridge with no regard for his personal safety." (A Study in Celluloid) Then he lies down in the dead woman's position to view the parapet, noticing the scuff under the lip in a noteworthy blemish. He was also able to see the relevant evidence of the empty gun-case which had held two pistols and the Brazilian artefacts in the schoolroom contributed by Miss Dunbar to the children's education showing Holmes more about the relationship between Gibson and the governess. It also provided a nod to Doyle's *The Lost World* in the photo of unscalable cliffs. The sparring between Gibson and Holmes continues with an archery contest between the two. Jeremy's skills with the longbow was something he had spent many years practising, although he tried not to beat his partner with too much flair and this scene was specifically written into the script to capitalise on his particular talent.

A return to the bridge and the parapet enables Holmes to try out a theory, with his familiar technique of imagining the circumstances. Miss Dunbar provides confirmation of the details regarding the note, the difficult meeting, and the hatred that his wife had felt towards the rival for her husband's affections, so that Holmes feels confident in his solution. The story of the pistol is finally proved with another visit to the bridge accompanied by the police officer and Watson's emptied revolver is the means of providing that proof. Holmes underlines the story of "a passionate creature of the Tropics" vindictive, ill-balanced and anxious to gain her revenge on the woman whom she thinks has wronged her, in reality an innocent victim of her plan. They have helped "*a remarkable woman and a formidable man*" with the assumption that they should soon join forces. Jeremy thought the solution to the problem was excellent, "The Problem of Thor Bridge *is my favourite of this new collection. It's about an American gold-mine millionaire and it's got the best piece of deduction in probably all the stories.*" (Jeremy to Louise Sweeney in Tracking the Master Sleuth Christian Science Monitor)

In interview Dame Jean Conan Doyle gave her opinion of Jeremy's interpretation of Holmes, first in *The Secret of Sherlock Holmes:* "I was consulted very early on. I was asked to a private view... I was sent a script. I heard it on a tape. I kept in very close touch with the author, Jeremy Paul and with the star Jeremy Brett. I could see nothing objectionable in it at all. I thought it was a very elegantly written little play. Fascinating in its way, something that would have amused my father greatly... It has been beautifully handled by people who obviously love Holmes and Watson and the acting is splendid." And she said of *The Casebook*: "Jeremy Brett's been appearing as Holmes in films for the television for a long time now but his performance has changed beyond measure. I didn't really like him in the early series. He was far too arrogant and too mannered, too highly strung altogether, whereas Holmes was a very cool character. It has been wonderful to see the change in him. In the last series instead of being a rather unpleasant man he became an endearing man in spite of his conceit: in spite of this, that and the other, he's somebody who you really care about. I think it is an absolutely great performance; he really holds you.... Edward Hardwicke is a splendid Watson just the sort of Watson my father would have envisaged unlike Nigel Bruce... Holmes would never have shared digs with a fool." (Interview with John Tibbetts)

140

Problem of Thor Bridge

Shoscombe Old Place

"This week brings a five week run of Holmes stories to a conclusion with *Shoscombe Old Place... Shoscombe* is no grand summing up of the Holmes myth – it's just a typical Holmes tale, the story of a chunk of bone found on the estate of a British nobleman (Robin Ellis). Holmes and the perpetually impressed Dr. Watson (Edward Hardwicke) are summoned to figure out who the bone belonged to and how that person died."

***Shoscombe Old Place* (Dramatised by Gary Hopkins: Directed by Patrick Lau fb: 7th March 1991)** is the final story (60th) of the Conan Doyle Canon and features a man who is not a villain but who is attempting to bend the law until the circumstances better suit him. Sir Robert Norberton, played by Robin Ellis, who appeared with Jeremy in *The Good Soldier*, is a man who is dependent on his horse, Shoscombe Prince, winning the Champion Stakes in order to pay off his debts, which are becoming a real threat to his security. Debt collectors had already visited in the person of Samuel Brewer, a well-known money lender, whom Sir Robert sent on his way with threats. When Brewer is declared missing, enquiries are made by the police. A visit to Baker Street by John Mason, Sir Robert's trainer, informs Holmes that his owner had "gone mad". He is reportedly down at the stables or in the old church crypt "at the dead of night" and is accused of mistreating his sister by giving away her pet spaniel. Another worrying fact is the discovery of a human bone, the upper condyle of a femur, found in the furnace on the estate. Norberton is suspected of foul play.

Watching Jeremy in action in this episode we become aware that this is as much Jeremy as it is Holmes. His movements and mannerisms no longer surprise us but they do amuse as we see him do the simplest things in a singular way. The scene opens with Holmes in his familiar task of searching for a particular piece of paper amongst his vast collection showering them aimlessly in his flamboyant manner, looking for the *Handy Guide to the Turf*, and a letter from Mason as he needs to know about Shoscombe and Sir Robert. Watson is able to provide details of the horse, Shoscombe Prince and the fact that Norberton had horse-whipped Samuel Brewer, the week before at Newmarket. William Baring-Gould in *The Annotated Sherlock Holmes* comments on the fact that Holmes has apparently lost his enthusiasm for the turf, which he had displayed so effectively in *Silver Blaze*, and now relies on Watson for his detailed knowledge of the horse owner and his widowed sister, Lady Beatrice.

Holmes responds immediately to an opportunity for distraction in following the trail of mysterious circumstances, and on this occasion seems to enjoy being in the countryside. He will protest loudly in the episode that follows with the comment that the fresh air will kill him. As he said in the very first Granada episode, *The Solitary Cyclist*, the centre of a community and local gossip is the local pub, thus *The Green Dragon,* becomes a suitable base for Holmes and Watson, to carry out their investigations posing as fishermen on holiday. The Lady Beatrice's spaniel, Jaspar, had been housed at the pub and as Jeremy has readily made friends with him, he has the Landlord's permission to take the animal along on their daily walks. With Sir Robert in York, lured away by a telegram, they might explore without interruption. The carriage scene is probably the highlight of Holmes's investigation and he shares his theories with Watson, "*Let us consider the data. The brother no longer visits the beloved invalid sister. He gives away her favourite dog. Her dog, Watson! Does that suggest nothing to you?*" However, Holmes is noted for his theorising and has already reached his conclusion and will test it by stopping the lady's carriage so that when the spaniel is released it would spring forward with "a joyous cry" in expectation of being reunited with his beloved mistress. The surprise and dismay of Beatrice's maid Carrie confirms his suspicions, as the carriage drives away before Jaspar can discover that his mistress is a stranger.

In carrying out his exploration of every possible theory to discover the truth he must explore the possibility that Sir Robert might have murdered his sister. As Holmes visits the cellar to explore the furnace, he finds nothing more than the remnants of an item which could possibly be Brewer's wallet. The solution to the problem is achieved with the break-in to the house whilst Watson has diverted the butler. Holmes's finds in Lady Beatrice's rooms are fairly small but enough, as he is interrupted by the unexpected return of Her Ladyship accompanied by her maid, giving him just enough time to escape through the downstairs window. An examination of the hair under the microscope in their rooms in the inn reveals a resin which suggests a wig.

The discovery in the haunted crypt is the stuff of nightmares with Watson unhappy about the thought of "*desecration*" of the grave. Holmes shows his mettle as he invades the house and confronts the Lady Beatrice stand-in with determination based on conviction and with Jeremy's customary flair. The revelation scene is particularly interesting due to the appearance of Jude Law in the role of Joe Barnes in which Holmes will uncover a man who would play a future Watson. Sir Robert excuses his behaviour in "If I told the truth I faced absolute ruin", but by delaying until after the race, there was a possibility of saving the situation. The whole deception is a source of distress but necessary. Laying his sister to rest in a coffin of one of her husband's ancestors in the family crypt in consecrated ground appeared to be the respectful thing to do.

The original story describes Norberton as an evil, notorious fraudster and as much of the dialogue has been preserved, his treatment of Brewer appears vicious "He nearly killed the man." He would appear to be a villain. Watson also calls him "a devil of a fellow" and yet Robin Ellis's Sir Robert does not create fear or menace. He is up to his neck in debt trying to borrow money on the horse, "his whole life is on it", but the conclusion brings him exoneration in that his deeds were carried out under a time of duress and can therefore be justified. The close of Doyle's story states that the eighty thousand pounds of debt was paid off in full when Shoscombe Prince won the Derby (Champion Stakes) which left enough to re-establish his position in life. Michael Cox says "Robin Ellis, fondly remembered from the BBC series *Poldark* in the 1970s, gives Sir Robert an air of romantic mystery, a man under pressure but not an obvious villain." (A Study in Celluloid)

Jeremy's performance was once more the focus of his fellow actors, and the critics. "I don't know what it was about Jeremy Brett but I fell in love with him immediately and unconditionally and have never reviewed it. He was so very, very special as Sherlock Holmes, a very special human being I think. So it was a beautiful marriage, between who the man was, his acting skills and this particular product." (Denise Black in Elementary my dear Watson ITV Documentary) "But really does anyone watch these things for the twisty plots or the invariably indignant suspects? No, you tune in to see Brett's performance which is a hilarious marvel. It's Brett's achievement to have taken the full measure of Conan Doyle's creation and to refuse to make this hero sympathetic and lovable in the modern manner; Brett plays Holmes as a cold, morose, arrogant man whose overriding genius makes him fascinating... Rathbone was elegantly understated, embodying the icy reserve of Holmes, but Brett has gone the other way — he is fearlessly florid, grandly melodramatic in a style that matches the tone of Conan Doyle's prose." (Holmes Improvement PBS)

"I used to watch the series with Brett as Holmes and David Burke playing Dr Watson, but I never read the books, so to suddenly be playing a stable boy was extraordinary.'"(Jude Law in The Telegraph)

The Boscombe Valley Mystery **(Dramatised by John Hawkesworth: Directed by June Howson fb: 14th March 1991)** opens with humour as Watson is pictured enjoying a fishing holiday when he is interrupted by his friend who appears unexpectedly at the riverbank initially unrecognised. Holmes has found his whereabouts in order to ask him if he would care to join him on a case, *"The newspapers are calling it* The Boscombe Valley Mystery. *I expect you have read something of it... A farmer, called McCarthy, Australian by birth, met his death by a mere at the bottom of his farm."* There is a *"very serious case"* against his son which is something Holmes would like to investigate and the request to join him is courteously phrased. Watson is pleased to accept with his customary *"well of course"*, but is then alarmed to find they have only thirty five minutes in which to catch the local train.

The gamekeeper who was a witness, believes James McCarthy is the guilty party as there was nobody else there and, on his arrest, James had said he was innocent of murder, but that he *"got no more than his deserts."* Holmes sees his *"contrition"* as the sign of a healthy mind and therefore dismisses the verdict made by the Coroner's Jury on the death of "wilful murder" as scandalous. The police case will be proven false with Holmes's evidence and the viewer will develop enormous sympathy for the accused and the girl he loves. The arrival of Miss Alice Turner is a breath of fresh air to Holmes and Watson especially as her assessment that Inspector Summerby, replacing Lestrade here, is only a policeman and cannot see the truth which is very much how Holmes himself sees it.

"Sherlock Holmes was transformed when he was hot upon such a scent as this. Men who had only known the quiet thinker and logician of Baker Street would have failed to recognize him." (The Boscombe Valley Mystery) Enthusiasm and vigour is the keynote of Jeremy's inspection of a crime scene as he throws himself to the ground in his search for trifles. His examination at the mere's edge brings evidence for so many people having been there, all traced in the ground surrounding the water. The discovery of tiptoes and a square-toed boot takes Holmes full length onto the muddy scene, "he would have made a rare blood-hound", says the Inspector as the detective crawls forward into the bushes. He identifies the murder weapon and the possible murderer with all the details necessary for identification. Jeremy explained, *"When Holmes hurls himself to the ground and wriggles through the bracken like a golden retriever, I felt a complete fool doing it and I thought the audience might laugh. But they didn't because it was perfectly in character – Holmes was using his animal intuition to find a clue and needless to say, he came up with one."*

John Turner played superbly by Peter Vaughan is both the villain and the most tormented as "a sitting duck for blackmail". The craggy and mortally ill land owner may have begun as a "highway robber" known as Black Jack of Ballarat in Australia, but since his arrival in England, his life had been an attempt to pay back for his wrong doing, to do a little good with his money. His daughter is a credit to him and a token of his redemption, but his nemesis, an Australian witness from his past, "the devil incarnate" William McCarthy is determined to keep Turner in his power, even using Alice as the means of marrying James into the family. Holmes clearly feels sympathy for him and listens with compassion to his story of bitter vengeance in the face of torment. The human reaction to pain and frustration can be seen passing across Jeremy's face as Holmes once more chooses to exercise his method of acting as judge and jury in this case. The murderer signs a full confession in anticipation of the authorities finding James guilty, but with Holmes prepared to speak up for him at the trial, with his expert evidence that was an unlikely outcome. It can be seen as a better bid for justice than the justice system would allow and both Holmes and Watson appear satisfied at the outcome. Michael Cox said, "He has a genuine sense of natural justice, a sense of honour. People wish that he did exist. They feel somehow that society would be a safer place if he did." (Heroes of Detection)

"When he does speak, Brett's line readings are a hoot – he mumbles whole paragraphs of Conan Doyle's fussy dialogue in a rude rush, as if he can barely deign to speak to the dimwits around him. This Holmes delights in being stubborn and perverse; last week in the *Boscombe Valley Mystery* the long-suffering Watson remarked on how pleased he was that the duo's investigation had taken them out of sooty London and into the bright English countryside. Holmes, however, responded by inhaling so loudly that his nostrils seemed to flap in the breeze, and then groaned, *'Oh Watson, all this fresh air will kill me'*. Whether you're a novice or a dedicated fan, there is enormous pleasure to be taken in watching an actor bring a myth to life the way Brett has done so consistently for so long." (Holmes Improvement)

Baker Street File - Boscombe Valley Mystery

113 - Has a keen questioning glance

114 - Like a dog picking up the scent

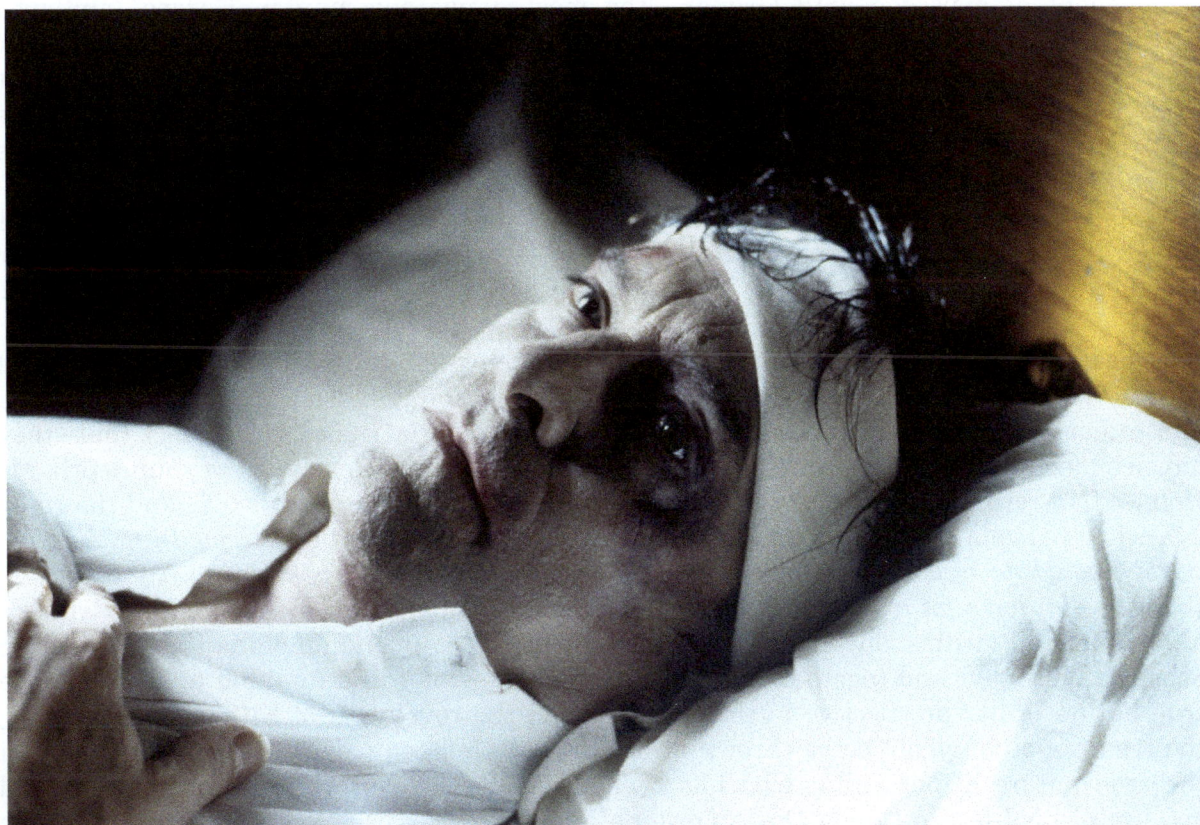

In the next episode, *The Illustrious Client*, the relationship between Mrs Hudson and her two charges comes into focus as she cares for the stricken Holmes in the most sympathetic manner and at the same time protects the overworked doctor. Rosalie Williams explained her closeness to Watson, "because they share an affection for Holmes and, in a sense, they manage him together. She's very fond, I feel, and very friendly with the doctor. She has great respect for him. It's a gentler relationship, but the main thing is that together they share this business of looking after Holmes... this man who can be so awful to deal with and at the same time so endearing." (Scarlet Street) ***The Illustrious Client* (Dramatised by Robin Chapman: Directed by Tim Sullivan fb: 21st March 1991)** features a ruthless and dangerous villain, Baron Gruner, played by Anthony Valentine, who "collects women" and features them in his book which he calls his "commonplace book," a locked diary. The Baron is among the worst of the villains that Holmes faces and the episode opens with a case of murder on the Italian/Swiss border as Gruner pushes his wife down the mountainside in order to be free to lure another wife into his trap. The introduction to Holmes and Watson follows the opening of Doyle's story. They are dressed in bathrobes in a Turkish bath, lying side by side on loungers with a hookah pipe between them in a brief moment of relaxation, a place where Watson sees his friend "less reticent and more human than anywhere else." However, their peace has already been broken as Holmes reveals a letter.

The formal request for Holmes's assistance is brought to Baker Street by Colonel Sir James Damery, in a bid to persuade the daughter of General Merville, Violet Merville, to end her engagement of marriage with Gruner, "the most dangerous man in Europe" and who Holmes recognises as *The Austrian Murderer*." Violet Merville will hear nothing bad about her intended husband because she is deeply in love. Sir James comes in his own person but he is clearly asking on behalf of a client whose identity he wishes to protect and Holmes is reluctant to work without all the facts at which Jeremy leaps out of his chair in protest, as precipitous as ever. Finally he is persuaded not to make specific enquiries about this elite personage who many Sherlockians believe is the Prince of Wales, later King Edward VII and to investigate the Baron who will prove to be a velvet tongued, diabolically clever opponent.

The meeting between Holmes and Gruner is one of two giants from opposing sides; good versus evil. He is a libertine who uses and abuses women. Holmes's attempt to persuade him to back off is unsuccessful and although the Baron is intrigued by the fact that "they have engaged the very best," he is unwilling to listen. "You are clearly out of your depth, Mr Holmes." In return he threatens Holmes with violence unless he "draws off", and the reply is a witty personal assessment, full of contempt. *"If you aspire to be accepted into English society, you'd do well to remove the band from your Havana before lighting it – otherwise you'll be put down for a bounder."* Shinwell Johnson locates Kitty Winter, one of Gruner's mistresses and victims, one of a hundred, maybe more, "Women and china they're his twin passions," she says and together she and Holmes visit Violet in a final bid to show her the true nature of her prospective husband. But even the revelation of Kitty's terrible scars, the result of oil of vitriol being thrown at her unprotected body, does not convince Violet of the true nature of her suitor who has been most clever in providing a carefully edited account of his life. In Conan Doyle's original story, Gruner uses hypnotism to mesmerize Miss Merville. At their first meeting, Gruner says to Holmes, "You have heard of post-hypnotic suggestion, Mr Holmes? Well, you will see how it works, for a man of personality can use hypnotism without any vulgar passes or tomfoolery." (The Adventure of the Illustrious Client)

Jeremy is supremely confident in his interpretation of Holmes in these episodes. He stands up to the bullying attempts from both Gruner and Gibson, both men of reputation accustomed to getting their own way. Holmes faces them down. He is secure in his responses to women, a significant adjustment from *The Adventures* and *The Return* where he would touch and then withdraw; here he is the confident mature man, charming yet remaining at a distance. His gaze is piercing, all-seeing and when it is linked to his genius mind it is formidable. Holmes makes a revealing comment in this episode when he tells Violet Merville, *"I am not renowned, Miss Merville, for the warmth of my affections,"* but here we see him showing a caring and sympathetic concern to each of the women, especially Kitty for whom he displays great sympathy as he seeks to understand why Gruner treated her as he did. Towards Violet Merville he will show respect but determination to show her that her love for the villain Gruner is sadly misplaced, but it is Holmes who suffers in her stead.

The scene in the carriage is very touching as Holmes comforts Kitty, and she provides the details of how Gruner gave her the dreadful scars, although she was less willing to describe the book, with its photographs, names, and details, which she sees as the ultimate humiliation. Gruner is a thug and a villain, a very dangerous man whose method of

148

defeating Holmes is to have him attacked and left for dead. Watson discovers the details in the daily newspaper, in the headline, *"Murderous Attack on Sherlock Holmes,"* and the scenes where he is cared for by Mrs Hudson and Watson are some of the most moving footage of the series. With the deliberate exaggeration of his injuries *"concussion, delirium, coma"* Holmes can recuperate from his injuries and prevent any further attacks. The friendship between the two men is highlighted once more as Watson is engaged to follow an intensive study of Chinese pottery and then sent to visit Gruner in the guise of a collector of fine arts.

"Holmes gets severely beaten up by two thugs in a very carefully choreographed sequence. Through all that follows, during which he is in bed with blood-soaked bandages and so on, we have been entirely faithful to the story. And it's a lovely bit for Mrs Hudson too. She is desperately worried about Holmes and Watson is studying the books on Chinese ceramics to prepare for his interview with Gruner. She comes in and says, 'You will remember to turn the lamp out, won't you? Don't stay up too late, Doctor, because we can't have you both ill.' It's all very human." (Michael Cox in The Armchair Detective 1992)

The *New York Times* gave their approval. "But the fun, as usual, is in watching Holmes move into action. In a meeting with the Baron, his contempt is bottomless as he reminds the nasty Austrian that in respectable society to remove the band from a cigar before lighting it... The Holmes plan to entrap the Baron involves a scheme to appeal to his passion for collecting, a scheme that requires Watson to spend 24 hours devouring books that will make him an expert on Chinese pottery. As always, Watson does what he's told with enviable competence. There is a resolution of sorts, and the identity of the 'illustrious client' is revealed with appropriate decorum. Holmes triumphs once again." (New York Times 14th November 1991)

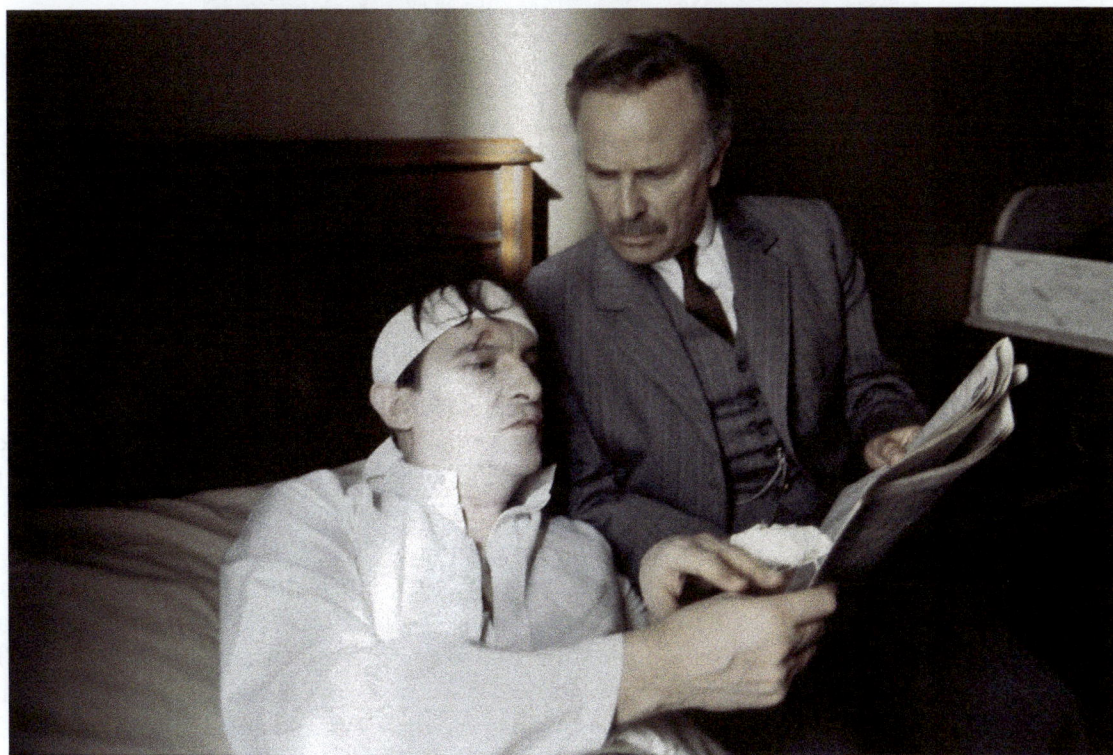

***The Creeping Man* (Dramatised by Robin Chapman: Directed by Tim Sullivan fb: 28th March 1991)** appears to be a story of Jekyll and Hyde, which presents a mystery to the reader, but not quite so effectively to the viewer who can recognise the actor if they watch closely. In his introduction for the showing of this episode on *Masterpiece Theatre* for PBS Vincent Price suggested the viewers should suspend their disbelief if they wished to enjoy a story which was more suited to science-fiction than the science of detection. Published in 1924 in *The Casebook* collection of stories it was Holmes's last official case as a consulting detective before his retirement to the Sussex Downs to take up bee-keeping. The case presented to Holmes by the victim's fiancé concerns the daughter of the eminent Professor Presbury who is frightened awake by a figure at her second floor bedroom window and as there is no means of a man climbing to that height it becomes a threatening situation. Her father, a distinguished natural scientist, doesn't believe his daughter and is violently against any investigations but the case becomes more intriguing with the discovery that several monkeys have been stolen from nearby zoos. "It was one Sunday evening early in September of the year 1903 that I received one of Holmes's laconic messages: *"Come at once if convenient – if inconvenient come all the same. – SH."* On arrival at their Baker Street rooms Watson found him waiting impatiently. This is one occasion when Watson does not show enthusiasm at some diversion and complains that he has left a full surgery but Holmes only sees the protest as evidence of his troublesome war-wound.

"Does Professor Presbury's daughter wake or dream?" is the problem which intrigues Holmes. He would like Watson to be present at an interview with Jack Bennett in order to take notes but also to hear his thoughts on the conundrum. Presbury, a respected man of learning, has been a cause for concern to his friends and family due to his strange behaviour since his return from a holiday to Prague. Bennett as the Professor's employee feels he should remain loyal, and is understandably reluctant to share his concern with a stranger. The divided loyalties stem from his engagement to his employer's daughter Edith, but eventually he does highlight some strange events worth investigating. In full understanding of his predicament, Holmes challenges him to choose where his true loyalties lie, with his employer or his fiancée.

Presbury's unexpected return home brings a tense meeting with Holmes providing an opportunity for the famous Professor, played with enormous poise and fury by Charles Kay, to show his disdain in the insult, "221-b Baker Street hardly an address to inspire confidence," which receives the expected reply, *"I have no need to inspire confidence in others as I have quite enough of my own."* The Professor seriously underestimates his opponent as Holmes will first explore the problem of Roy, *"Why does Professor Presbury's faithful wolfhound, Roy, endeavour to bite him?"* He considers it curious that the staid, elderly professor should behave in such an erratic manner that it should antagonise his devoted wolf-hound. He will also provide an explanation for the theft of six mature male apes from different zoos and when the facts of the case are tied into the delivery dates of packages which have arrived secretly for the Professor the unnatural behaviour of the dog is finally made relevant.

Watson may suggest that the case is unworthy of Holmes's skills as a detective and he is probably right, however, Holmes does save Presbury's daughter from a terrible attack from the tree-swinging figure. Half way through this case Holmes proclaimed that Edith did not dream but was in serious danger but *"from whom or from what?"* and does he realise that the danger comes from her father? Lynne Truss in *The Times* analysed the reason for Professor Presbury's fall, "The source of this nastiness is arrogance, of course. As Jeremy Brett averred in *The Casebook of Sherlock Holmes*: 'When one tries to rise above Nature one is liable to fall below it. The highest type of man may revert to the animal if he leaves the straight road of destiny.' Unfortunately, he said this in the context of a preposterous story called *The Creeping Man,* in which an elderly Professor injects himself with monkey glands, and acquires, through side effects the climbing skills of an orang-utan – but these were wise words, none the less. Incidentally, he also advised Watson, 'Always carry a firearm east of Aldgate,' which may be of no little interest to colleagues on *The Times.*" (Lynne Truss The Times 30th March 1991)

Watson reveals that Holmes possesses "a photographic memory" for facts and details and it is this skill which gives him the information he needs to memorise a century of murder and to alert him to anomalies. He also said, "It was not merely that Holmes changed his costume. His expression, his manner, his very soul seemed to vary with every fresh part that he assumed." In fact these words could be applied to Jeremy's performance as each new episode brought a fresh interpretation of the famous detective. Sherlock Holmes had become a real person of flesh and blood in his very capable hands. *"Holmes could be rude, impatient, abrupt, and his intolerance of fools was legendary. I tried to show all this, all of the man's incredible brilliance. But there are some cracks in Holmes's marble, as in an almost perfect Rodin statue. And I tried to show that, too."* (Jeremy) When asked what he enjoyed the most about playing Holmes, his sense of humour was very much in evidence, *"We're all very well-mannered people, aren't we?... It's heaven to be rude. I loved that. I loved being able to say, 'Thank you!' dismissively. That was great fun! All that cutting of all the rhubarb! I enjoyed all of those times when Holmes walks away without even saying goodbye. He just hasn't the time to go through all that polite behaviour."* (Jeremy in The Armchair Detective)

A letter from Dame Jean Conan Doyle expressed her appreciation of the *Casebook* series: "What a wonderful success you and all concerned made of *The Casebook*. It was a joy to watch and then to read the acclaim of the critics. As you know, I was worried about *The Creeping Man*, but I was wrong. The changes from the original didn't spoil it. I find that Jeremy gets closer and closer to the Holmes of my childhood and the final episode left me longing to see him in further adventures. Edward Hardwicke is a perfect Watson. Very sincere congratulations and also gratitude in that you have brought my father's works so splendidly before millions of viewers one hundred years after they were written." (Dame Jean Conan Doyle)

"If Rathbone was the seminal Holmes, the classic must be Jeremy Brett on UK television (1984-94). Those shows were played without camp or irony. Brett was tall, dark and handsome, but also eccentric and moody. Surely a generation will never get him out of their heads..." (The Guardian, 2nd December 2011) "With his dry, wind-blown hair, thin gold necklace and diamond stud in one ear, he bore no resemblance to the slicked-down, hawkish detective who has become so familiar to *PBS* watchers. To achieve his mordant Holmes look, Brett said he has to spend an hour in the make-up chair. *'The worst part is the eyebrows. S.H. had arched eyebrows, so they had to glue mine up. Then my hair has to be glued and gelled.'* Whatever humiliations he has to undergo, the results are surely worth it, to judge by the response of viewers. As one critic typically put it, Brett is "the king among all the players who have ever slipped on a deerstalker cap." (John Blades in Chicago Tribune 12th November 1991)

Doctor Who enthusiasts regret that Jeremy never played the role. A recent article records the expectations. *"Jeremy Brett is the Lost Doctor.* At least in our universe which celebrates alternate possibilities and adventures for our favourite Time Lord, his name was oft-cited by fans as potential casting for the role, and in 1994 he was long-listed for the part... imagine a performance infused with more of the actor's warmth and charm that are self evident in interviews – characteristics that he stripped away to deliver a more austere performance as the world's greatest consulting detective. Consider this a tribute of sorts to one of our favourite actors, then, as the quintessential Holmes becomes our latest incarnation of the Doctor." (Dwaitas.wordpress.com)

Jeremy

On occasions Jeremy had the ability to be philosophical about the loss of his wife as in 1991 he told the Dallas press, *"I'm here for public television. My wife (Wisconsin native Joan Wilson, who died of cancer in 1985) devoted her life to it, and I'm here… in memory of her… My wife was, you see the founder of Mystery!"* In the same interview he watches a hawk which was circling the sky and goes on to say, *"She built a delicate bridge between our two countries. God bless her soul. I'm sure that hawk was her."* Joan was part Native American. Jeremy here is expressing the Native American belief that everything is connected and that a hawk or any animal sighting can be a message. But in 1986 he had completely lost that acceptance, *"I was advised that the way to get over it was to get back on my bike, and get back to work. That is what I did, but I think it was wrong. I was worn out, but I went into a kind of overdrive. It wasn't manic depression: more of a manic high. Then when I had finished filming, I was so thrilled to be free and resting, but I couldn't sleep. And then it began to go wrong. I think I probably should have gone on Valium, but as we all know that also has its dangers."* (Jeremy Brett the ultimate Sherlock Holmes looks forward to his last case)

He suffered a major breakdown and entered the Maudesley Hospital where he stayed for ten weeks. Seeing his son at his bedside in tears made him determined he would get better and learn to live again. Jeremy was dismissive about his experiences and not ashamed to talk about his condition. *"One good thing that has come out of it all is that, because I'm well-known, I can say I've been desperately ill and give others some hope… There's a terrible stigma about mental illness. People become isolated, but what they really need is some company."* Loneliness and depression can ambush anyone who has lost a loved one and Jeremy had succumbed to his natural feelings of loss of his beloved wife Joan. However, within two months he was back in front of the cameras and filming the next episodes of *Sherlock Holmes* in *A Sign of Four* and his courage had a positive effect, *"I have been flooded with letters from people in similar circumstances to my own, who tell me that hearing about my own recovery has given them the strength to struggle on."*

Jeremy always loved classical music, especially opera, and told one interviewer, *"I gave myself a tremendous treat – a week at the Salzburg Festival, where I heard some of the most brilliant musicians and the most wonderful singers, like the great Marilyn Horne. I saw the opera* Carmen *and also* Capriccio *by Richard Strauss. My ears were still tingling with all the magnificent music after I came back – I think I had probably too much. I needed to sit in silence for about a week afterwards to absorb all that I'd heard. But it was one of the most exciting, beautiful weeks of my life."* (Secret of Success by Christine Palmer 17th January 1987)

Interviews over the years would centre on his love for Joan and the possibilities of a new relationship. . 'Mr Brett began to tell us as he listened to the music every detail of that last happy night together, her last good day… *"I remember the last time we danced together, it was in the Rainbow Room on the top of the Rockefeller Centre… she was wearing silver and looking absolutely supreme. Delicate. Fragile. And we danced for the last time there… and I lost her…"* One of these had the heading, *"I had the perfect wife. Five years after her death I can't even decide what age a new girlfriend should be."* In it he said again that he was overwhelmed by grief and his life fell apart when she died. His self-confidence died when he lost his perfect wife and *"to get to know someone that well again is going to be difficult. I can't ever imagine having that closeness again…"*

The Casebook of Sherlock Holmes

"He was a tremendous realist, I'm a romantic. He was an introvert, I'm an extrovert. He was immensely serious, I'm rather a jolly chap. It's difficult for me to say what I may have given to the image of Holmes. Faithful to Conan Doyle's text, certainly. Also, I've tried to bring out the emotion that is there in Holmes." (Jeremy)

The three two hour episodes which follow are under *The Casebook* title but link with the final series of *The Memoirs* especially as the man that Jeremy creates is one who is prepared to show his feelings, where there were only hints in *The Adventures* and *The Return*. He will be shown responding to the charms of the girl, Aggie, in *The Master Blackmailer*, struggling with nightmares in *The Eligible Bachelor* and openly crying at the death of a good man at the close of *The Red Circle;* instinctive responses to these situations but hitherto alien in other interpretations of Holmes.

The *TV Times* listing introduced *The Master Blackmailer* with the following description: "From London's underworld creeps Charles Augustus Milverton, intent on destroying the society wedding of the year unless his blackmail demands are met. Sherlock Holmes who himself is engaged to be married, mounts an investigation." (TV Times 21st December 1991)

Serena Gordon as Lady Eva Blackwell in The Master Blackmailer

"It was his search for perfection that underlined Jeremy's portrayal of Holmes. His sole intent was being true to Doyle…"

***The Master Blackmailer* (Dramatised by Jeremy Paul: Directed by Peter Hammond fb: 2ⁿᵈ January 1992)** is based on the story *Charles Augustus Milverton* and the script used as much of the original dialogue as was possible. "*Do you feel a creeping, shrinking sensation, Watson, when you stand before the serpents in the Zoo, and see the slithery, gliding, venomous creatures, with their deadly eyes and wicked, flattened faces? Well that's how Milverton impresses me…*" Holmes describes the blackmailer as "*the worst man in London.*" He was based on a real person, rumoured to have blackmailed a friend and patient of Conan Doyle. William Baring-Gould suggests that Charles Augustus Howell, an art dealer who died in suspicious circumstances nine years before the story was written, was the person on whom CAM was based. June Wyndham Davies explained the approach to *The Sherlock Holmes Gazette* "The story is intact and correct. Jeremy Paul has invented some characters and put weight behind those that were already there. I spoke to him beforehand and said we want as much downstairs as upstairs – we need to see the lower and the higher ranks in this. Our story starts twelve years before, in which we show how several people have been affected by Charles Augustus Milverton. Bertrand, his servant, will eventually become another Milverton."

If Milverton is the revolting villain of the episode, feared by everyone, Holmes becomes the hero, the only lifeline in whom the victims are able to trust. This episode opens in Paris with secret love letters being retrieved from the fire by Bertrand (Nickolas Grace) and then handed over in exchange for a great deal of money. The blackmailer had waited for 12 years before demanding an extortionate sum of money and had chosen a time when the stakes were at their highest. Her Ladyship may beg for mercy but there was none. Holmes was informed of the case of the Viscount Croft who was caught *"in flagrante"* in the bed of a prostitute and his brother, Edward, who took a revolver to the footman and left him disfigured for life. The young men were consequently living abroad in disgrace and their grandmother can now provide Holmes with a clue to the identity of their oppressor in the hope of some retribution. The monster "lives and breathes, Mr Holmes, with a smiling face and a heart of marble," the signed page of a book of poetry *"CAM Devil"* and the comment "a man who preys upon weakness" is all she can offer. *"And I had a wonderful leading lady in this last film. Dame Gwen Ffrangcon Davies. She's 101, which is intriguing because Doyle, of course, would have seen her... and she said, 'That lady is improperly dressed.' And I said, 'What do you mean, Dame Gwen?' And she said, 'Well I know because I was there. She would have on a Hessian petticoat... very starched petticoat - and she would lift her dress as she walked across the gravel.' Can't knock that, can't question that. She was there. So, that was thrilling. Lovely, lovely, lovely, lady."* (Jeremy)

Holmes follows his familiar method of investigation when there are no clues to follow; the gossip columns are examined and Watson is assigned the task of reading out possible cases for scandal and blackmail. They are very much a team in this film, with Holmes asking more of his friend than usual. The next victim is shown in a male brothel watching a theatrical performance of a haunting air from Debussy, then refusing to pay a penny to the blackmailer whilst his traitorous boyfriend looks on smirking. The tragedy that follows is reported in the newspaper as "The Hon. Miss Miles calls off her marriage to Colonel Dorking two days before the wedding," with consequences which are *"tantamount to murder."* Holmes speaks for us all when he says, *"I have had to deal with 50 murderers in my career but the worst of them never gave me this sense of revulsion that I feel at this moment towards Mr Charles Augustus Milverton."* This tone of indignation is in evidence throughout the episode as Holmes tries to control his feelings.

Holmes's announcement that he has become engaged to Milverton's housemaid is given substance by Granada's decision to show the detective in disguise as the plumber Ralph Escott with his natural, ungreased hair across his eyes, flat cap, walking and sounding like a tradesman. Scenes of Aggie chasing Escott out of the living room with a cloth in her hand and then walking with him, hugging him and asking for a kiss is something he has little experience of. *"Oh Aggie, you've touched my heart"*, and the touching reply, *"I could make you a gift of mine"*, accompanied by the tentative kiss, is totally convincing. This is an awkward, yet sensitive Holmes who comments, *"Watson, you will be interested to hear that I am engaged to be married... to the Milverton's housemaid... a most necessary step."* The romance is certainly fascinating but perhaps one which should have been left for the imagination. Holmes has discovered the identity of the blackmailer's next victim and his approach to her godmother brings rewards as Lady Eva Blackwell's imminent marriage to the Earl of Dovercourt causes her to visit Baker Street seeking his help. Holmes may be sensitive to her situation, but the practical concerns of gaining the necessary funds for negotiating with the blackmailer remains his focus. The subsequent confrontation with

Milverton at Baker Street is fraught and tentative, almost a game of chess, whilst each explores the lengths to which the other is prepared to go.

The concluding act of burglary and murder presents an excellent opportunity for Holmes to finally take control of the case which hitherto has been out of his range, needing no sleuthing or use of his brain. The working out of justice in this episode is different from similar cases in the Canon in that murder is the means of achieving justice, "as the woman poured bullet after bullet into Milverton's shrinking body I was about to spring out, when I felt Holmes's cold, strong grasp upon my wrist. I understood the whole argument of that firm, restraining grip – that it was no affair of ours: that justice had overtaken a villain; that we had our own duties and our own objects which were not to be lost sight of." (Charles Augustus Milverton) *"When you read something that says, 'Lady Diane empties six shots into Milverton's chest, and rams the heel of her shoe into his mouth and screws it to the ground...' that's fine, but when you do it, it's not pretty."* (Jeremy)

Alas, one change that Granada made to the original story is the omission of the final scene in which Lestrade visited Baker Street to ask Holmes for help in pursuing the two burglars who he believes had murdered Milverton. As Lestrade describes them Holmes makes a humorous comment about one of them, *"That's rather vague!... Why it might be a description of Watson!"* The scene was filmed and then unfortunately cut from the final version. It is a supreme piece of comedy from the master himself, Conan Doyle. Holmes and Watson are faced with the possibility of arrest from their old friend Lestrade. There is also one guest appearance of interest and that is of David Scase in the role of Art Gallery Owner. He was Jeremy's Director at the Library Theatre in Manchester in 1955.

Several of Jeremy's flourishes remind us of his physicality which is at the heart of his interpretation; his movement around Baker Street which is almost balletic on occasions and his little jig to the music during the ball for Lady Eva which one feels is rather un-Holmesian. We smile at his exclamations of exasperation as he searches through his wardrobe for the necessary disguise for the burglary which results in chaos as clothes flung onto the floor are left there. The image of the burglars who walk across the night scene with Holmes striding out in front in military fashion with Watson limping behind remains in the memory. Altogether it is a very impressive episode with so many treasured moments.

The Kiss became the most celebrated scene in this episode. And the main thing is Holmes seems to enjoy it. *"Ah yes the kiss,"* chuckled 56 year old Jeremy mischievously, *"If I say it's bending the willow in terms of what Arthur Conan Doyle originally wrote in the story then I only hope it doesn't actually break it... At one point she clasps my face in her hands and says, 'Oh, you poor, poor boy!' and plants this smacking kiss on my mouth. She has glimpsed the lonely man beneath the mask. Of course, Holmes is never the same again."* Jeremy grins. (TV Detective Special) The *TV Times* reported that "the famously chaste sleuth actually falls for a woman! He has been targeted by a hot-blooded housemaid called Aggie, and he seems to enjoy it... *"I went home after shooting to my little bar I go to in London and they said, 'How are you doing today?' I said. 'Fine, I had to kiss Sophie Thompson all day. I'm exhausted.' They were all so jealous. Can you imagine going to work and being kissed by a 22 year old at my age? It was magic."*

"The casting is splendid with Robert Hardy playing rather against type as the repressed Milverton. Brett has rarely been better as Holmes, his distaste for the repellent extortionist being plain in every scene. Daringly, he's given a sort-of-love interest... having inveigled himself into the fortress-like Milverton household in the guise of a plumber, Holmes is required to romance Milverton's flighty maid, Aggie, and his heartfelt reply to her *'Give us a kiss'* – *'I don't know how'* is all too believable. Watson has a big moment too – being moved to strike Milverton in a lengthy 221B scene pregnant with menace." (Sherlock Holmes On Screen) Another review applauded the performance, "Jeremy Brett, as the famed detective, is in his element here, showing off the various aspects of the great mind that is Holmes. Holmes is always driven by the prospect of a challenge, a particularly adept criminal, but in this case, there is nothing to work his mind around. Everyone knows who the criminal is, but there is simply no way to stop him without risking scandal. Holmes is so disturbed by the evil that this man is sowing, that when all seems lost, he decides to stoop to the ways of the petty burglar... the best scenes are the ones in which Brett expresses his indignation and his helplessness." (Parama Chaudhury in Film monthly.com)

The bathing scene as he washes away the grime of the plumber Escott, restoring the real Holmes was memorable for its picture of him in a bathtub. Jeremy Paul explained his frustrations with the financiers at Granada who held the purse strings tightly closed, "We were carrying Granada's flag through most of the countries of the world. But each new series had to tough it out against the money... I felt for mood and quality... Right then, could Granada afford a bath for Holmes? And perhaps a samovar with Watson drinking tea? Play it all in a cloud of steam. I like to think it was my shaft of sarcastic wit that came up with this bright idea, but it may have been June. I was not too pleased when several well-meaning friends said later. 'Did you do that one – can't remember the story, but that one with the marvellous scene with Holmes in the bath?'" (Jeremy Paul in Granada Television: First Generation)

This performance would be Dame Gwen Ffrangcon-Davies's last. She was the oldest working British actress who had her first performance backstage at the age of 15 with Ellen Terry and her career had lasted 80 years. "The first take was all over the place. She watched Jeremy Brett's lips and took her cue from that. The second went like a song... The film itself is a gorgeous business. Thickly buttered, not to say jammed with mist and mirrors, greenery and tapestry, reflections of reflections. And a group of girls like a Fragonard on the grass. *The Master Blackmailer*, Charles Augustus Milverton, lives in Hampstead in premises of unparalleled grandeur with his own rain forest, which suggests that business is encouragingly brisk. As Sherlock Holmes remarked there are hundreds in this great city who turn white at his name...." (Nancy Banks-Smith; Holmes and the playful dowager The Guardian 3rd January 1992)

The Last Vampyre (Dramatised by Jeremy Paul: Directed by Tim Sullivan fb: 27January 1993) was filmed at Pitchford Hall in Shropshire and is another glossy two-hour film shot in 35mm based on *The Sussex Vampire*. Conan Doyle wrote to Bram Stoker in August 1897 in congratulation for his book *Dracula*, "I think it is the very best story of diablerie which I have read for many years." They were reputed to be friends and his story of vampires was written in homage to Stoker. June Wyndham Davies would recommend the episode as an intriguing combination of *Holmes* and *Dracula*, two attractive iconic literary figures of the twentieth century. The prologue concerns an event in local history of a hundred years before, in which a young girl was made pregnant by an evil landowner. She was brought to the sanctuary of the church with bite marks on her neck suspected to be those of a vampire and as she lay dying he was burned alive by the villagers in an act of vengeance. The fire was staged in a model mansion built at a cost of more than £30,000 on the footings of a ruined house in Warwickshire.

Holmes has been consulted about a case that appears to involve vampirism and plays a humorous trick on Watson as he enters their Baker Street rooms. It is very much in the style of Conan Doyle who loved practical jokes. *"I'm slumped at my desk and Watson comes in. I'm wearing a pair of false fangs. I turn with my teeth in and Watson is shocked. I say: 'Your reaction is very interesting, Watson. You believe in these things, then?' Watson is horrified. It's the kid inside Sherlock Holmes that I love."* (Jeremy) The appeal to Holmes for help comes not from Bob Ferguson as in the original tale but from the Reverend Merrydew, the vicar of the village of Lamberley, and he is able to provide a pastoral view of the Ferguson family who are at the heart of the matter. Bob has returned from Peru in South America with a new wife and son but problems clearly exist in the relationship with Jack, his fifteen year old son by his first marriage, who had been left disabled in a childhood accident. The presence of Stockton, a newcomer to the village has upset the family and the villagers too who fear that he is a vampire. The vicar would like Holmes's presence in the village "as a steadying effect" and the detective sees it as an interesting case with the possibility of preventing the crime of a stake driven into man's heart. Peter Cushing was offered the part of Merridew but, unfortunately, was not able to accept. It would have been very satisfying to see two Holmes together onscreen.

Whether vampires exist is at the heart of the action. The strange paralysis of the family dog and the death of the child, Riccardo, bring fears and accusations to the surface which should have remained unspoken. The report of Bob's wife Carlotta found sucking blood from the neck of her injured maid seems to confirm that the gossip has foundation although the reasons these things happen is understood later, but does anyone want to listen to reason. Nevertheless, Holmes dismisses the idea of vampires as lunacy. *"What are we to do with the walking corpses who can only be held in their grave by stakes driven through their hearts? It's pure lunacy."* He states categorically, *"This Agency must stand flat-footed upon the ground, and there it must remain. The world is big enough for us. No ghosts need apply."* (The Adventure of The Sussex Vampire)

The Vampyre in this tale is embodied in John Stockton, a cold pale man dressed in black, played by Roy Marsden and although he proves to be a troubled man with a troubled past, he is not a vampire. The villagers think otherwise as his piercing stares appear to be the cause of a neighbour's injury and, more seriously, the death of a strong, healthy blacksmith. He never sleeps and haunts the graveyard so they avoid him wherever possible. In this volatile situation we see Holmes explaining away every mystery with common sense and confidence, the voice of reason in a disintegrating community but after speaking to the locals in the public house, admitting that there is *"a dangerous mood in the air."* Watson adds, *"but no fresh evidence against Stockton."* Watson has greater responsibility in this episode, firstly as a friend to Holmes with whom he reasons for the possibility of vampirism but also acting as a general practitioner, called in to substitute for the local doctor, who is himself sick from the outbreak of influenza in the village. It is most likely the Russian Flu which was virulent and killed millions in Europe at this time.

Holmes seeks to discover more about Stockton by accompanying him on a visit to the ruin of his home where he tests his theory that the man is innocent. At the same time he is showing his lack of fear to the villagers. But this atmospheric scene is more suited to horror films and creates questions which remain unanswered, as the man suddenly disappears from Holmes's sight and then is shown in another area of the ruin sobbing uncontrollably. Holmes is visibly affected by the experience and will tell Watson, *"I got too close"* and believes he has seen a ghost, but not a vampire. Ghosts and gothic myths of vampires don't fit our expectations of Holmes who represents factual knowledge and truth. He seems out of his depth in these circumstances, as his deductive powers and logical reasoning cannot explain what is happening. *"To make the great detective grapple with characters invested with a mysterious evil which defied rational explanation was a nonsense."* (Max Davidson) The pace of the action also brings a disadvantage as his great talent is to think more quickly than everyone else, never giving up the investigation until he arrives at the only possible solution. We expect him to show certainty and action and Jeremy has shown remarkable activity in his interpretation, always rushing to challenge danger. His eventual discovery of the use of the poison curare helps to identify the attack on the maid and the dog, but some events remain unresolved, however, Jack's jealousy of his younger brother Riccardo is finally revealed.

June Wyndham Davies described the attraction of putting two of the biggest box office subjects into one film, the world's greatest detective and *Dracula*. "The Last Vampyre was very short and we worked out that we could turn this into a film, particularly as there has been a lot of media pressure to do something like this... the two biggest audience pullers in the world are *Sherlock Holmes* and *Dracula*, so it was a very good idea to make this film. We got a lovely cast, we went to the most marvellous village for it, and I thoroughly enjoyed it – and people were frightened when they saw the film." (June Wyndham Davies) *"The reason it's called the* Last Vampyre *is because we couldn't shoot it in Sussex... Sussex is so overgrown with people that we had to get away from them. But Cotswold stone is a particular colour and we'd have been the laughing stock of England if we had called it The Sussex Vampyre."* (Jeremy in Scarlet Street 20)

There may have been some reservations amongst the critics about the liberties taken in these later two-hour productions, but Jeremy and Edward continued to be applauded for their performances. Max Davidson in *The Daily Telegraph* once more recognised Jeremy's masterly interpretation of Holmes in "Jeremy Brett's Holmes is quite as fine a creation in its way as John Thaw's *Morse*. It is a hypnotic performance, mannered in the best sense and veering excitingly between introspection and extroversion... Brett's Holmes bristles not simply with intelligence, but with a strange psychic energy that transfigures his whole being. But it is one thing to have 24 carat stars, another to use them properly..." (Max Davidson in The Daily Telegraph) "The Granada series was beautifully shot and well-acted throughout but kudos must be given to Brett and Hardwicke who make a fantastic Holmes and Watson. Brett in particular is superb, at times arrogant, perhaps distracted and yet always keying in to the most pertinent facts, he is totally believable as the master detective. Purists may baulk at this episode though not at the series as a whole as I'd imagine, because it isn't accurate to the original story but to me the changes were welcome and, despite the fact that there were unanswered aspects, the story telling was superb..." (taliesintttlg.blogspot.co.uk)

"Totally absorbing. Jeremy Brett is the definitive Holmes incomparable as always." *"My relationship with Sherlock Holmes has changed over the ten years... But now I can wear the make-up and the black costume without getting upset. The role doesn't invade me any more. I've found a way of getting into him without screwing up my own existence."* (Alec Lom in Nothing – Holmes haunted me, says Jeremy)

"(Laurence) Olivier was a little perverse about 'the method' but he's the only one I ever saw actually become a part – and I know because I was there when he did it... he was not an external actor. He was a primitive. You can't leave blood out of the primitive. He could be so outrageously frightening, wonderful, so powerful! Fearless! He could whiplash his voice. Nothing he could not do. You couldn't put him down. I tried to do something similar with Holmes." (Granada's Greatest Detective Keith Frankel)

"*A great girlfriend of mine, Sue, who has known me for a long time, recently said, 'Who would have thought it would have been Sherlock that you would be most remembered for?' I never thought it would be this; in fact I thought it would ruin my career. It has been like a very small hew stone rolling away from the sepulchre and the air has got in now. But for a long time we have been shut up. Now I am seeing the light - and am enjoying it.*" (The Sherlock Holmes Gazette)

The Four Oaks Mystery 1992 - Telethon

The Four Oaks Mystery was filmed immediately following *The Last Vampyre* as part of a *Telethon* in aid of charity and transmitted on 18th July 1992. The Independent Television production gave the viewers a two day presentation of detective dramas in four episodes of ten minutes with a detective murder mystery that the public was invited to unravel. Van der Valk in Amsterdam, Taggart in Glasgow, and Inspector Wexford in Kings Markham would each investigate a murder linked to the Roman treasure which began in Tunlow but it was Holmes and Watson who were the first team on the case. Written by Jeremy Paul, directed by Tim Sullivan and produced by June Wyndham Davies the presentation was enhanced by the gloss and expertise of the Granada series. The filming was carried out at Adlington Hall in Cheshire with the appearance of Phyllis Calvert in the role of Holmes's godmother, Lady Cordelia, with whom they were visiting at Great Tunlow Hall, whilst on a fishing holiday. Two murders in the village will require their expert attention and Holmes will once more be in his true atmosphere. Watson's skills as a Doctor would also be essential here, alongside his role as companion to Holmes.

The initial investigation uncovers information about the murdered coach driver and his passenger Colonel Harrison, a cartographer, supervising the latest ordinance survey of the district who has possibly found the location of a huge hoard of Roman treasure. Holmes is particularly intrigued by the story told by his godmother of a similar murder a hundred years before with the reference to treasure, "a fortune under the Four Oaks by a river." Colonel Harrison's two colleagues appear suspicious and when they are put under scrutiny by Holmes, they depart from the inn where they were staying leaving behind an exotic ring which seems to confirm that the Roman hoard was discovered. Further investigations are left for the other detectives as Holmes is called to an urgent case before the fateful journey to the Reichenbach Falls.

Kevin Jackson wrote in *The Independent*: "Mr. Brett's true brilliance is overlooked not because no one says that he is splendid but because everybody does. What Brett offers is a combination of fidelity and audacity. Everything he does can ultimately be justified by chapter and line from Conan Doyle's stories, but he has taken liberties with the myth so confidently that he has also, over the last decade, taken possession of it, and displaced the literary Holmes. Brett's is a richly comic performance. His Holmes is composed of sudden wild stares, dreamy vacancies, hoarse exclamations, dulcet murmurs which wilt into silence. He holds his body stiffly yet languorously, like an opium eater who has held a commission in the Guards, and his accent is patrician enough to make Sir Kenneth Clark sound like Danny Baker. Into this potent brew go a jigger of remorse, a dash of sheer lunacy and a strong whiff of camp – though the camp is held firmly in check by sincerity... What other actors have represented in Holmes is the superbrain, the overgrown swot. What Mr Brett has given us for our own *fin de siecle* is a portrait of the Detective as a crazed aesthetic. Conan Doyle did not only borrow the format of the detective story from

Poe's doomed artist-heroes, which is why Holmes is a drug addict, why he plays and composes wild music on his Stradivarius, why he dreads ennui and oscillates between lassitude and frenzy... and indeed, why he often quotes Poe."

As he approached the completion of *The Casebook* Jeremy was interviewed by the *TV Times* for an article entitled *It's Holmes and Away* in which he said, *"My Sherlock streaks through the night sky – not naked, you understand, but like a magnesium flare, with all the world trying to keep up with him. A man of utter genius, not a depressant... there is another Holmes: the thinking man's Holmes, who works things through logically – spasmodically puffing on his pipe, as ash tumbles down his waistcoat. That's the one I've never been able to capture."* But he was grateful. *"Playing Holmes is hard going, but it has done me sterling service. I'm vey grateful. When I go shopping, people stop and talk to me. You have the feeling that the hard work you've done has not gone unappreciated. A good feeling."* (Jeremy)

The Eligible Bachelor **(Dramatised by T R Bowen: Directed by Peter Hammond fb: 3rd February 1993)** based on *The Noble Bachelor* is a slim tale adapted and expanded to create a totally different story and a glossy production. The eligible bachelor in question is a Lord Robert St. Simon played by Simon Williams and his prospective bride, Henrietta (Hetty) Doran, an American heiress. In the original story Holmes reads the newspaper accounts of the engagement with a comment on the passing of the noble houses of Britain into the hands of "our fair cousins across the Atlantic" with a further note that Hettie is the fascinating daughter of a Californian millionaire" with a dowry running into "considerably over six figures." The great house of Glarvon, the ancestral home which has been in the family for around 500 years with its wild cats and baboons roaming freely is at the centre of this relationship as much as the bride's money, which is shown in the bridegroom's dealings with money lenders, insistent on the payment of his debts. Some event has taken place during the wedding ceremony, unnoticed by most of the people present, but it has been significant, and as the family gathers for the reception, the bride has disappeared.

The episode opens with a series of unsettling images, references to the mental home, the unruly noise of the London streets and in this version Holmes is not well; he is suffering from nightmares which keep him awake at night and although he wanders nightly amongst the tumultuous streets of London in order to gain some peace, he gains none. A depressed and defeated Holmes suffering from nightmares offers a new insight into his multi-faceted character in Jeremy's hands. There will be a moment in this case when he runs into the street in the pouring rain in his nightclothes in order to make contact with a veiled woman he has seen on the opposite side of the street. He tries to stop her carriage and winds up sitting in a puddle on the kerbside muttering, "*Damn! Damn!*" Jeremy saw this as a comic moment but the picture of Holmes in this condition is unsettling. However, it was not going to last long and as the mood changes, he is able to recover himself sufficiently to investigate and solve the mystery of the disappearing bride.

In the original Conan Doyle story *The Adventure of The Noble Bachelor*, Lord St Simon certainly has his problems but he is no villain. Yet in Granada's radical re-creation of the story he plays both victim and villain. With his increasing debts and with no prospect of remarriage he will pursue Hetty's wealth ruthlessly. His arrival at Baker Street asking for Holmes to help find his bride has already been prepared for, however, the great detective is in need of sleep so Watson agrees to take the preliminary notes of the case. The delivery of a note by the woman in a veil: "*What of the Ladies Maude and Helena?*" during the interview brings questions for St Simon who reveals that they were the names of his first wives. Holmes cries in disbelief, "*Married! But you are known, even celebrated, as one of the most eligible bachelors in the country!*" to which there is no satisfactory answer other than signs of personal discomfort. As the veiled lady, played by Anna Calder Marshall, comes finally to Baker Street, her terrible story at the hands of St Simon is revealed. Her sister Helena had been his second wife, whom he had committed to an asylum after stealing her fortune. In her attempt to find clues to her sister's disappearance at Glarvon, Agnes too had been attacked and left for dead. It is her story which brings about the re-energising of Holmes who, now out of his nightshirt and back in his traditional black city costume, follows his investigation of Miss Flora Millar. The West End actress has been arrested for the attempted shooting of Lord St Simon and as his discarded mistress she is suspected of involvement in his wife's disappearance.

Holmes may be unwell, suffering from an unexplained malaise yet he manages to find the husband, Frank Moulton, who was thought lost, murdered by Apache Indians in the American Southwest. The extortionate price of a glass of sherry is the one piece of evidence that Holmes thinks worthy of investigation amongst the best hotels and with his success, Hetty's future looks much more secure. She will not be under the control of the rapacious Lord St Simon but she must survive his attempt on her life first as he seeks to keep control of her money. The concluding scenes are played out with tension and drama at Glarvon as Hetty faces up to a husband not prepared to let her go.

"Damn! Damn!"

The secret of the estate has already been solved by Holmes in his dreams and Watson helps Holmes in his attempt to understand his recurring nightmare when he refers to Sigmund Freud's *Interpretation of Dreams*, published in 1899. Holmes adds the possibilities of "prophetic and precognisance". Conan Doyle was an avid proponent of the Spiritualist Religion which included such beliefs, amongst others and this may have been added to the story in homage to him. Though he was ridiculed for this belief in his day, it became the precursor to today's New Age Religion. "*It's a departure. We are moving into a space we have never been in before. We now have a Holmes picturing the future, when he's actually on a case. It becomes really gripping. I don't know what Doyleans will think about it.*" (Jeremy in Bending the Willow)

There is no humour in this episode, only drama in a secret marriage, confinement in horrific and unimaginable circumstances, murder and insanity and each person wanting something from another without receiving any satisfaction. We also miss Inspector Lestrade who is reputedly in Leamington Spa "taking the waters" but despite his disparaging manner towards Holmes Inspector Montgomery does a sterling job. Jeremy may have been unwell during the making of *Bachelor* but Holmes proves to be the hero throughout the investigation, defeating the villain Floutier and finding the imprisoned Helena. His suffering was shared only by Anna Calder-Marshall, but the viewer catches an occasional glimpse of his lack of energy in a physically demanding episode.

"(Jeremy) was such a very dear friend to my husband, David Burke, they had a very special relationship. There was something like Garbo about him. The face was never blank. So many thoughts would pass over his face, but subtly. It was packed in; it was rich... He was very generous; he wasn't just locked in his own psyche. He was always perceiving things in other people. His generosity, vision, his enthusiasm – he was a star. I was disappointed by the obituary, because it kept on saying what he wasn't. Maybe he didn't have the chances that he should have done, but in every way, in working with him, he was a star." (Anna Calder Marshall in Scarlet Street Winter 1996)

"I made a science of instability, and I succeeded." That line comes near the end of *The Eligible Bachelor*, but it could sum up Jeremy Brett's run nicely: a portrayal of the detective as a man whose genius pushes him to the brink of insanity, though one which doesn't extend to caricature, even when the writers go a bit overboard. The plot device of Holmes's strange dreams is an odd and controversial choice to make; as in *The Last Vampyre*, it pulls Holmes away from one of the things that makes him appealing. That, although Holmes's abilities may appear supernatural, everything he does is comprehensible (even, dare I say, elementary) after it has been explained... On a certain level it seems as though these nightmares were created for the sole purpose of keeping Holmes visible in the first act... And if you can do it well, there are far worse things to do when making a Sherlock Holmes movie than giving Holmes and Watson more face time." (Jay Seaver efilmcritic.com)

The American critics recognised the fact that he was the "quintessential Holmes". "More than any other actor since Basil Rathbone, Mr. Brett was regarded as the quintessential Holmes: breathtakingly analytical, given to outrageous disguises and the blackest moods and relentless in his enthusiasm for solving the most intricate crimes. The actor regarded the detective as a 'black-and-white figure moving through a world of colour,' as a 'man without a heart,' but within those parameters he performed with a demonic intensity..." (Mel Gussow in The New York Times 14th September 1996)

Jeremy and Linda

Jeremy thought he would never find love again; however, he did find someone else he could care for, and she was to bring the comfort he so badly needed in the last years of his life. The relationship began with his generous response to her request for help with her bid to raise money for Cancer Research by running around the coast of Britain. His surprise phone call with the promise *"Darling, I will do all I can to help,"* was followed by a meeting in his dressing room at Richmond Theatre where he shared with her his sorrow at Joan's death, *"I did not give up hope until the moment she died. There are success stories and there are miracles, and one always thinks you're the one who is going to get away with it, even right up to the very last minute. There are cases, of course, where people do. But I think what is extraordinary is that the human spirit is so strong that one doesn't really give up hope, right up to the end."* (On The Wings of Paradise) "That evening Jeremy held a collection at the theatre, which paid for ten pairs of running shoes. This was followed by a photo shoot with the press to initiate interest in the run and get a back-up driver." (The Road is Long) The headline and accompanying picture showed him in Holmes's costume running alongside Wyndham's Theatre, "Holmes goes on the run. Here's Sherlock Holmes, hot on the trail of a missing fortune but without his trusty henchman Watson. Instead the super sleuth – in the person of TV star Jeremy Brett – has sped to the rescue of charity runner Linda Pritchard, who plans to raise £25 million for cancer research by running 5,000 miles round Britain... She has named her marathon 'Keep Hope Alive', but to set off on April 12th, she needs back-up drivers as support. But with Holmes on her side the solution should be, well, elementary." (The Daily Express) Ted, a throat cancer sufferer, responded to the article and volunteered to become Linda's driver on her run.

Jeremy continued to support her and joined her at the launch of her run from the Cutty Sark at Greenwich. "My parents cried, I cried and even Jeremy shed a tear as I set off on this journey of a lifetime..." (Linda in The Road is Long) During her run they would keep in touch by telephone; he was almost telepathic as so many of his phone calls were when she was in need of support. When Linda phoned him to ask for advice about visiting Ireland as her personal safety during the Troubles was an understandable concern, "Jeremy told me it was my run and no one should try to influence me. He said, *'You know why you are doing this run and you know what God wants you to do, so you do what feels right.'* He then told me how proud he was of me and that meant a lot." (ibid) On another occasion when Linda was at a low ebb and needing extra support, he said, *"Remember what you are doing is right. Sometimes our hopes and dreams do not go the way we planned, but we must never let despair overcome us. We have to try and we have to care. We must never give up hope when we still have something to give. Nothing is really over until the moment we stop trying."* (On The Wings of Paradise) Linda would raise £50,000 in her six month run and her relationship with Jeremy would resume when she returned to everyday life. In an interview in 1993 he told of their meeting and how much Linda meant to him. He also explained how she had helped him recover from his latest attack of depression and the contribution he had made to the start of her fund. In 1989 he had been voted *Pipesmoker of the Year*. *"I'd just won a prize of £3,000, so I gave her that." "She used to drive a Hoppa bus in Ealing but, bless her heart, she's given that up to help me. When I was desperately ill... this angel, this pixie was sitting at the foot of my bed. She began to question every medicine I'd been on. She saved me. A miracle occurred. I remembered I'd had rheumatic fever when I was 16, which left me with an enlarged heart and a weak valve...."* Will that include marriage? *"I think I am probably married in heaven. I am reborn."* (Radio Times March 1994)

In another report he said he had found love with Linda, *"an avid fan."* His help with advertising her run around Britain had brought them together. An unnamed source revealed that, "They are both so happy, it's lovely. Jeremy's life fell apart when his wife died. I don't believe he thought he would ever find happiness again." Linda explained, "I can never be, nor would ever want to be, a replacement for Joan. She was an amazing lady and they were so in love. Jeremy truly believed she would recover. The anger he felt when she didn't was just immense." Life with Jeremy was never going to be easy. He told one reporter how difficult he was to live with, especially when he was working: *"I'm certifiable."*

172

He was also suffering from a very difficult illness which affected his personality. In her book *On The Wings of Paradise* concerning the last years of Jeremy's life, Linda summed up how bipolar disorder had affected him: "The real Jeremy... was sensitive and compassionate, full of feeling for others, never saying or doing anything to hurt anyone deliberately. He was jolly and playful, a positive thinker with a marvellous philosophy on life, a joy to be around. His effervescence rubbed off on others and infused them with the same joy and playfulness. People wanted to be around him because he made them feel so good about themselves."

Linda then goes on to describe the other Jeremy that showed itself when the manic depression emerged. Severe mood swings could make him unable to sleep, or even keep still. "No longer the gallant and golden-hearted gentleman he would become edgy, impatient, snappy of tongue, saying hurtful things, crushing things, so out of character for him." In retrospect, he considered this aspect had been affecting his life for as long as he could remember. However, as is typical of these disorders, it had not presented any real problems until his second wife died. The severe shock and grief of this traumatic event in Jeremy's life led to what he called "A good old fashioned nervous breakdown." And it seemed to unleash its power upon his life. "How brave he was... I never heard him moan about his condition once. He never turned round to me and said, 'I can't cope.' Or 'Why me?' He just got on with it." (Linda in Sherlock Holmes: The Detective Magazine) In spite of the miseries that this condition created, Jeremy would show immense courage in his ability to pick himself up and bring comfort to so many others who were suffering. *"My illness has certainly widened my compassion. When I meet people now I can see the stresses and strains they are all under. Life just isn't easy."*

The Memoirs of Sherlock Holmes

The final six episodes of *The Memoirs* would represent Jeremy's goodbye to the role. They would return to the one hour slot in the schedules as everyone felt a return to Conan Doyle was preferable to the two-hour films. The length of approximately 55 mins of the originals seemed to fit the format better. However, it was clear that Jeremy's health was failing and he was no longer able to fight for authenticity of dialogue and interpretation. Even one or two inaccuracies appeared, for instance, Mycroft's talking to Lord Cantlemere in The Diogenes Club where talking is forbidden in *The Mazarin Stone*, which Jeremy would surely have commented on, if he had appeared in this episode.

The critic in *The Guardian* commented on the first episode and compared the latest incarnation with the previous series, "A few instalments ago Jeremy Brett was the best Holmes ever – a slightly camp drug addict allaying his boredom with the solving of supposedly insoluble crimes. His was an essentially comic interpretation, perfectly suited to Doyle's character. Brett is shouting his lines these days, to no one in particular, and the effect is operatic." (Paul Bailey Holmes Flares up again The Guardian 8th March 1994) One memorable comment showed Jeremy had not lost his outrageous sense of humour, "*Holmes has really become a semi-permanent job. But the time is coming when I'm going to have to wash off my mask, show people what I look like and say: 'What do you think?' First though, I've got to think of a way of publicising this series. Perhaps, I could streak naked across Lord's cricket ground with S and H painted on my backside..."* (Why Sherlock Holmes nearly killed JEREMY BRETT by Adam Furness TV Times 1993)

And, after all, he was proud of the success of his interpretation. *"Why should I mind being typecast as a genius?"* Brett laughed. *"It's been hard going at times but I'm very grateful for the opportunity to be recognized for a role that is so close to people's hearts. When I am out in public, people come up and tell me how much they enjoy the series. Many of them tell me they appreciate the fact that we've been so reverent to the original stories. That's a marvellous affirmation for an actor."* (Holmes: Brett Still Essential Sherlock)

The Three Gables

The Three Gables (Dramatised by Jeremy Paul: Directed by Peter Hammond fb: 7th March 1994) has remained faithful to the Conan Doyle story with only minor adaptations. It was the third episode to be filmed and would have an impact on Jeremy's health for the rest of the series. It is a very glossy and beautifully filmed drama with rather too many reflective surfaces. As Watson arrives at Baker Street, Holmes is in danger of his life at the hands of the boxer, Steve Dixie who is threatening to push him through the window with the chilling directive, delivered with significant menace, to stay away from Harrow.

It is a strange case for Holmes as there is no crime involved, only a general feeling of something amiss. Mrs Maberley, played memorably by Mary Ellis, has received an over-valued offer on her house which she had accepted until her Solicitor warned her that nothing could be removed, not even her personal possessions. The story of her recently deceased grandson who had been an attaché at the British Embassy in Italy is an important detail although at this stage she does not connect the incident with the offer for her house. The young man had become a moody and "worn-out cynical man" before he died and his possessions remained forgotten in her house. Her story is interrupted as Holmes loudly and dramatically confronts the housekeeper who has been listening to everything that was said and he recognises her as a member of Barney Stockdale's boxing establishment. Her presence validates Holmes's suspicions, and finding Steve Dixie lurking in the bushes outside confirms his conviction that Mrs Maberley is in danger.

One change the Granada team made to this episode is in the assignment of Watson to remain at the Three Gables to protect her and as Mrs Maberley is burgled in the night Watson, who threatened Dixie to a fight at Baker Street, is here savagely beaten by him. On his arrival the next morning Holmes finds his friend black and blue from the beating and uncharacteristically tells him, *"Physician heal thyself"* which raises the question; where is the more sympathetic and caring Holmes of *The Devil's Foot* and *The Three Garridebs*? The only consolation lies in the rescue of the final page of the forgotten manuscript by the injured Mrs Maberley which incriminated Mrs Klein.

The villain of the episode is revealed as the wealthy Isadora Klein, played by Claudine Auger, a woman who preyed on men. She is exotic, beautiful, of Spanish Gypsy descent and although she was considerably older than he, it is no surprise that Douglas Maberley had been wildly in love with this fascinating creature. His lack of fortune meant she would not accept his offer of marriage, so she would have him severely beaten in a bid to discourage him and these injuries would bring about his death from a ruptured spleen. Her plans to marry the Duke of Lomond, another young man, but this time in possession of a fortune and a title, has put her into Holmes's power and he has accused her of murder. In a dramatic scene of confrontation Holmes will fend her off and preserve his position with the comment, "*You are a destroyer of men. You destroyed Douglas Maberley, and very nearly my friend John Watson.*"

The final accusation is an unforgivable offence and receives considerable gravitas from Jeremy. His final demand of a breakup from the Duke of Lomond and a £5,000 cheque to send Mrs Maberley around the world appears to be the right price for her crimes. Whether Holmes should have involved the authorities in the case is raised when Watson accuses him of compounding a felony by letting Mrs Klein go without paying the just price for her crimes. But Holmes thinks they will meet again. "*You can't play with edged tools for ever without cutting those ageing hands,*" substituted here for Doyle's "*dainty hands*" and provides a fitting symbol for the story. The other consideration of this decision could be attributed to the changes the Granada team had made to the original story where Douglas Maberley had died from pneumonia brought on by a broken heart, and not the ruptured spleen displayed in this episode. No crime had been committed.

One addition made by Granada, was the development of the role of gossip columnist Langdale Pike, played by Peter Wyngarde, whom Holmes approaches for the identity of Douglas Maberley's love interest, and the scenes between Pike and Holmes are full of wit and humour. The midnight masque with revels and fireworks was filmed at Lyme Park in Disley and due to an unseasonable frost Jeremy caught pneumonia and just escaped being hospitalised. "*I thought I was a goner. I should have known better than to stay out there. I was very ill when I was young and I've never fully got over it.*" (Why Sherlock Holmes nearly killed JEREMY BRETT by Adrian Furness TV Times 1993) "I knew Jeremy for a long time, but I'd never worked with him until I was asked to in this episode. What I found absolutely fascinating was his hold on the whole production. He'd become Sherlock Holmes – totally and utterly, he'd become this man. It was quite extraordinary. He had this wonderful ability to know what was good for the series and what wasn't, and he always hit the nail on the head." (Scarlet Street 21)

"A lot of sweeping gestures have been made, many a wild shout has rent the air since Jeremy Brett's Sherlock first swept into view. It was a fairly extraordinary characterisation in 1984 and in the new series, a six-parter that began last week with *The Three Gables*, reaches new extremes of extravagant performance: long meaningful glares, much lip-curling, arms outstretched as if summoning spirits from another world. When Ed Siegel of *The Boston Globe* wrote in 1985 that Brett's portrayal lifted "the curse of Basil" from the English speaking world he was putting it mildly: in all the Holmes films he made, including those dire wartime ones, Basil Rathbone never went so recklessly over the top as Brett, never made the great detective's genius seem so akin to madness. It's thoroughly enjoyable, even the make-up goes too far, and Edward Hardwicke is the best Dr Watson yet, even better than Nigel Stock..." (Critics Choice by Richard Bruton)

***The Dying Detective* (Dramatised by T R Bowen: Directed by Sarah Hellings fb: 14th March 1994)** is the fourth episode to be filmed featuring a harrowing case in which Holmes is infected with a deadly tropical disease. "Mrs Hudson... was a long-suffering woman. Not only was her first-floor flat invaded at all hours by throngs of singular and often undesirable characters, but her remarkable lodger showed an eccentricity and irregularity in his life which must have sorely tried her patience. His incredible untidiness, his addiction to music at strange hours, his occasional revolver practice within doors, his weird and often malodorous scientific experiments, and the atmosphere of violence and danger which hung around him made him the very worst tenant in London. On the other hand... the landlady stood in the deepest awe of him, and never dared to interfere with him, however outrageous his proceedings might seem. She was fond of him, too, for he had a remarkable gentleness and courtesy in his dealings with women. He disliked and distrusted the sex, but he was always a chivalrous opponent. Knowing how genuine her regard for him, I listened earnestly to her story when she came to my rooms... "He's dying, Dr. Watson," said she. "For three days he has been sinking, and I doubt if he will last the day." (The Adventure of the Dying Detective)

Mrs Hudson goes on to say, "He has been working at a case down at Rotherhithe". The case may have begun in Rotherhithe amongst the opium dens; however, Granada had chosen to focus on the relationship between Culverton Smith and his cousin, Victor Savage, a director of the Oxford and Lombard Bank with an opium addiction. This had begun when he wanted the kind of inspiration that comes only from a drug-induced state in order to write poetry. By frequenting these dangerous establishments he has put himself into the hands of

Culverton Smith, *"the well-known resident of Sumatra,"* the authority on tropical diseases, and strangely enough, the man who will inherit the banker's estate and fortune on his death.

Holmes is called in to help when Savage becomes ill and he and Watson are there as dinner guests as the banker has a fatal collapse from which he subsequently dies. The scene is a tense affair and Holmes points to the different human vices on display, of fever, gluttony, acute irritation and envy, all encapsulated in the different guests. Smith shows his spite and lack of compassion as he has Savage's wife and children evicted from Summerly, the family home under the entailment of the will and watches their suffering from a distance. Watson, who is present in the role of protector, makes a direct appeal on their behalf. As Holmes appears he warns Smith loudly and publicly that he will pursue him until justice is done. This will affect Smith's professional reputation and is designed to draw him out. *"It is a singular coincidence, is it not, that you should inherit so much from a man who dies of a disease upon which you are the sole expert. Coincidence, bordering on the unbelievable. Let me tell you, the doors of your profession which have been closed to you, will now be locked and bolted against you. It is my mission."* (The Adventure of The Dying Detective)

The infection of Holmes represents the dramatic centre of this episode. Mrs Hudson and Watson certainly believe he is mortally ill, and delirious, as does Culverton Smith. Jeremy's acting is convincing and very dramatic and Michael Cox says, "Most actors enjoy nothing more than a part which allows them to die in agony or go mad. Jeremy Brett was no exception and clearly relished the opportunity to don his nightshirt again and succumb to Sumatran River Fever." William Baring-Gould wrote, "It is of considerable interest to note that the first account of the isolation of the etiologic agent of oriental plague, *Pastuerella pestis*, was published in 1894... Thus Smith's unpublished studies, performed at his Sumatran plantation, preceded the recognised work by several years..." Mr Hugh L'Etang holds that "... Snake venom would be a most convenient poison with which to load the box..." (The Annotated Sherlock Holmes) It is sufficiently convincing to say the delivered box which held the infection would be an efficient method of infection, had not Holmes been alert to the risk. He had been watching and waiting for such an attack and his perfect presentation of the symptoms is enough for Smith, the only expert in this particular fever. Three days after infection, he would experience delirium, and an enormous thirst followed by intense stomach cramps, "Painful, is it? Yes, the coolies used to do some squealing before the end." (Smith) And as the darkness begins to fall, to signify the last minutes of life, Smith is giving himself away and confessing his responsibility for the box, the infection, and his guilt of murder. Unknown to him, Watson is in the room, hiding behind the curtain and with instructions to listen carefully to every word, but not to make a sound. The phrase which Holmes uses as the gas lamps are turned up, could almost be Jeremy's when he says, *"Three days without food and water is one thing. But to be without tobacco I have found most irksome."*

The title of this episode *The Dying Detective* was almost prophetic as Jeremy fainted into the arms of Roy Hudd in his cameo role as Gedgrave during filming. Between scenes he had been confined to a wheelchair and needed to use oxygen to relieve his breathing difficulties so that Linda wanted him to go to hospital to receive treatment. He continued to be unwell on occasions, suffering from "whiteouts" until filming finally ended when he was persuaded to go into hospital again. He was diagnosed with heart failure. (On The Wings of Paradise) *"I thought there was something seriously wrong, but like an idiot I soldiered on. Suddenly I was fainting all over the set. They had laid on a birthday party for me* (his sixtieth) *and I just said, 'I can't go, take me to hospital...' (A heart specialist) realised straight away it was nothing to do with the mind. I had heart failure brought on by rheumatic fever I had as a child. They drained five litres of fluid from my chest cavity just for starters."* (Adam Furness TV Times 1993) As Jeremy was hospitalised for this new complication he missed the next episode to be filmed and Granada had made the strange decision to film a Sherlock Holmes film without their Sherlock Holmes star. One must ask why the series couldn't delay filming briefly to allow Jeremy to recover his health! The next two episodes in the *Memoirs* had been filmed earlier so we can see Jeremy at his best in the final series. The absence of Edward in the first of these was mainly due to the lack of go-ahead from Granada and the fact that Dr Watson was committed elsewhere when final decisions were made.

***The Golden Pince-Nez* (Dramatised by Gary Hopkins: Directed by Peter Hammond fb: 21st March 1994)** was the first episode filmed in *The Memoirs* series and follows the original Conan Doyle story with only the occasional adaptation. The timing had been pushed from 1894 into the twentieth century to include the origins of the revolution in Russia and the suffragette movement. Unfortunately, Edward Hardwicke was not available to play Dr Watson as he was engaged in filming *Shadowlands* playing the brother of C.S. Lewis. Thus the episode was rewritten to bring back Charles Gray as Mycroft. The appearance of Mycroft here enabled the relationship to be explored in much the same way as the friendship between Holmes and Watson had been developed throughout the series. The opening scene with the shared analysis and clarification on an "original inscription upon a palimpsest", a reused 500 year old manuscript was an erudite one as the two siblings have a similar intellect. Mrs Hudson is much more in evidence too as she sticks up for Doctor Watson reminding Holmes that he is missing his companion but also putting herself underfoot and inviting more complaints from Holmes for being in the way.

Inspector Hopkins, played by Nigel Planer, is a methodical representative of the law; he explains the Yoxley Case with every relevant detail. It is a murder "without motive" as the

Inspector can see no reason why anyone should wish to harm Professor Coram's secretary, Willoughby Smith. The secretary was "a quiet, well-educated fellow with hardly any weak spot in him at all." The pince-nez found in the victim's hand offers Holmes and Mycroft an opportunity to examine the spectacles for information about the owner. The scene with Holmes wearing the spectacles whilst rubbing the attached cord beneath his fingers is indicative of his search for the scent of the owner. They each contribute to the portrait of a lady of refinement with poor eyesight, almost blind, but it is Mycroft who makes the largest contribution as Charles had been given more of Jeremy's lines. *"I was thrilled to have Mycroft... I asked the powers that be if I could switch my speech about the deduction of the pince-nez and gave it to Charles Gray. And he did it brilliantly. Because after all Mycroft is the brains of the family."* (Jeremy to Scarlet Street Number 20)

At the scene of the crime there is the business with the magnifying glass, where Sherlock immediately recognises it as once belonging to his father, *'That's father's magnifying glass. He gave it to you?'* brings humour as they each show their competitive spirit mingled with mutual respect. Holmes needed someone to share the investigation with and his elder, equally observant brother was an ideal substitute, especially as Mycroft seems to be one step ahead in his observations and deduction and even leaves the primary clue of the empty snuff case for Sherlock to ponder on. Mycroft will also remind his brother of their father's axiom (taken from *The Sign of Four*) *"after eliminating the impossible whatever remains, however improbable, must be the truth."*

Frank Finlay as the Professor is an unlikely villain. He is guilty of telling terrible lies against his wife and brother-in-law which resulted in their imprisonment in the Siberian Gulag and he is guilty of crimes against the Brotherhood for which he will eventually pay with his life. In the murder of Willoughby Smith he has hidden the killer from the Police and is therefore guilty of withholding important information. His relationship with Holmes is one of evasion yet companionship as they enjoy smoking together. The scene with the invalid lying on his bed totally immersed by the smoke of Alexandrian tobacco of his and Holmes's cigarettes is amusing, made even more humorous as Holmes sees himself as *"a connoisseur"* of fine tobacco and he smokes four cigarettes in succession, lighting each from the stub of his last. Surprisingly, it is this shared pleasure in smoking which will help Holmes discover a solution to the difficult case as the two men create a great deal of ash.

The reveal of the Professor's wife is dramatic and as she staggers from her hiding place behind the bookcase she tearfully tells her story of the Brotherhood who had revolted against the Russian authorities with their own Bloody Sunday and provides a convincing explanation for accidental murder. The Professor, Sergei is her Russian husband and she has a story of betrayal during their struggles with the Cossack soldiers, the means of putting down the insurrection. Her search of the bureau for letters to save her brother, Alexis, results in the death of Smith but justice was guaranteed as Anna dies at her own hand from poison.

Jeremy shows a mixture of responses in this episode, some of them are familiar and others offer a new impression of Holmes. We hear him shouting at the policeman who was falling asleep on duty as watchman and showing his customary rudeness to the housekeeper, Mrs Marker. But we also see his sensitive and sympathetic treatment of the maid, Susan Tarlton. Willoughby Smith had bled to death in her arms so it is no surprise she is unable to take her eyes from the blood stain on the carpet until Holmes covers it with his scarf and tells her, *"now you can look at me."* His sensitive questioning brings him the valuable information he needs to proceed. She had heard the dying man's final words, "Professor – it was she." Curious words which at this point in the proceedings have no meaning but which will later bring illumination. Jeremy's moment of hesitation at accepting the return of his scarf pushed onto him by the weeping girl is a touching moment in these final episodes.

"One of the best of the late Jeremy Brett Holmes films, this one is particularly distinguished by its use of colourful, self-consciously arty cinematography to heighten an eccentric mood, I love it. This one is a visual delight. Brett is fine as always, so is Charles Gray as his sharp brother, Mycroft, who comes along to investigate as well... All of Brett's films are notable for their period detail and engaging neurotic take on its lead character." (Amazon.com)

The Red Circle **(Dramatised by Jeremy Paul: Directed by Sarah Hellings fb: 28th March 1994)** the second episode to be filmed remains faithful to the original story and was one of Jeremy's favourites in the final series. Watson introduces the story with the two antagonists, Gennaro and Black Gorgiano, both who loved Emilia. In Baker Street the appeal of Mrs Warren accompanied by Mrs Hudson is something Holmes is unable to dismiss even if he would like to, and the mention of Enrico Firmani convinces him that there might be something of interest for him in her story. The mystery of a lodger whom the landlady has never seen, yet hears moving around in the room above frightens her, especially as her husband is at work during the day and Mrs Warren is becoming hysterical. However, Holmes can be a magician in circumstances like these, "He had an almost hypnotic power of soothing when he wished." As he lays his fingers on the lady's shoulders her fears eased, "The scared look faded from her eyes," and he requests to hear every detail. Her concerns began when a young man, under thirty, clean shaven and with accented English had offered her more than double the usual rent on a room in exchange for being left alone with no interruptions. He had gone out on the first night and returned much later, but since then he had not been seen. He wanted a copy of *The Daily Chronicle* every morning and left a piece of paper on a chair outside his door when he wanted anything extra. The White Star sticker on the luggage suggests he had arrived from New York as a sailing had arrived ten days before.

Granada introduced a new character in Firmani, from the Italian city of Naples, working as a backstage technician at the Royal Opera House. Holmes describes him as a good man who stands as "a beacon of light, if you will, in a dark web of devilry." However, Black Gorgiano, a member of the Brotherhood, the Mafiosi, is a man of different reputation "the name of death... red up to his elbows in blood" and extremely dangerous. Firmani is murdered by Gorgiano and Watson claims responsibility for visiting him at home and leading him to the victim. Nevertheless, Watson has found a link to the Red Circle, with details of other atrocities and a mention of Gorgiano which will prove useful in the solving of the case.

Holmes appears to be at the mercy of events here. They come faster than he can deal with them. Initially he pursues the idea that the personal column in *The Daily Chronicle* was used for communication *"what a chorus of cries and groans!"* and very soon the repeated messages with the signature G prove him right.

"Be patient. Will find some sure means of communication. Meanwhile, this column. – G."

"Am making successful arrangements. Patience and Prudence. The clouds will pass. – G."

These brief messages help to make the case appear "more intelligible". But then the kidnapping of Mrs Warren's husband, played by the *Carry On* actor Kenneth Connor, appears as the next crisis. He was attacked outside his home as he left for work as a timekeeper, taken into a cab and some time later left on Hampstead Heath which causes Holmes to assume the kidnappers who were heard speaking Italian had mistaken Mr Warren for the secretive lodger. The discovery of how Emilia Lucca and her husband became caught up in the criminal exploits of the Red Circle is achieved by Holmes's adoption of the observer hiding in the box room but unfortunately he will also alert the murderer to their whereabouts.

This is a very tight action-packed episode accompanied by high drama as Holmes and Leverton, the American agent, attempt to thwart the attack by Gorgiano but fail to capture him. Jeremy can be seen once more climbing confidently on roofs and crawling through the loft space seemingly without fear or concern about safety. Michael Cox pointed out the anomaly of a watched house with a top-hatted man coming and going through the roof without being noticed, however, he seems to achieve it without interruption. The fight on a fire escape between Leverton and Gorgiano which ends in a wounding for the American means there is much blood and although he is splattered by it, Holmes remains uninjured. *"The brute got away."*

Justice is done where Gorgiano pays the ultimate price but Emilia and Gennaro are not immediately free to leave for Australia. "He will be arrested and tried for the murder of Gorgiano. That is the law." The authorities must go through the procedures and have their final judgement on them first, even on a crime committed in self-defence. The Inspector points out that if Holmes had been alone no doubt he would have found a different solution. *"The law is what we live with, Inspector. Justice is sometimes harder to achieve."* (Sherlock Holmes) It is interesting to hear Holmes remind us of the correct formula, "What you say may be used in evidence" rather than the frequently used "in evidence against you." It is also a reminder of all those instances where he has been the true source of justice because he has intervened and rescued the offenders who might have ended in the unsympathetic hands of the law courts.

Jeremy has created a sympathetic Holmes in this episode, a sensitive man beneath the cold exterior, able to express his deep regret for the loss of Firmani, a man who had represented a point of refuge for the Italian community in London and his words *"Golden lads and girls all must, as chimney sweepers, come to dust"*, taken from Shakespeare's *Cymbeline*, expresses the depth of his feelings for the loss of a good man. During the filming of the final scene during Wagner's *Tristan and Isolde* at the Buxton Opera House he said he was much happier with the one hour productions in which he could stay closer to the original stories. *"We moved so far away from the canon in the last two films that I could not bring my book with me and say 'This is how it should have been.' I lost control. They were interesting but they were not Doyle... The one-hour format is much tighter, I can turn to Doyle and bring a little bit of him in because we are so much closer to the substance of the series - and we can call them by their proper names."* (Jeremy to Elizabeth Wiggins in Sherlock Holmes Gazette) One of the houses in a Moravian settlement in Fairfield, Manchester was used for filming in this episode and the *Manchester Evening News* spoke to Jackie Hammond, 72, who grew up in the settlement with her family. "The team filmed it in my house. I think they were here for about two weeks. Jeremy Brett... loved it, he really got involved with the community. After he left he sent a big bunch of daffodils to the church because he loved it that much."

"In the last series, his Holmes is older, often sad, sometimes moody but he remains the brilliant Holmes we have come to know and love, not only as a genius consulting detective but as a man with all his weaknesses, fears and his inspirational reflections about the meaning of life." (www. jeremybrett.info) After his death a year later Edward highlighted his struggles in the final series. "Jeremy was quite ill in the last series. It was a real test of strength for him, but he battled through. He was an actor who needed to work and was at his happiest on set." (Edward Hardwicke in The Daily Mail 14th September 1995)

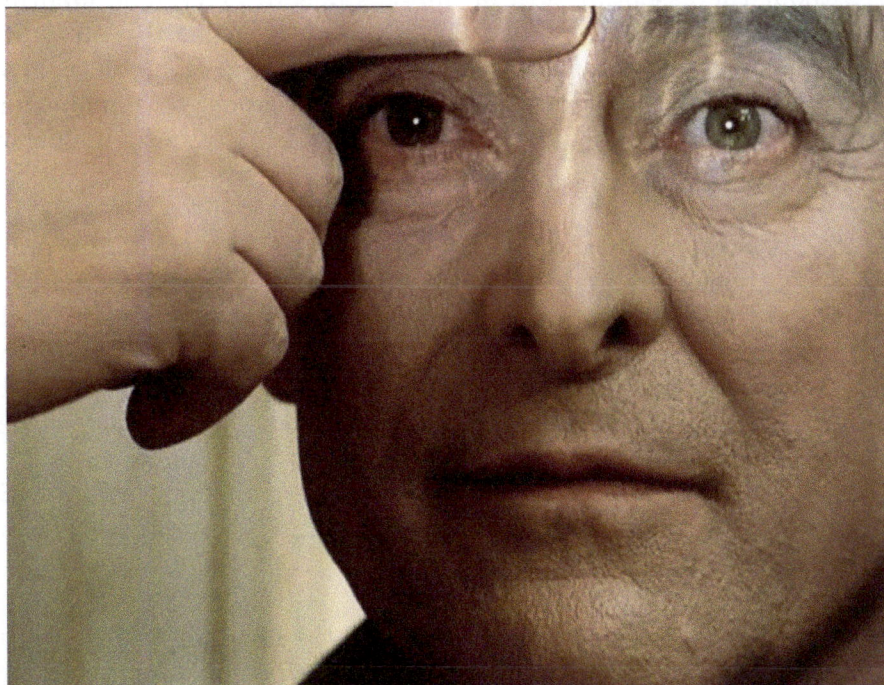

The Mazarin Stone (Dramatised by Gary Hopkins: Directed by Peter Hammond fb: 4th May 1994) incorporates *The Three Garridebs* within the story. The fifth to be filmed in the sequence seriously lacks the presence of Jeremy. He appears at the opening of the story and as a concluding image which reminds us of his genius portrayal of Holmes. Watson also needs him when he is wounded with the splitting tool, which is a missed opportunity for Holmes to finally show him how much his friend and colleague is loved. It has been called the supreme moment when a serious wound had revealed to Watson the depth of Holmes's devotion to him. "'*You're not hurt, Watson? For God's sake, say that you are not hurt!*' It was worth a wound – it was worth many wounds – to know the depth of loyalty and love which lay behind that cold mask. The clear, hard eyes were dimmed for a moment, and the firm lips were shaking. For the one and only time I caught a glimpse of a great heart as well as of a great man." (The Three Garridebs)

Mycroft was chosen as the person to fill in for Jeremy's Holmes who was seriously unwell, so after a brief scene at the beginning in which he demanded that Watson provide "*the medical term for obsession,*" he retired to the High Lands to "*lay to rest the ghost that has haunted me for some time*" and promised to watch him with his "*third eye.*"

Sherlock's help is requested by Lord Cantlemere in his meeting with Mycroft at the Diogenes Club, "It is the Prime Minister's personal wish that your brother should employ his detective skills, find the Mazarin Diamond and return it to Whitehall without delay." Mycroft has been accused of letting his younger brother have too long a leash as he was unavailable to investigate the daring theft of the famous Mazarin Stone; which at 110 carats in weight is "bigger even than the Koh-i-Noor." Count Sylvius was the last person to leave the Museum so he becomes the focus of attention. Mycroft will pursue his suspect in disguise, but without the essential skill of hiding himself, Mycroft is identifiable in each appearance. The Count, unsettled by all this attention, becomes threatening and takes a pot shot at his oppressor on several occasions, just missing him, but when challenged, excused his behaviour as "the hair trigger" on his weapon. A famous gameshot and sportsman with a keen eye would surely not have missed his target which shows Mycroft's life is very much in danger.

Another case for Sherlock Holmes, *The Three Garridebs*, is presented simultaneously to Watson in his consulting rooms by the two elderly, eccentric Garrideb sisters with a story about the promise of immense wealth. Their brother Nathan believes he will inherit five million dollars from Alexander Hamilton Garrideb of Kansas USA if another male called Garrideb can be found, but it is sensibly dismissed by his younger sisters as the bringer of the news, an American called John Garrideb, "doesn't have the bone structure" which identifies a true member of the family. They were unable to persuade their brother that he was chasing moonbeams and sought Watson's help to investigate. Nathan had been one of Watson's university lecturers and persists in calling him Watkins which is amusing and Watson, ever the gentleman, doesn't correct him.

Inspector Bradstreet as Mycroft's assistant, is as ever the efficient representative of the law and provides an update on Presbury, the only jeweller who could cut the diamond, (in the original story he is "The greatest counterfeiter London ever saw") but he was murdered five years ago, for which James Winter (Killer Evans) went to prison. This detail will bring the two investigations together, as James Winter is identified by Watson as the American, John Garrideb, and Holmes has provided further evidence in a letter to Watson where he writes to warn his friend about Presbury's lodger. Mycroft and Watson stake out the Garrideb house and challenge the thief as he breaks into Presbury's workshop in the cellar where his tools remain, looking for a forger's tool to cleave the diamond so it can be transported to Amsterdam. The removal of Nathan Garrideb from his study to Birmingham is also brought into context. Drama and excitement is central to this scene as the evil Winter first aims his cleaving tool at Watson but then holds it to his neck. There is humour too as the two elderly sisters who had been sent to bed for their safety, unexpectedly defeat the criminal by dropping the cellar door onto him, rescuing Watson and then attending to his injuries.

A successful conclusion is achieved by the final confrontation with the Count as Mycroft has pursued him relentlessly until he meets him on the mudflats of the River Thames, identifies the hiding place of the diamond and restores it to its owner, the Princess of Wales. *"Brother mine. Bravo!"* The words of congratulation from a slimmer and more vigorous Holmes reminds us of what might have been if Jeremy had been well enough to appear. As a piece of detection it doesn't disappoint and the scriptwriters had achieved an exciting action packed adventure with all the gloss and expertise the Granada Studios could achieve. But a Sherlock Holmes story without its star couldn't escape being an anticlimax.

Charles Gray in Mazarin Stone

***The Cardboard Box* (Dramatised by T R Bowen: Directed by Sarah Hellings fb: 11th May 1994)** is the final appearance of Jeremy as Sherlock Holmes and for many it is the best of *The Memoirs*. Although the original story is set on "*a blazing hot day in August,*" the filming was done in winter so Christmas was chosen which gave the opportunity for Mrs Hudson to put up Christmas decorations and for Holmes, on Mrs Hudson's advice, to buy Watson a Christmas present from Gamages, The People's Emporium. Snow and festivities provide the backdrop for a startling story of a macabre present, two human ears, severed and preserved in salt which the unsuspecting Susan Cushing opens on Christmas Eve. Her little dog is fascinated by the box and has probably smelt the contents, but Susan has no idea and as she discovers the horrors within, she is overcome and faints.

When Miss Cushing arrives at Baker Street seeking Holmes's help to find her missing sister, he is dismissive as it is a personal matter when he preferred to focus on the unusual. He suggests she tries the Missing People's Agency. She may be hurt by his lack of sympathetic concern, especially as she feels her family is beset by difficulties, but she has no idea whether Mary is truly missing or not. The macabre present of human ears bring Holmes back into the affair as investigating agent. At the same time he is helping Inspector Hawkins, who replaces Lestrade here, to look into a number of grave robberies. They have been reported in the Police News as *Grave Robbed again – Body Snatchers Strike in North London,* "a modern version of Burke and Hare." Holmes wishes Hawkins to continue in his search of the records for details of the crimes and at the same time, to watch Murdoch Gull who could be involved. A possible link with these events is suggested by the dismembered ears which Hawkins thinks is "a nasty little joke and therefore unrelated". Watson agrees that medical students can often be unthinkingly callous when involved in post-mortem anatomy, which appears to give evidence for the link. However, the two ears are from two separate people, a woman and a man.

The relationship between the sisters, especially between Sarah and her married sister Mary, reveals the tensions in the household. Holmes's sympathetic and searching questions persuade Susan to describe the reality of the situation. Jeremy presented the Holmes of Doyle where, "Holmes listened attentively to everything". When Susan mentions Sarah's temper and that, "she was always meddlesome and hard to please," his survey of the situation will include this element. Sarah spent far too much time within the Browner household making herself indispensable to her sister but also causing distrust within the marriage. It is Sarah who is the villain and her brooding, malevolent presence seems to dominate the episode; she is obsessed with Browner but is piqued by his rejection and in her hatred "spits poison" into her sister's ear, causing the breakdown of their relationship. The murder can firmly be laid at her door and the two ears, boxed and preserved, were meant as a present for her and not Susan. The sympathetic and compassionate Holmes is a highlight of this episode. He can recognise the truth of how Browner was driven to murder, how emotional outbursts can spill over into violence and love can turn to hatred, *"I believe I wish you had committed this deed in France. They acknowledge the crime of passion there."* He also shows an instinctive understanding for Browner's need of company and the desire never to be left alone with his guilt

Meanwhile, Holmes has effortlessly solved the body-snatching crimes by pointing out that it is only the graves of pugilists which are disturbed, as boxers often suffer from brain injury. Scarring of the brain creates people who are punch drunk and an examination of such specimens would probably be carried out by Sir Marcus Lanyon, who is reputed to be a ruthless man. The arrival of Murdoch Gull to Baker Street provides Holmes with the evidence about Browner's ship putting into Harwich on the date around Mary's disappearance, and in return he is promised that the involvement with the grave robberies will be halted but a scandal can be avoided.

The final *Sherlock Holmes* episode acknowledged the two people that Holmes lived with, worked with and depended upon. And as always they contained humour, first in Holmes's choice of a Christmas present for his friend, the bicycle cape from Gamages which will go over the handlebars, and then mimed by a delighted Watson. Secondly, Holmes's interchange with his landlady about the aspidistra, *"Mrs Hudson how dare you move my aspidistra?"* And her reply, *"I do dare!"* is an outburst that has been criticised. Rosalie explained Mrs Hudson's response in *Scarlet Street*, "When he throws a tantrum, she can come back at him. She may win or she may lose, but at the end of it, there will be a twinkle between them as if to say, 'Well, you won that time. But I'll get you next time.' It may only be a glance, you know, or a gesture. They're still—not good friends; that's not the right way to put it—but they understand each other and they live together in a sort of harmony." (Rosalie Williams)

The final scene of the whole series was presented by a view of the two dead bodies caught and preserved in the ice, presenting a fitting image for Holmes's lifetime's work. It seemed to sum up his response to the human misery that crime creates, *"What is the meaning of it Watson? What is the object of this circle of misery and violence and fear? It must have a purpose or our universe has no meaning and that is unthinkable. But what purpose? That is humanity's great problem. For which reason so far has no answer."* Michael said, "Quite properly, Jeremy Brett was allowed to complete his portrait of the great detective with thoughts which are typical of the Canon and its creator." (A Study in Celluloid)

Jeremy's performance in this episode was much improved as he was able to move more freely and swiftly climb the stairs to the Baker Street rooms. *"It was a dark story, but a true story. It happened at the time. I thought June was particularly clever, as was her brilliant director on that one, Sarah Hellings. They set it at Christmas to make it look a little less dark. I was particularly pleased with* The Cardboard Box, *partly because I'd lost a lot of weight and I looked better, and I thought it was very well put together. It was a dark and sinister story and seemed to belong to my attempts at the earlier stories. It did originally come from* The Memoirs *after all."* (Jeremy to David Stuart Davies in The Sherlock Holmes Gazette 1995)

These episodes of the final series underscored Jeremy's professionalism and his courage. It is true that his confidence had been shaken by the decline in his health but this brought another facet of his interpretation to the fore as this reviewer highlighted. "When taken in its entirety Jeremy Brett's *Sherlock Holmes* series stands the test of time as the definitive telling of the stories, the later episodes underscoring Brett's courage as he faced personal tests that shattered his emotional and physical well-being. I would argue that it is that very human element in Brett's portrayal that makes his Holmes so breathtakingly accurate, compelling and poignant. Holmes denied his humanity and in so doing became more vulnerable as a human being, exposing deep character flaws and weaknesses. In Brett, we not only see but feel those shortcomings and something deeper too, each person's ultimate struggle to find his or her place in life..." (Amazon.com)

"He certainly included more of the man's moods and manners than any other actor I can remember in the part. He ran the whole gamut from the deepest gloom to the most outrageous laughter." (Study in Celluloid)

"Just as the adaptation is applauded for its faithfulness, so is Jeremy Brett considered to be the best Holmes ever presented and he plays the part with huge authority... Ascetic, ascerbic, ironic and sarcastic, his mercurial performance is literally a joy to watch and I defy anyone to watch the series and then read a Holmes story without visualising Holmes as Brett (or the other way round...). David Burke and (later) Edward Hardwicke do Watson to a tee; always a step behind (literally and mentally) his good friend Holmes... Let's not forget Rosalie Williams' doughty Mrs. Hudson - always there to remove a sopping cloak and bowler and deliver a hearty breakfast (curried fowl and some piping hot coffee) after a night's adventuring." (Amazon.co.uk)

Jeremy

Sherlock Holmes – By courtesy of Marcus Tylor

As Jeremy was forced to retire from his ten year commitment to Holmes through his recurring ill health, the plaudits came in and they were overwhelming: "Everyone from the scriptwriters, actors and directors, to the production team, the designers, costumers, and make-up people, not forgetting the cameramen, technicians and grips – even the secretaries – all have made a contribution. But if anyone deserves special praise, it has to be Jeremy Brett for being like a father figure to the whole company. He created a family feeling in which everyone wanted to do well. The success was very much theirs." (Michael Cox) "Jeremy had a touch of genius and was a master craftsman in the art of television. I miss him as a dear friend and the theatre has lost one of its finest actors - too soon." (Rosalie Williams)

"Jeremy Brett's Holmes is fundamentally faithful to Doyle's original. The magnetism of his bravura performance attracts a new generation of admirers to the stories. In the years to come it will be his face they see when they read the books, and it will be his voice they hear when the great detective speaks. A part of the monument, that is the legend of Sherlock Holmes, now has Brett's name indelibly carved on it." (Gunner54.wordpress.com)   "I have no doubt that few performances in the history of television drama were as perfect, as passionate, exquisitely realised and definitively delivered as that of Jeremy Brett's extraordinary Sherlock Holmes." (Stephen Fry)   The critics universally agreed, "Jeremy Brett's Holmes offers a combination of fidelity and audacity. Everything he does can ultimately be justified by chapter and line from Conan Doyle's stories, but he has taken liberties with the myth so confidently that he has also, over the last decade, taken possession of it, and displaced the literary Holmes." (Kevin Jackson. The Independent)   Jeremy's visit to America after filming *The Adventures* an admirer paid him the same extravagant compliment that Booth Tarkington paid William Gillette, the first actor to play the part: *"I would rather see you play Sherlock Holmes than be a child again on Christmas morning!"* Praise does not come much bigger than that. Jeremy was always humble in response to the accolades. *"It's utterly thrilling! I mean it is wonderful. I can't tell you how happy it makes me. I'm thrilled to bits. Who would have thought that Jeremy Huggins of Warwickshire, the son of a soldier, would win such an accolade. It's absolutely bizarre!"*

He was often finding explanations for his own success rather than seeing it as a reward for his hard work; in reality a ten year commitment which took away his freedom to live his life as the zestful Jeremy Huggins, the romantic with love his *raison d'etre*. The dark brooding nature of Holmes worried him and he found it a very difficult part to play; the man consumed his very existence at times and the demands were enormous. *"I suppose the only thing that I do have in common with Sherlock Holmes is enthusiasm: mine is for life, his is for work. He's dead when he's not working – in that sense, he is like an actor. But I've had a fascinating time playing him. I said to Dame Jean Conan Doyle: 'I've danced in the moonlight with your father for 10 years.' The moonlight, not the sunlight – Holmes is a very dark character."*

Jeremy admitted that playing the part had made his career. He may have had a long and successful career on the stage and in television, but it was Holmes which had made him a household name. He always responded to the plaudits with sensitivity and grace. *"I've always felt that I could never, ever convey to anyone the thinking man's Holmes. Then this gentleman, who was giving a party, suddenly stood up and said, 'Thank you Mr Brett for giving us the Thinking Man's Holmes'. And I had to step out, to cry. I was so touched. That is what I thought I would never be able to do."*

So many people commented and still comment on the fact that Jeremy never received an award or any official recognition for such a remarkable piece of acting. BAFTA had received the nomination of Jeremy's name year on year from Ellen Dean, the make-up artist throughout the series and herself a member of BAFTA, until finally she had resigned in disgust at the lack of recognition. In spite of the snub, Jeremy was proud of his achievement, *"Now I think it's time to take lots of rest and think about what I actually want to do myself, not about what other people want me to do. But it will be a great comfort to me as I get older to be able to look back and say: 'Oh well, I did Holmes and I managed to do it not completely badly'"*

"Bless your darling hearts. Much love, keep warm and dry and if you see him whisking around the corner – you know who, SH – then wave, because that's all you'll see of him. Bless his darling heart, isn't he wonderful, streets ahead of us – still." (Jeremy Brett 1995)

Richmond Theatre

Even before reading this book I knew what an extraordinary actor Jeremy Brett was, but having now read the full list of parts, I am more in awe at the diversity of his acting skills. He was truly a star and I am so glad I got to know him and to see him perform live.

The first time I saw Jeremy was in September 1988. He was appearing as Sherlock Holmes opposite Edward Hardwicke as Dr. Watson in the play, *The Secret of Sherlock Holmes* at the Richmond Theatre in Surrey. The theatre, originally known as the Richmond Theatre and Opera House is a beautiful theatre built in 1899, which was most fitting for the play as it was set in Victorian times.

Jeremy oozed confidence on stage. He was the ultimate showman who loved a live audience. He was able to show off his skills that he had honed over many years as a performer. He was quick to ad lib when something went wrong, which is exactly what happened during one stage performance. Jeremy as Sherlock was holding a magnifying glass to inspect a watch Dr Watson had given him to test Holmes's power of deduction. After Holmes deduces a lot of information from the watch, Watson, unable to accept that so much detail could be gathered, becomes annoyed and believes that Holmes is a charlatan and has looked into his background. Holmes hands Watson the magnifying glass and as he does so, the glass falls out. As the glass hits the stage and begins to roll away, the audience holds its collective breath. Edward then promptly puts his foot on it. Jeremy without a second thought said, "Watson, well done, your reactions are quick, but you fail to see the obvious," and then carries on with the next line from the script, which was to explain to Watson how he had uncovered so much evidence. Naturally the audience gave a big round of applause.

The Secret of Sherlock Holmes, ran for a year in London before going on a nationwide tour of the UK, and with each performance, Jeremy would add something extra, either a mannerism or extra dialogue. Edward Hardwicke enjoyed working with Jeremy a lot but said to me once, "You had to have your wits about you when playing opposite Jeremy. When he went off script, I would have to be ready to add words of my own. Sometimes, he would go a little too far and afterwards I would tell him off, but he just gave one of his mischievous smiles and promised not to do it again. But Jeremy being Jeremy always did." Having seen, *The Secret of Sherlock Holmes* many times, I can vouch for everything Edward said. I never got bored of watching the show over and over again as no two shows were exactly the same.

What was most disappointing and unjust about Jeremy's role as Sherlock Holmes was the lack of recognition he received. At the very least he should have won a BAFTA. The only excuse for the lack of any award was best summed up by Kevin Jackson in *The Independent*: "It might seem perverse to suggest that Jeremy Brett's portrayals of Sherlock Holmes are in any way underrated: The Granada series has, after all, proved immensely popular not just in Britain but in more than 70 other countries (it's huge in Japan), and reviewers regularly commend its leading players, its high production values, strong supporting casts, atmospheric scores and so on. Moreover, only die-hard Basil Rathbone fans will resist the proposition that Brett makes a fine Detective, and Edward Hardwicke an engaging Dr Watson. But even the most widespread acclaim can still be insufficient if it does not try to address its object, and popularity is not quite the same thing as recognition. The case of Mr Brett is a little like the case of the purloined letter in the Poe tale which was one of the influences on Conan Doyle. In Poe's yarn, a filched letter was overlooked precisely because the villain had not hidden it at all. Similarly, Mr Brett's true brilliance is overlooked not because no one says that he is splendid but because everybody does."

Of course Jeremy was not only brilliant at playing Sherlock Holmes. I admired his portrayal of William Pitt the Younger, Captain Ashburnham in *The Good Soldier*, Maxim de Winter in *Rebecca*, Bassanio in, *The Merchant of Venice*, D'Artagnan in *The Three Musketeers* and the list goes on and on.

Jeremy had a presence when he acted. One was always drawn to watch him, even when he was not the main speaker in a scene. A look, or a stare would speak volumes and a smile would almost tell you what he was thinking. The fact he is remembered and admired more than 20 years after his death says a lot about Jeremy as an actor and a man.

My own personal memories of Jeremy, was his storytelling. He would tell me moments in his life that had me laughing so much that my sides hurt, or concerned at how he managed to survive an incident. On one such occasion he told me that some poor woman ended up in a ditch in her car when they were both trying to outmanoeuvre each other at speed on a country lane. Before I continue I would like to add that the women was not hurt and they sorted things out amicably thanks to Jeremy's charm. It seems he pulled up alongside the lady at a set of traffic lights. He looked across and thought she looked attractive, but at the same time, his foot pressed heavily on the accelerator. The lady looked across, saw that his was the better car and assumed Jeremy was showing off and was going to speed off when the lights changed. As the lights turned green she took off like a bat out of hell leaving Jeremy still admiring her beauty. He went after her hoping to ask her out for a coffee, but soon realised she had no intention of letting him pass as she moved the car from side to side. He saw this as a challenge and took the next opportunity to overtake. However, the lady lost control and ended up with the car in a ditch. Unhurt, she got out of the car and chastised him for his bad driving. Jeremy pointed out that it was her car in the ditch and not his. Before the lady could further the argument, he explained how her beauty had caused him to hit the accelerator pedal and that he was only chasing her down for a coffee. I asked him if he ever got that coffee. The answer was no, but he did get an apology and a radiant smile.

After listening to this story I was glad Jeremy no longer drove. I was never really sure why he stopped driving. It may have been because of his illnesses but it never bothered him as he enjoyed trips on the bus. His favourite journey was from Clapham into the heart of London. The bus took passengers over the Battersea Bridge and Jeremy would always sit on the top deck so he could see across to the Albert Bridge, which was his favourite bridge in London. For me the bridge is best seen lit up against the night sky.

Another of Jeremy's favourite places was Richmond Park. It is the largest of the capital's eight Royal Parks and is a National Nature Reserve. I would drive there and we would very slowly make our way around the park to see who was quickest to spot the herds of Red and Fallow deer. I remember those days with such happiness. Later we would make our way to a local café for coffee where I reminded Jeremy that it was the nearby Richmond Theatre where we first met. Afterwards, we would buy French loaves from the local bakery and consume them that day with different cheeses we had also bought.

On another day we would do crosswords together and one crossword we did was huge and took days to do. We did not have access to the internet in those days so we relied on our memories. Of course some memories take a while to emerge, hence the reason it took us so long. I made the huge mistake of writing in the final question thus finishing it. I thought Jeremy would be pleased that it was finally complete, but no, he wanted to be the one who answered the last question. I wouldn't say he sulked; it was more him telling me off over the next few hours. From then on I made sure Jeremy always answered the last question.

Living with Jeremy was never dull. He would make a drama out of the smallest incident. One afternoon, I returned to the flat a couple of hours late after visiting a friend. When I walked in, Jeremy was on the phone, pretending to be talking to the police about my disappearance and whereabouts! *"Oh, thank you, officer. You needn't bother with the patrol car and the all-night search. She has just walked through the door. But I do appreciate your willingness to put the entire force on the alert."*

Jeremy was a magical person and incredibly courageous in his battle with bipolar and heart disease. Even in the darkest moments of his illness his strength of character shone through. He deserved a knighthood for the way he inspired and helped people with the same illnesses. Although he never won any awards, he remains an inspiration to so many people. More than twenty years after his death, he is remembered for his ability to overcome so many obstacles in order to realise his dreams.

Linda Pritchard 2017

Jeremy on Clapham Common

Tributes to Jeremy

"He was a very wonderful man, a giant of the profession and a great friend to those that loved him. Above all, he was quite unique and there will never be anybody like him again, at least for me in my lifetime. He was a best friend perhaps to too many and I shall always miss him..." (Sue Locke)

"Offstage, Brett was a complex and dazzling personality, whose life was troubled with manic depression. His life and work encompassed strange opposites – he seemed to find pride in treachery, freedom in front of the cameras or on stage in a theatre, beauty in ugliness, and saintliness in sin. But he was, above all, a loving, sympathetic and wise man and a true star of British theatre." (Patrick Newley in The Stage)

"In 1988, when I had had no acting work for some time and felt more than adequately rested, I took a job as a day person at Wyndham's Theatre, where the *Secret of Sherlock Holmes* was about to open... Once the first night had passed successfully, it was arranged that the cast would go out for a meal after the show with everyone who was working backstage. At the restaurant, Jeremy was exuberant and flamboyant, but he was the first to leave. When at the end of a thoroughly enjoyable evening, the rest of us asked for our bills, we were told that he had paid for us all. The following night he accompanied all the front of house staff to the same restaurant and paid for their meal. This seemed to me an extraordinary act of generosity, and I will always remember him not only as a very fine actor, but also as a delightful and warm hearted human being." (British Newspaper Archives)

"He was a sweet person, and in some ways a sad person. He switched between great gaiety and moods of depression – but never on the set. This was the extraordinary thing. When he was working, he was bubbling with joy and enthusiasm and drive. And it's funny – I think Sherlock kept him alive in some ways." (Rosalie Williams)

"We were on location somewhere and he serenaded me at a restaurant table in the middle of a very crowded restaurant in the evening... He wasn't taking the mickey, it was absolutely serious as only Jeremy could be serious in a situation like that... suddenly his voice was floating out all over this restaurant, and he improvised this song all about me and my beautiful wife and my beautiful son. I was absolutely crimson with embarrassment. But it didn't make me love him any the less." (David Burke)

"He was charming. He was the only actor who has played Sherlock Holmes who took the trouble to get in touch with me and to come and see me. All along, he would ring me up and ask my opinion. Jeremy was trying to do his very best to be faithful to my father's stories." (Dame Jean Conan Doyle)

"Jeremy's favourite outfit in which one usually found him was a black cashmere sweater and white cotton trousers. One day I was arriving at the studio and Jeremy was getting out of a taxi. As he leant forward to pay the cabby, the waistband of this particular much-laundered pair of white cotton trousers parted company with the legs, which fell to the floor. Jeremy then struggled into Wardrobe where his laughter could have been heard in Liverpool. Whenever I think of him - I think of him laughing. I cannot pay him a greater compliment than that." (Edward Hardwicke)

"Whatever the conversation was about, it would have ended with Jeremy's motto, 'Onwards and upwards!' It's hard to think of a simpler expression of his attitude to life or a better clarion call to remember." (Michael Cox in Sherlock Holmes Gazette Tribute to Brett)

"The funeral was a moving occasion, and all Jeremy's close friends came, and one realised what a loved person he was. People had found comfort and warmth in his company, even though at times he behaved most strangely, for his manic depression was so severe that there were periods when he went completely out of control. But throughout all his troubles not one friend had deserted him. This must illustrate the magnetic qualities that he possessed... generous, warm, larger than life, and often quite crazy. A light went out in many people's lives when he died, for he was one of life's true originals." (Anna Massey)

'Twenty (five) years on and Jeremy still touches and inspires the lives of many. He is and always will be the special being that made us all realise that our dreams and wishes can be accomplished. I still marvel how he overcame heart disease and Bipolar and had an incredible career. Even in the darkest moments of his illness, his strength of character shone through. His inner strength and spirituality is a shining light that has reached out to us all. God bless you Jeremy.' (Linda Pritchard 2015)

Highest Honours

Jeremy may not have received a BAFTA for his definitive performance of Sherlock Holmes but he was assured of the highest award from two different sources. His name appeared as a nominee on the New Year's Honours List but at his untimely death was regrettably removed. Another award was the Knight of the Legion of Honour (Chevalier de la Legion d'Honneur) by the French President which Jeremy accepted at the tenth anniversary celebration of the Granada series in Manchester. Other recipients of the honour include Audrey Hepburn, Seamus Heaney, Marilyn Horne, T.S. Eliot and Christopher Lee.

This fitting memorial was presented by Thierry Saint-Joanis President of the Société Sherlock Holmes de France. "The 58 year old actor, who is still being treated in hospital following a mental breakdown, left his hospital bed last night to be guest of honour at the glitzy Granada shindig marking the programme's 10th anniversary – and heard he is to receive the coveted Legion d'Honneur in Paris for bringing the detective to life on the TV.... Looking frail but cheerful... (Jeremy) said he was overwhelmed by the accolade, created by Napoleon... 'I am very grateful to the team here at Granada, who have made this programme one of the best experiences in my many years of acting. I feel a great warmth from everyone here tonight and can honestly say this is the best night of my life.'" (The Case of the Highest Honour May 1994)

"Unfortunately, our dear Jeremy died too early. The presentation of a medal requires several steps. After our own request to the French State, it is mandatory that the recipient accepts the decoration. This is what Jeremy did in May 1994, in public, at the closing night of the series in Manchester.

It was then necessary to organize an official ceremony in France (or at the French Embassy in London). Jeremy's state of health and the administrative formalities delayed the event which could not take place before the disappearance of the recipient. The rank would have been that of knight. In a way, the Canon has been respected since Sherlock Holmes, too, receives a letter informing him that France has decided to award him the Legion of Honour, but, nowhere in Watson's texts, we have an account of the official presentation of the decoration (a scene that we see however in the Granada series).

Having alerted the French State about this aspect of the life of the hero of Conan Doyle, I had the mission, as president of the Sherlock Holmes Society of France, to choose a living person worthy of receiving the detective's medal in our reality. For me, there was only one man: Jeremy Brett, the one who embodies (still today) Sherlock Holmes to perfection. After Jeremy's death, I still had the right to offer this medal to another "living" person, but I chose not to do it in memory of the one who remains unique in his embodiment of the character of Sherlock Holmes." (Thierry Saint-Joanis President of the SSHF, BSI 2020)

Appendix

When you get what you want in your struggle for self,

And the world makes you king for a day;

Just go to a mirror and look at your self,

And see what that man has to say.

For it isn't your father, or mother, or wife,

Who judgement on you must pass.

The person who's verdict counts most in your life,

Is the man staring back from the glass.

He's the fellow to please never mind the rest,

For he's with you clear to the end.

And you've passed your most dangerous, difficult test

If the man in the glass is your friend.

You may fool the whole world down the pathway of years,

And get pats on the back as you pass,

But your final reward will be heartache and tears,

If you've cheated that man in the glass.

'Anon'

Dear Mr and Mrs Pritchard.
This was given to me the other day.
I like it so much; I thought you might like a copy?
Linda will tell you all the news.
Sincerely J.B.
(February 15th 1994)

I am most grateful to Linda Pritchard for her invaluable help in so many different ways and especially for the photographs, the majority of which are taken from Jeremy's personal collection. Without her encouragement this book would never have been written. I am grateful to Severine Rubin for her valued assistance, to Louise Cotulla for her support, to Marcus Tylor for his friendship, and to Gretchen Altabef and Bonnie MacBird for their encouragement. Grateful thanks are also due to National Theatre Archives, BBC Written Archives, BFI Archives for access to unpublished films and Manchester Library Archives for access to the Library Theatre Archives. The Times Archive Database and British Newspaper Archives have proved to be invaluable sources. The ProQuest Observer/ Guardian sources have been used and the BBC genome site. Not all the sources are so clearly marked so in these cases I have given the author the credit. If anyone can provide the missing information to enable full credit, then that would be much appreciated.

Bibliography

A Study in Celluloid: A Producer's Account of Jeremy Brett as Sherlock Holmes by Michael Cox: Rupert Books 1999

Bending the Willow by David Stuart Davies: Calabash Press 1996

Granada's Greatest Detective by Keith Frankel: Fantom Publishing 2016

Mystery! A Celebration by Ron Miller KQED Books 1996

Sherlock Holmes On Screen The Complete Film and TV History: Titan Books 2011

Telling Some Tales by Anna Massey: Hutchinson 2006

The Annotated Sherlock Holmes by William S. Baring-Gould: Clarkson N. Potter 1977

The Illustrated Sherlock Holmes Treasury by Arthur Conan Doyle: Avenal

The Jeremy Brett – Linda Pritchard Story On The Wings of Paradise by Linda Pritchard: Rupert Books 1998

The Man Who Became Sherlock Holmes The tortured mind of Jeremy Brett by Terry Manners: Virgin 1997

The Road is Long by Linda Pritchard: Amazon Kindle

The Television Sherlock Holmes by Peter Haining 1994

BBC genome site - bbcgenome.co.uk   Brettish Empire site - brettish.com

jeremybrett.info.co.uk   Kaleidescope Database

Radio Times   TV Times 1955-1995

Scarlet Street Numbers 8, 20, 21, 22

Stage Struck pub. Penguin   BFI Sight and Sound Magazine Archives

British Newspaper Archives: The Stage Magazine, Illustrated London News:

ProQuest Historical Newspapers: The Observer, The Guardian, New York Times

Lightning Source UK Ltd.
Milton Keynes UK
UKHW050318101120
373107UK00005B/173

9 781787 056688